Marketing Due Diligence

WITHDRAWN

With thanks to all my friends and colleagues at Cranfield
– Malcolm

For Lindsay, Eleanor and Catherine
– Brian

For Angela, Sam and Rob
– Keith

Marketing Due Diligence

Reconnecting Strategy to Share Price

Malcolm McDonald

Brian Smith

Keith Ward

ELSEVIER

AMSTERDAM • BOSTON • HEIDELBERG • LONDON • NEW YORK • OXFORD
PARIS • SAN DIEGO • SAN FRANCISCO • SINGAPORE • SYDNEY • TOKYO

Butterworth-Heinemann is an imprint of Elsevier

Butterworth-Heinemann is an imprint of Elsevier
Linacre House, Jordan Hill, Oxford OX2 8DP
30 Corporate Drive, Suite 400, Burlington, MA 01803

First published 2006

British Library Cataloguing in Publication Data
A catalogue entry for this book is available from the British Library

Library of Congress Cataloguing in Publication Data
A catalogue record for this book is available from the Library of Congress

ISBN-13: 978-0-7506-6727-2
ISBN-10: 0-7506-6727-3

For information on all Butterworth-Heinemann publications visit our web site at http://books.elsevier.com

Typeset by Charon Tec Pvt. Ltd, India
www.charontec.com

Printed and bound in Great Britain by MPG Books Ltd
06 07 08 09 10 10 9 8 7 6 5 4 3 2 1

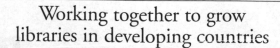

Working together to grow
libraries in developing countries

www.elsevier.com | www.bookaid.org | www.sabre.org

ELSEVIER   BOOK AID
            International   Sabre Foundation

Contents

Foreword

by Sir Michael Perry, GBE

A few years back I was asked to address an Economist conference for senior marketing people on the questions – 'Why do so few CEOs of major UK companies come from a marketing background? Do marketing people make bad CEOs?'

To start with I was puzzled by the questions. I had spent thirty nine years working in a company, Unilever, where marketing was virtually the default background for the CEOs of successful operating companies. Every such subsidiary had a Marketing Director on its board as well, whose voice carried more weight than anyone's when it came to business strategy. Even at parent company level, of the ten Executive Chairmen of Unilever plc since the company was formed in 1929, four were marketing men – more than from any other discipline.

A little research soon revealed that this pattern did not by any means hold true for most FTSE 100 companies. Worse still, too many of them did not even have a marketing person on their executive boards. That really got me worrying. In such companies who represents the interests of customers? Where is the analysis of markets and market segmentation done? What about the detailed understanding of competitors and sustaining competitive advantage? Where does the prime responsibility lie for optimizing crucially important shareholder values such as intangible assets – like brands, or good-will? No wonder so many companies run into difficulties.

In the absence of a Marketing Director, it has to be the CEO himself who shoulders this prime responsibility, and since he or she typically comes from a financial, or perhaps a technical or operations background, he needs all the help he can get from his marketing specialists if he is to deliver sustained success. That's where the experience so skilfully displayed in this book comes in. It is precisely aimed at Chief Executives from non-marketing backgrounds, and it sets out simply and with great clarity what their marketing departments should be capable of delivering for them.

CEOs who have spent their entire earlier career in marketing would also do well to peruse these pages carefully. Shibboleths abound in the marketing trade, and most of us have been guilty at one time or another of keeping alive the myth that much of what we do is neither quantifiable nor expressible in the demanding terms of measured change in shareholder value. Scholarly attempts have been made in the past to find language and techniques for marketing metrics, most of which have helped improve marketing's accountability to some degree. But this book goes a step further, by insisting that the ultimate test of measurable impact on shareholder value is as relevant for marketing investment, in the widest sense, as for any other deployment of shareholders funds.

All of this begs the questions I posed at the outset, of why there are so few marketing people on the boards of major UK companies. At the heart of the matter, sad to relate, is the fact that many companies either do not put the constant search for long-term competitive advantage at the centre of their thinking, or if they do, they do not believe their marketing departments have much to contribute. For many business leaders today, marketing is synonymous with advertising and sales promotion, and marketing people are caricatured as the flamboyant and not very numerate folk down the corridor who love to remind them, on impeccable historical authority, that half the money they spend is undoubtedly wasted. Not a very promising basis for a relationship grounded in mutual respect and trust.

The third group, therefore, who should take this book very seriously indeed are those Marketing Officers who understand the strategic elements of their role, and who need to break down the barriers that prevent their voices from being heard clearly enough in the boardroom. Marketing people typically do not speak the language of finance and investment, and this book makes a major contribution to the bridging of a gap that has become a major source of business under-performance in the increasingly competitive and globalized world in which we operate.

My advice to Chief Marketing Officers is very simple. You should be responsible for generating the value propositions that achieve sustained customer preference for your company's products or services. If your CEO does not recognize that, it is up to you to persuade him otherwise, or move somewhere else, where your proper role is fully understood.

The authors of this book rightly refer to the prime importance of measuring shareholder value creation. In recent times the concept of shareholder value has come to mean different things to different people and in different circumstances. The prime responsibility of boards is to secure and safeguard the longer-term prosperity of their business, for the benefit of its owners and its other stakeholders, most especially its customers and employees. Shareholders often see things differently. Owners of public companies, notably institutional investors, have less interest in the longer term than they publicly profess, or indeed demonstrate by their day-to-day trading behaviour on the world's exchanges. They also accept less of the responsibilities normally demanded by society in return for the benefits of legal ownership. Boards of public companies are therefore always obliged to bear the short-term needs of markets in mind, as they focus strategic thought on their wider responsibility of building longer term prosperity.

Marketing specialists are subject to the same pressures, and all too often they yield to the demand to sacrifice the long term interests of building brand equity, or other intangible asset values, to short term expedience. Careful examination of the contents of this book will remind them of the consequences of so doing. If they and their Chief Executive Officers are equally well informed, perhaps fewer businesses will be crippled by the inevitable results of the short-termism that we all profess to deplore.

A note for busy people: how to get the best out of this book

This book is written for directors and managers of firms operating in the real world. By definition, such readers will be busy people and may not have the luxury to read this book from start to finish before returning to review parts of the book that are especially relevant to their situation.

In recognition of this, we offer some suggestions as to how to gain an overview of the book and the subject of Marketing Due Diligence before attempting to understand and apply it in detail.

Each chapter begins with a short 'fast track' section which summarizes briefly its contents. These provide a succinct way to acquaint oneself with the content of each chapter before reading and when returning to it.

In addition, these 'fast track' sections are consolidated, with a little editing, into Chapter 10. This chapter therefore provides a good overview of the book and can be read before and/or after reading Chapters 1–9, depending on your learning style.

The main body of the book is split into three parts:

Part 1: What is Marketing Due Diligence?
This is intended for those who need an explanation of why this new process is needed, what it involves and what its implications are.

Part 2: The Marketing Due Diligence Diagnostic Process
This is intended for those who wish to assess the shareholder value creation of their marketing strategy.

Part 3: The Marketing Due Diligence Therapeutic Process
This is intended for those who wish to improve the shareholder value creation of their marketing strategy by acting on the outcomes of the diagnostic process.

By means of this structure, it is hoped readers will be able to understand the concept and process of Marketing Due Diligence as quickly as possible. Be warned, however, that Marketing Due Diligence is intended as a route to creating sustainable competitive advantage. Our readers will appreciate that it is naive to expect that outcome to be either quick or easy.

List of figures

List of tables

What is Marketing Due Diligence?

Chapter 1

Why Chief Executive Officers must demand a revolutionary new approach from their Chief Marketing Officers

| Fast track |

Many CEOs despair of their senior marketing colleagues. There is a disparity between what boards see marketing doing and what they need from this critical function. CEOs and senior non-marketers perceive marketing's focus to be on promotional activities rather than on the key issues of strategy which create shareholder value. What they need is good decisions about which customers to target and with what value propositions in order to create sustainable competitive advantage. Above all else, boards need to know if the planned marketing strategy is going to make returns, above the cost of capital, that take account of the risks associated with the strategy. Marketing as a discipline has failed during the past 50 years by concentrating on promotion rather than on developing world-class marketing strategies. The result is that, in most companies, marketing has been relegated to running promotional campaigns and designing T-shirts and does not deserve a place at the high table, i.e. the board of directors.

The result of this sad lack of marketing leadership is the demise of many of our erstwhile famous organizations. Most of the highest earning Return on Investment plcs during the decade up to 1990 have since gone into liquidation or were acquired in desperate circumstances, while many of the leading companies in different sectors up to the year 2000 also got into financial difficulties or were acquired.

All of this happened against a background of three major challenges that industry was facing during this period and still faces.

The first is maturity in demand in many markets. Since most consumers already have most things, market growth is no longer a natural expectation and suppliers have been forced to understand the needs of their customers as a route to growth in sales and profits. Alas, since their so-called marketing colleagues were obsessed with promotion, many failed in this fundamental task and subsequently went bust. This sad trend began first and is clearest in consumer markets, but the same argument applies and will apply in business-to-business markets.

The second challenge is globalization, the result of mature national markets combined with political and macroeconomic change. Today, we have a situation of a declining number of global mega-companies, with only eight car companies in the world, only four major firms of accountants whilst, in the UK, only four supermarkets account for nearly 80% of all grocery product sales. The result of this is that many second-tier companies face a bleak future, having to compete with companies whose global reach gives them enormous economies of scale and scope. Again, the only hope for such companies is an increasing focus on customer needs.

Finally, all of this has resulted in a massive shift of power to customers away from suppliers. Today, customers are destroying old make/sell business models, whilst entrepreneurial, technology-enabled competitors unfettered by the baggage of legacy bureaucracy, assets, cultures and behaviours have raised customers' expectations. Technology has empowered customers to have more information about their suppliers than their suppliers have about them. This customer pressure is, of course, in addition to new business metrics and pressures from institutional shareholders to report meaningful facts about corporate performance. Other stakeholders demand exemplary corporate behaviour. All these pressures have resulted in a need for strategies other than downsizing and cost-cutting as a route to increased profitability. Never before has the need for real marketing professionalism been greater and the challenge facing Chief Executives is to drag their marketing colleagues away from the trivia they are engaged in to a central, board-driven, strategic role.

This raises the question of what marketing is. It is a function, just like finance, with its own professional standards, institutes and body of knowledge. The role of marketing is to define markets and to understand the needs of the segments within these markets, then to formulate strategies for meeting these needs. Furthermore, they need to do this in a way that enables the company to create long-term, net-free cash flows which, having taken account of the associated risks, represent a financial return over and above the cost of capital, thus creating shareholder value.

CEOs need a way of holding marketing accountable, despite the obvious complexity of the process. At the lowest level of promotional effectiveness, tools for this have existed for decades. They can, however, only tell us about the effectiveness of promotional activity, which is far removed from understanding the effectiveness of the entire marketing process. It is perfectly possible to communicate effectively with the right customers and still fail to improve sales or profit. At the next level of assessing the degree to which the whole mix of tactics creates advantage, existing and new tools allow us to predict and measure the degree to which that mix creates customer preference and hence sales and profits. It is, however, perfectly possible to create sales and profits whilst destroying shareholder value. What CEOs and the board need is a way of measuring the risk associated with a marketing strategy and hence its likely shareholder value creation. That is the aim of Marketing Due Diligence.

Why many CEOs despair of marketing

When the Chief Executive Officer asks the Chief Marketing Officer what was the return on the company's $20 million invested in marketing, he expects more than to be told that the organization has achieved an increase in awareness, or a change in attitude. Hiding behind this kind of insubstantial half truth is likely (and with some justification) to result in the Chief Marketing Officer being sacked without any remorse whatever!

There is no question that we have well-established econometric models that spell out clearly and unequivocally the impact of promotional campaigns on certain measurable outcomes. However, the same rigour fails to be applied to the real issue, which is marketing's strategic role of ensuring return on investment and an increase in shareholder value. The problem lies in the deeply held belief by some marketers and others that marketing is principally about promotion. This explains why, in the majority of organizations, the marketing function has been relegated to designing T-shirts and running money-off sales promotion campaigns. But more about this later.

Even the renowned Professor Philip Kotler of Northwestern University has admitted that most CEOs have finally lost patience with their senior marketing colleagues:

'They (CEOs) feel that they get accountability for their investments in finance, production, information technology, even purchasing, but don't know what their marketing spending is achieving.'

Supporting this, a survey at Cranfield University School of Management in 2000 found that senior non-marketers believe that marketers are:

'Unaccountable, expensive, untouchable and slippery.'

Furthermore, the 2004 Research International Survey of disciplines in the USA and the UK has shown that marketing as a discipline has slipped disastrously to the bottom of the pile in terms of reputation, with a massive gap between it and the next worst.

Let us be unequivocal for those CEOs, General Managers, Chief Financial Officers and other justifiably frustrated directors reading this book. Marketing is principally about developing strategies for what is sold, to whom it is sold, why these target customers should buy it from us rather than from a competitor offering something similar. Above all, marketing is about proving that these product/marketing strategies result in sustainable shareholder value added, i.e. that they make returns over and above the cost of capital, having taken proper account of the risks associated with the strategy.

Such fundamental, shareholder value-enhancing activities must be evaluated, audited and proved, and this is what this book is about, so anyone hoping that it will be about promotion should return it immediately and ask for their money back!

However, before detailing what we call the Marketing Due Diligence process, let us elaborate on why marketing has lost any appeal it ever had and what Chief Executives must do to drag it out of the tactical cul-de-sac it has got itself into.

The remainder of this chapter is organized as follows:

● The challenges facing all organizations today
● How these challenges have changed the corporate landscape
● An introduction to the role of marketing in creating shareholder value added.

Challenges facing all organizations today

Research by leading business schools and other prominent research organizations world-wide have together reached the conclusion that the most pressing challenges facing all organizations today are:

- Market maturity
- Globalization
- Customer power.

Market maturity

Figure 1.1 shows what is known as the diffusion of innovation and its impact on markets.

The point of drawing the reader's attention to this and the short explanation that follows is that today, in most developed markets of the world, the easy days of growth have gone, with the result that the customer has finally become king. This is true both in product and service industries, and applies as much to business-to-business (B2B) as it does to business-to-consumer (B2C), so much so that any company that doesn't put the customer at the centre of their business strategy is doomed to failure.

Briefly, the bell-shaped curve shows that, over time, different categories of consumers adopt new products or services. A fashion might take three months before everyone who could adopt it will have done so and another fashion takes its place, whereas the time of adoption of a technology like microwave ovens was about 30 years.

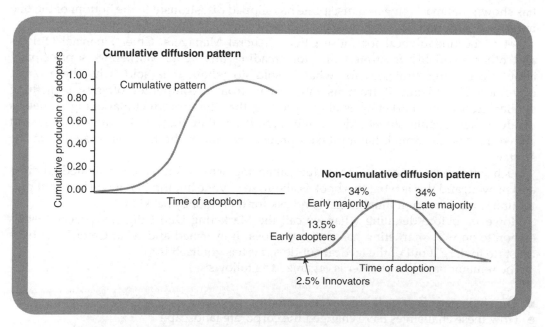

Figure 1.1 Diffusion of innovation patterns (after Rogers, 1976)

Put simply, a very small group of innovators will try anything new, simply because it is new, but such people are not typical of society as a whole. So it doesn't mean that there is a long-term market for it. However, when the next group (often called 'opinion leaders' or, in more popular parlance, 'the Joneses') enters the market, this signals that there is indeed a market for the new product or service, and market growth begins, fuelled when the early majority adopt it. The early majority group is often referred to as 'the Smiths', proverbially determined to keep up with the Joneses. Subsequently, the late majority enter the market and prices tend to fall, reflecting the fact that consumers in this group are often less affluent and also that suppliers have geared up production to meet demand in a growing market at a time when there are fewer and fewer new consumers entering the market (clearly indicated by the shape of the curve). Hence growth begins to decline. Finally, the so-called 'laggards' enter the market, until everyone who could use the product does so, with the result that the market is now dependent for growth on factors such as demographics and GDP.

Figure 1.1 also explains the well-known life cycle effect. Thus, in Western Europe, every potential customer already has cars, TVs, washing machines, insurance, banking facilities, etc. Business customers already have photocopiers and fax machines, PCs and office cleaning or facilities management services. So suppliers of these and similar goods and services are forced into competing for market share, which is extremely difficult, as customers now have the upper hand by dint of enjoying a wide choice between suppliers who are vying for their attention.

As stated above, the point of drawing the reader's attention to this phenomenon is that, whatever we think marketing is (and an introductory explanation of what marketing is follows later), it should be driving any organization's strategy, not residing in some remote, self-contained area of the office, fiddling with T-shirts and promotional campaigns!

Globalization

Figure 1.2 explains what had happened to most markets by the millennium.

Briefly, when a market is new, there are often just a few, smallish competitors. When the market is rapidly growing, there are often some big leaders, some smaller second-tier

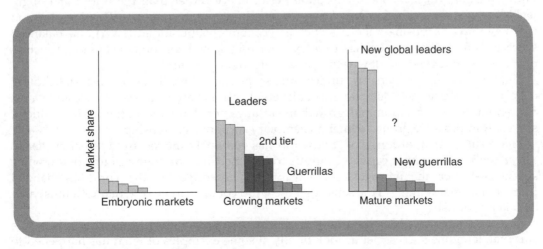

Figure 1.2   Globalization and market share

companies and lots of 'guerrillas', or very small ones. As the market matures, a shakeout occurs and the second-tier companies often disappear, because they can't match the economies of scale and scope of their very large competitors, whereas the very small competitors can still behave like hunters, finding profitable niches in the market.

Hence, in the UK, there are four supermarkets accounting for the sales of about 80% of consumer goods. There are only eight car firms remaining in the world. There are only four global firms of accountants, etc. The same is true in B2B markets. Although B2B lags behind fast-moving consumer goods (FMCG), these markets are nonetheless showing the same trends.

It is possible, of course, to become a global niche player, like American Express, but generally organizations that are 'stuck in the middle' are in for a very difficult time, as more markets follow this pattern.

Customer power

This trend towards market polarization, which sees markets occupied only by the very large and the very small, has given customers enormous power over suppliers. This power is manifested in two ways.

Firstly, key account management has now become a fully fledged corporate discipline in its own right, with the equivalent of general managers taking on the role of developing strategies with dedicated multi-disciplinary teams for major global customers.

Secondly, organizations which stick to the old 'make and sell model', as opposed to building their offers around the researched needs of their customers, find themselves being rejected by more powerful customers and, consequently, doomed to failure.

Meanwhile, the rules of competition have changed. The make and sell model referred to above has been killed off by a new wave of entrepreneurial technology-enabled competitors, unfettered by the baggage of legacy bureaucracy, assets, cultures and behaviours. The processing of information about products has been separated from the products themselves and customers can now search for and evaluate them independently of those who have a vested interest in selling them.

On top of all these pressures, there is greater pressure from institutional shareholders to report meaningful facts about corporate performance rather than the traditional, high-level financial reporting that appears every year in corporate accounts. This pressure and the new wave of business metrics such as economic value added (EVA) and balanced scorecards force business leaders to re-examine established corporate behaviours such as cost-cutting, mergers and downsizing as a route to profitability.

Finally, business leaders are under intense pressure to deliver against stakeholder expectations. Customers demand greater levels of customization, access, service and value. Shareholders expect continuous growth in earnings per share and in the capital value of shares. And pressure groups demand exemplary corporate citizenship.

The result is that, at long last, the world has genuinely moved from *caveat emptor* to *caveat vendor*. No longer can we continue to hammer into the soggy brains of erstwhile supine customers the messages that *we* want them to receive. No, the world has changed forever and 'marketing' (in the sense that the word contains the word 'market') must now be taken seriously.

Lest the reader should harbour any doubt that a robust strategy is essential to business survival, let alone success, let us look briefly at some examples of what has happened to some companies whose strategies may have been less than entirely sturdy.

Impact on business from lack of customer focus

What better place to start than with the famous Tom Peters's *In Search of Excellence*? According to Richard Pascale, of Peters's original 43 excellent companies, only six were still excellent eight years later!

As the old saying goes, experience is something you don't have until just after you need it. Similarly, the kind of insight needed here can only be gained with some years' perspective on the situation. Table 1.1 shows clearly that many of Britain's best performing companies during the decade up to 1990 subsequently collapsed. Similarly, Table 1.2 shows a selection of leading companies in different sectors during the decade up to 2000 and what happened to them.

Table 1.3 shows a real company (disguised here), which apparently has performed extremely well over a five-year period. Table 1.4, however, shows clearly that its performance is extremely poor when set in context.

Likewise, Table 1.5 also shows that one apparently high performing company is really poor when the kind of non-reportable items shown in the table are taken into account.

Table 1.6 shows the retention rate of a real company by segment, whilst Figure 1.3 (from a Cranfield database of leading European companies using an anonymous Audience Response System) shows that, almost ten years after the famous Reichheld and Sasser (1990) article, spelling out the major impact customer retention has on profit, very few companies measure customer retention by segment.

Table 1.1 Britain's top companies (*Management Today*, 1991)

Year	Company[a]	Market value (£ million)	ROI[b] (%)	Subsequent performance
1979	MFI	57	50	Collapsed
1980	Lasmo	134	97	Still profitable
1981	Bejam	79	34	Acquired
1982	Racal	940	36	Still profitable
1983	Polly Peck	128	79	Collapsed
1984	Atlantic Computers	151	36	Collapsed
1985	BSR	197	32	Still profitable
1986	Jaguar	819	60	Acquired
1987	Amstrad	987	89	Still profitable
1988	Body Shop	225	89	Still profitable
1989	Blue Arrow	653	135	Collapsed

[a]Where a company has been top for more than one year, the next best company has been chosen in the subsequent year, e.g. Polly Peck was rated top 1983, 1984 and 1985.
[b]Pre-tax profit as a percentage of investment capital.
Source: Professor Peter Doyle, Warwick University.

Table 1.2 Britain's top companies (*Management Today*, 2002)

Year	Company[a]	Market value (£ billion)[b]	ROI[c] (%)	Subsequent performance
1990	Maxwell Communications plc	1.0	5	Collapsed
1991	Imperial Chemical Industries plc	8.6	13	Collapsed
1992	Wellcome plc	8.3	40	Acquired
1993	Asda Group	1.6	7	Acquired
1994	TSB Group plc	3.7	20	Acquired
1995	British Telecommunications plc	22.2	17	Not profitable
1996	British Steel plc	3.3	19	Collapsed
1997	British Airways plc	6.1	7	Not profitable
1998	National Westminster Bank plc	19.6	14	Acquired
1999	Marconi plc	29.8	22	Acquired
2000	Marks & Spencer plc	5.3	7	Not profitable

[a]Each company was a FTSE100 when selected.
[b]Market values as of 31 December of each year.
[c]Pre-tax profit as a percentage of equity and long-term debt.
Source: Professor Malcolm McDonald.

Table 1.3 InterTech five-year performance – sales revenue based

Performance	Base year	1	2	3	4	5
Sales revenue (£ million)	254	293	318	387	431	454
– Cost of goods sold	135	152	167	201	224	236
Gross contribution (£ million)	119	141	151	186	207	218
– Manufacturing overhead	48	58	63	82	90	95
– Marketing and sales	18	23	24	26	27	28
– Research and development	22	23	23	25	24	24
Net profit (£ million)	16	22	26	37	50	55
Return on sales (%)	6.3	7.5	8.2	9.6	11.6	12.1
Assets (£ million)	141	162	167	194	205	206
Assets (% of sales)	56	55	53	50	48	45
Return on assets (%)	11.3	13.5	15.6	19.1	24.4	26.7

Figures 1.4 and 1.5 (also from a Cranfield database of over 500 leading European companies over a five-year period) show clearly that very few organizations measure market or customer profitability, in spite of the fact that, for most mature product and service markets, it is the cost of dealing with customers after the 'product' leaves the 'factory' that determines profitability.

Figure 1.6 indicates what marketing information the financial community needs to make sensible investment decisions. It also shows very clearly that very little of this is reported in annual accounts.

Table 1.4 InterTech five-year performance – market based

Performance	Base year	1	2	3	4	5
Market growth (%)	18.3	23.4	17.6	34.4	24.0	17.9
InterTech sales growth (%)	12.8	17.4	11.2	27.1	16.5	10.9
Market share (%)	20.3	19.1	18.4	17.1	16.3	14.9
Customer retention (%)	88.2	87.1	85.0	82.2	80.9	80.0
New customers (%)	11.7	12.9	14.9	24.1	22.5	29.2
Dissatisfied customers (%)	13.6	14.3	16.1	17.3	18.9	19.6
Relative product (%)	+10	+8	+5	+3	+1	0
Relative service (%)	+0	+0	−20	−3	−5	−8
Relative new product (%)	+8	+8	+7	+5	+1	−4

Table 1.5 The importance of the source of profit

	Virtuous plc (%)	Dissembler plc (%)
Sales revenue	100	100
Cost of goods sold	43	61
Profit margin	57	39
Advertising	11	3
R&D	5	–
Capital expenditure	7	2
Investment ratio	23	5
Operating expenses	20	20
Operating profit	14	14
Key trends	• Past 5-year revenue growth 10% p.a. • Heavy advertising investment in new/improved products • Premium priced products, new plant so low cost of goods sold	• Flat revenue, declining volume • No recent product innovation, little advertising • Discounted pricing, so high cost of goods sold

This table is similar to a P&L with one important exception – *depreciation*, a standard item in any P&L, has been replaced by *capital expenditure*, which does not appear in P&Ls. In the long term, Capex levels determine depreciation costs. Capex is a percentage of sales in an investment ratio often ignored by marketers, and it has been included in this table to emphasize its importance.

Factor	The make-up of 14% operating profits	
	Virtuous plc (%)	Dissembler plc (%)
Profit on existing products over 3 years old	21	15
Losses on products recently launched or in development	(7)	(1)
Total operating profits	14	14

Source: Davidson, H. (1998). *Even More Offensive Marketing*. Penguin Books.

Table 1.6 Retention rate by segment

	Total market	Segment 1	Segment 2	Segment 3	Segment 4	Segment 5	Segment 6
Percentage of market represented by segment	100.0	14.8	9.5	27.1	18.8	18.8	11.0
Percentage of all profits in total market produced by segment	100.0	7.1	4.9	14.7	21.8	28.5	23.0
Ratio of profit produced by segment to weight of segment in total population	1.00	0.48	0.52	0.54	1.16	1.52	2.09
Defection rate (%)	23	20	17	15	28	30	35

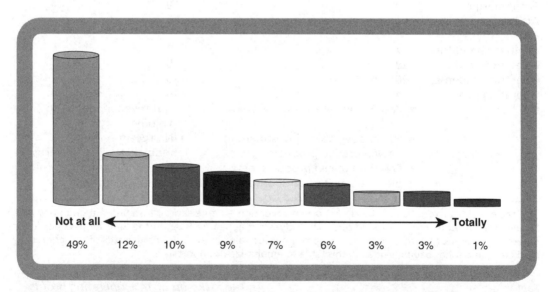

Figure 1.3 Companies that measure customer retention by segment
Source: Cranfield School of Management (2000)

Finally, and also from a Cranfield database, Figure 1.7 reveals a depressing honesty amongst senior marketing practitioners about their lack of knowledge about the financial impact of marketing expenditure.

In short, notwithstanding that the above represents a somewhat random and biased selection of examples of the state of practitioner marketing, most readers will in their heart of hearts recognize that they are not far from the truth. The reality of the situation is that

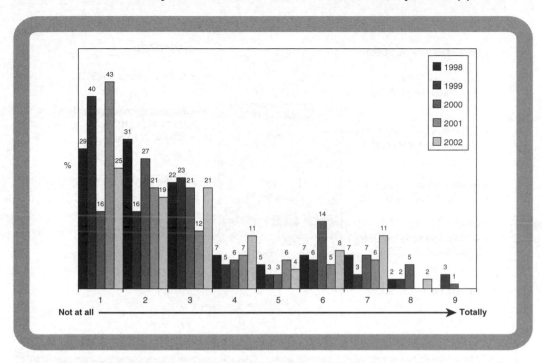

Figure 1.4 To what extent do you allocate attributable costs (interface costs) to individual accounts (not apportion costs across the whole customer base)?
Source: Cranfield School of Management (2002)

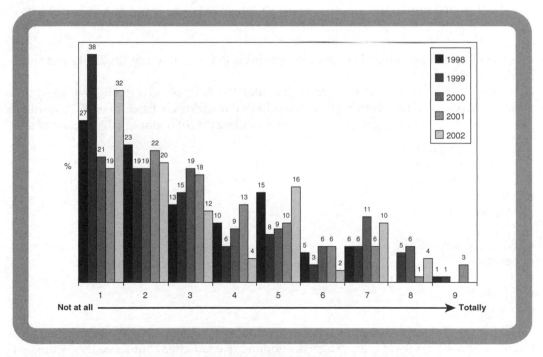

Figure 1.5 How well do you know the profitability of your top ten accounts?
Source: Cranfield School of Management (2002)

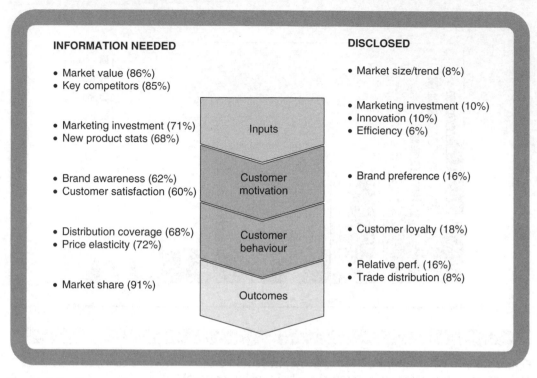

Figure 1.6 External investor marketing disclosure
Sources: Information needed – Brand Finance (1999); Disclosed – Professor Hugh Davidson
(Cranfield visiting professor)

most companies have little idea about the contribution of marketing to results and share-holder value.

Turning briefly to consultants, which includes the likes of advertising agencies, they appear to have fared little better. The authors have painstakingly listed over 300 consultant initiatives developed during the past 30 years, including the following small selection of fads:

- In search of excellence
- Marketing warfare
- One-minute manager
- MBWA
- Skunk works
- TQM
- Balanced scorecard
- Seven Ss
- Business process re-engineering
- CRM
- Six sigma.

During the past ten years, many companies have sought a remedy for their declining fortunes by retreating into faddism, eagerly adopting one fad after another as they were peddled by fervent consultants. In most cases these initiatives have failed, as organizations

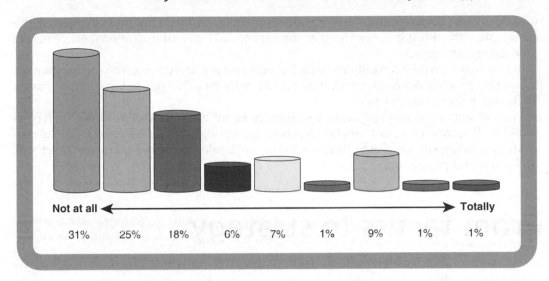

Not at all ◄───────────────────────────────► Totally

31%   25%   18%   6%   7%   1%   9%   1%   1%

Figure 1.7   We know the financial impact of all the elements of our marketing strategy and we measure and report them to the board
Source: Cranfield School of Management (2002)

have treated them as a quick-fix bolt-on, without addressing the underlying problems. The International Standards Organization's ISO 9000 quality initiative, for example, laudable when used sensibly, has, in the main, only been a guarantee that organizations can produce rubbish perfectly and consistently. We use the word 'rubbish' judiciously, because there is little point in producing perfectly something that people do not buy.

Another fad has been business process re-engineering (BPR). This has been an outstanding success in those companies which have used it to redesign their processes to create value for customers. But in those organizations which have not grasped the nettle of customer satisfaction, it has achieved merely cosmetic productivity improvements.

Yet another has been balanced scorecards. This too, for CEOs who need to balance the requirements of all the stakeholders in a company delivering customer value, has been very successful. It is a strategy used with great success by BAA, for example, for managing its complex web of stakeholder relationships. But for those CEOs who do not understand the importance of being market driven, it has proved to be just another fad.

Of course, all of these initiatives are fabulous when they work. And they do work, but only when set in the context of providing superior customer value as a means of providing superior shareholder value. Alas, even in those organizations committed to 'relationships' and 'one-to-one' marketing, customers too often remain the Cinderellas. As Harvard Business School's Susan Fournier pointed out in 1998, rapid development of relationship techniques in the USA has been accompanied by growing customer dissatisfaction. The much vaunted relationship that companies were so eager to forge with their customers involved not so much delighting them as abusing them, suggested Fournier.

The problem is that companies have become so internally focused, they have got carried away with supply-side issues and taken their eye off the customer ball. Until organizations make a serious effort to lift their heads above the parapet and understand their markets and their customers better, all the great initiatives such as ISO 9001, BPR, balanced scorecards, knowledge management and the like will amount to expensive, time-consuming mistakes. Most boards spend too much of their valuable time on internal operational efficiency measures (doing things right) at the expense of external operational effectiveness (doing the right things).

In conclusion, whilst consultants have, not surprisingly, fared somewhat better than the marketing practitioner community, they could hardly be adjudged to have had a consistent positive impact on practice.

The net impact of this sad neglect of marketing by business communities is that, as stated earlier, marketing as a function has been increasingly relegated away from the core strategy-making engine of organizations to become a sales support department, in charge of T-shirts and promotion.

From tactics to strategy

So, what can Chief Executives do to begin to drag the marketing community out of the sorry state in which it finds itself?

Firstly, we must work hard to recapture the high ground – the strategy domain. This, however, means reaching some kind of consensus about what marketing is. Serious damage is done to marketing's cause when senior people in the Chartered Institute of Marketing declare: 'Marketing isn't a function. It is an attitude of mind.' There will be many amongst us who wonder how an attitude of mind can be measured, researched, developed, protected, examined, etc., all of these being the avowed purpose of the professional body. Add to this the hundreds of different definitions of marketing to be found in books and papers and the confusion is complete.

Let us be unequivocal about marketing. Just like finance, or HR, or IT, it is a function, but described in terms of what it actually entails.

According to McDonald and Wilson (2003), marketing is a process for:

● Defining markets
● Quantifying the needs of the customer groups (segments) within these markets
● Putting together the value propositions to meet these needs, communicating these value propositions to all those people in the organization responsible for delivering them and getting their buy-in to their role
● Playing an appropriate part in delivering these value propositions (usually only communications)
● Monitoring the value actually delivered.

For this process to be effective, organizations need to be consumer/customer driven.

This is shown diagrammatically in Figure 1.8, which shows a consolidated summary of the marketing process.

In Figure 1.8, it can be seen that boxes 1 and 2 are clearly about strategy determination, whilst boxes 3 and 4 are about tactical implementation and measurement. It is these latter two that have come to represent marketing as a function, which is still principally seen as sales support and promotion. One of the authors recently drove through a new housing estate, where a neon sign above an up-market prefab blasted out the following words: 'The Marketing Suite'. This could be loosely translated as: 'Where you come to get sold to'. And when government bodies, charities and the like say: 'We need marketing', what they mostly mean is: 'We need some promotion'.

The way forward, then, is clear. Chief Executives must wrest the marketing community from where it currently is (sales support) and take marketing centre stage, with a major impact on corporate strategy development.

There is more than enough evidence that correct market definition, market segmentation and positioning is one of the fundamental determinants of corporate success. There is equally enough evidence that this is poorly understood in the corporate world at large. So, let us begin by looking in a little more detail at each of the boxes in Figure 1.8.

The process is clearly cyclical, in that monitoring the value delivered will update the organization's understanding of the value that is required by its customers. The cycle may be predominantly an annual one, with a marketing plan documenting the output from the 'understand value' and 'develop value proposition' processes, but equally changes throughout the year may involve fast iterations around the cycle to respond to particular opportunities or problems.

We have used the term 'determine value proposition' to make plain that we are here referring to the decision-making process of deciding what the offering to the customer is to be – what value the customer will receive and what value (typically the purchase price and ongoing revenues) the organization will receive in return. The process of delivering this value, such as by making and delivering a physical product or by delivering a service, is covered by 'deliver value proposition'.

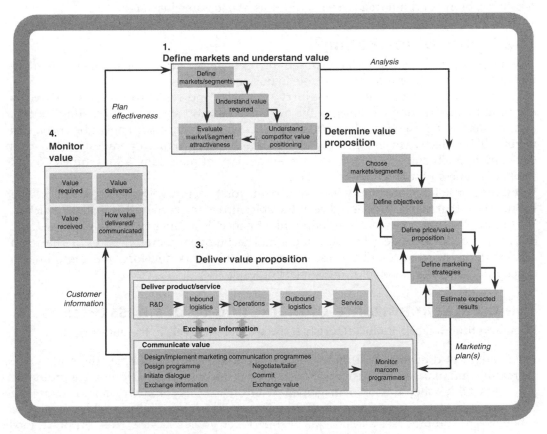

Figure 1.8 Summary of marketing map
Source: McDonald and Wilson (2002)

Thus, it can be seen that the first two boxes are concerned with strategic planning processes (in other words, developing market strategies), whilst the third and fourth boxes are concerned with the actual delivery in the market of what was planned and then measuring the effect. Throughout, we use the word 'proposition' to indicate the nature of the offer from the organization to the market.

It is well known that not all of the value proposition-delivering processes will be under the control of the marketing department, whose role varies considerably from organization to organization. The marketing department should be responsible for, and central to, the first two processes, 'understand value' and 'determine value proposition', although even these need to involve numerous functions, albeit coordinated by specialist marketing personnel. The 'deliver value' process is the role of the whole company, including for example product development, manufacturing, purchasing, sales promotion, direct mail, distribution, sales and customer service.

The various choices made during this marketing process are constrained and informed not just by the outside world, but also by the organization's asset base. Whereas an efficient new factory with much spare capacity might underpin a growth strategy in a particular market, a factory running at full capacity would cause more reflection on whether price should be used to control demand, unless the potential demand warranted further capital investment. As well as physical assets, choices may be influenced by financial, human resources, brand and information technology assets, to name just a few.

The failure of marketing?

This surge in customer power has exposed the irrelevance of traditional views of marketing and the gross ignorance about its role in business.

What is most worrying about the flurry of articles and reports in the last few years claiming that marketing has failed is the evident confusion about the marketing concept and the marketing function. The marketing function (or department) never has been and never will be effective in an organization with a technical, product, operations or financial orientation. Such enterprises adopted the vocabulary of marketing a long time ago and applied a veneer of marketing techniques.

But the marketing community itself is its own worst enemy, with its vapid, tear-jerking insinuations that marketing should be at the epicentre of the corporate universe, which is, of course, absolute nonsense. Marketing, like finance, is a functional discipline, with its own body of knowledge, processes, tools and techniques, represented by a chartered organization, which proscribes, researches, examines and develops the discipline in exactly the same way as other professional bodies do.

The pivotal importance of marketing to business leaders

For marketing to work, it must flourish at three different levels in the enterprise:

1 The board of directors must understand and enthusiastically embrace the notion that creating and maintaining customer satisfaction is the only route to long-term profitable success. Only when the top management team shares this common vision is there any chance of inculcating an organization-wide, market-driven culture where everyone believes in and practises the concepts of superior customer service. This corporate, top-down, driven vision can create significant and sustainable success, as companies like General Electric, 3M and Unilever have demonstrated.

2 The business strategies of the company must start with and be evaluated against the needs of the market. Unless marketing has a strategic input in order to ensure that the future of the company is planned from the marketplace inwards, then any subsequent marketing activity is likely to be unsuccessful.
3 Tactical marketing activities must be implemented within the context of the market-led strategies. They must meet high professional standards across the spectrum of functions, such as market research, product development, pricing, distribution, advertising, promotion and selling.

In summary, satisfying customers is not the concern of only the marketing department, but of the whole organization. However, given the challenges of market maturity, globalization and customer power, and given the almost total failure of total quality management, business process re-engineering, knowledge management, customer relationship management and other faddish outpourings from the world of corporate consultancy, the time has never been more ripe for professional marketing as a function to earn its spurs.

Marketing's role in value creation

There is one final, but crucial, piece of the jigsaw to put in place. Professor Keith Ward, one of the authors of this book, has stated publicly on many occasions that marketing can and should have a central role to play in creating sustainable competitive advantage:

'The overall purpose of strategic marketing, and its principal focus, is the identification and creation of sustainable competitive advantage.'

Figure 1.9 shows a typical array from any stock exchange of the relationship between risk and return, the diagonal line showing the capital market's required rate of return.

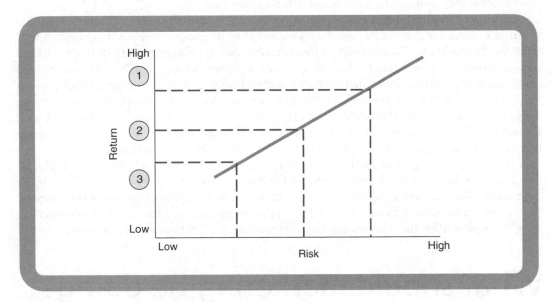

Figure 1.9   Financial risk and return
Source: McDonald and Wilson, 2002

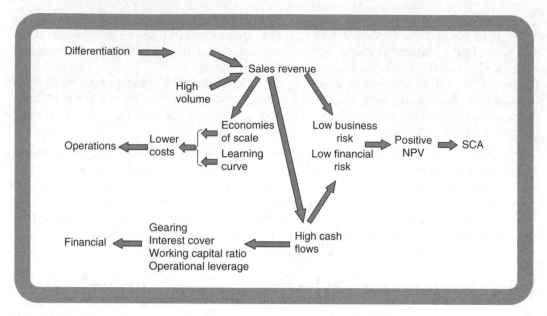

Figure 1.10   The route to sustainable competitive advantage (SCA)

Any firm positioned on the line will only be generating 'acceptable' returns for its share-holders, given its industry risk profile. In other words, such a company is producing returns equal to the shareholders' cost of capital. Firms consistently producing returns greater then the risk-adjusted cost of capital are creating real shareholder wealth, known gener-ally as shareholder value added, economic value added, positive net present value, super-profits, sustainable competitive advantage and so on. Figure 1.10 shows diagrammatically how sustainable competitive advantage can be achieved.

This idea of shareholder value, which is considered in more depth in Chapter 3, can be restated in terms of the future cash flows expected to be generated by a proposed invest-ment by the business. These expected future cash flows are discounted by the appropriate risk-adjusted required rate of return to generate a present value, which can be compared to the level of required investment. Shareholder value is generated when the net present value of the cash flows is positive. Hence expenditures to develop marketing assets make sense if the sum of the discounted cash flows they generate is positive. Also, it is well known that, whilst accountants do not measure intangible assets, the discrepancy between market and book values shows that investors do take them into account.

A little thought will indicate that every single corporate activity, whether it be R&D, IT, purchasing or logistics, is ultimately reflected in the relative value put on a firm's offer by its customers. The marketing function, as defined in Figure 1.11 (but particularly the strategic roles outlined in boxes 1 and 2), is central to this, as every aspect of the value proposition can only be improved by the whole organization focusing its attention on its customers.

What should marketing be doing?

The crux of the matter is failure to align marketing with the fundamental shareholder value objective. Marketing objective setting is, in practice, murky or, at worst, downright

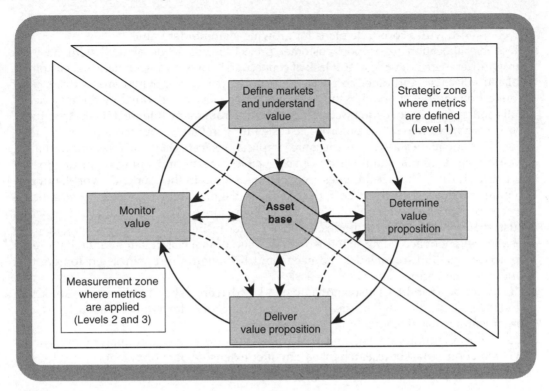

Figure 1.11   Map of the marketing domain

wrong. Increasing sales volume, the most widely cited marketing objective, can easily be achieved by sacrificing profitability, for instance. Increasing the coming year's profit, another commonly cited marketing objective, can also be attained in the short term by relinquishing investments for future growth.

Perhaps more worrying than comments about lack of alignment between marketing strategies and corporate objectives are charges of poor marketing professionalism. There is widespread evidence from research that very few marketing professionals actually understand or know how to use the widely available strategic analysis tools that would help them to dovetail their plans with what is going on in the wider marketplace, and elsewhere in their organizations.

There are numerous tried and tested tools that would be of immediate value in improving marketing's contribution to the main board agenda. For example:

- Financial rigour in appraising marketing objectives would be a useful start. Financial managers have used sophisticated discounted cash flow-based tools for many years to support investment appraisal and resource allocation. However, these methods are mainly applied to major capital projects and acquisitions. Although DCF is occasionally used to calculate brand valuations, it is not widely used to support marketing decision making.
- Marketing planning methods should be more strategic. Unfortunately, the annual budget cycle has a stranglehold over marketing objective setting. Studies of marketing planning processes reveal that less than 20% of marketing professionals use strategic

objective setting methods. Objectives are predominantly short term and have little connection with wider corporate plans for growing shareholder value.

- Resource allocation to support customer projects needs to be aligned with business growth. Yet there is a widespread lack of connection between value-enhancing, customer-related objectives and other corporate cost-cutting objectives. Symptoms of this lack of connection can be observed in the exceedingly poor service provided by the majority of call centres, and the inadequate customer response from many Internet business ventures, which are very often set up as corporate cost-cutting initiatives. Surprisingly few marketing plans adequately assess their resource implications (especially not cross-functionally).
- Market segmentation should be driven by customer needs and wants, according to best practice studies. These techniques are well understood in the academic world, but corporate practice still seems to be in the dark ages. Segmentation in practice is dominated by easily available demographic data, rather than more difficult to obtain data on actual customer behaviour and attitudes. In business-to-business marketing, managers most usually segment according to industry and occupational classification data that is easy to access and fail to consider the needs and behaviours of business customers that underlie true segmentation.
- Customer profitability is also known to be a key driver of shareholder value, according to academic studies. Again the state of marketing practice is poor. Remarkably few organizations use this vital tool.
- Customer retention analysis and root cause customer defection analysis are widely written about. Market research firms can offer extensive data on retention and loyalty. Once again, the take-up by practising managers is pitifully low.

The low value that marketing places on measurement is brought home when we look at what marketing spends on market research. Currently this stands at about 700 million euros annually in each of the major Western European economies. Compare this with the 70 billion euros that engineers spend on research. Or compare it with the 700 million euros spent recently by a single oil company on a new financial information system – the same figure that each Western European market spends on marketing information.

It is in response to the challenges outlined above that the authors have developed a process for appraising the main elements of marketing investments and for linking these investments to shareholder wealth. We have named this process 'Marketing Due Diligence' in order to indicate that marketing should be treated in exactly the same way as an organization's other major financial investments, with the board, through their marketers, held accountable for the investments made in building shareholder value.

Virtually no company would consider making a significant acquisition without going through a comprehensive, formal 'financial due diligence' process, which normally includes the use of outside expertise. Similarly, large organizations now have sophisticated internal audit departments and external audits, which are focused on assessing the risks faced by the business. Yet the greatest risks for most organizations lie in their largely poorly reviewed marketing strategies.

It is clear that the time has come for a similar process of due diligence to be initiated for marketing processes. This is the role of the Marketing Due Diligence process and the way that this works is explained in the next two chapters.

Before we go on to an explanation of the Marketing Due Diligence process, however, it is worth putting it in context. As already mentioned, there have been, for many years, approaches to measuring the effectiveness of marketing in its narrow, promotional, sense.

As useful as many of these approaches are, there is a risk of confusion between these measures of essentially tactical activity and Marketing Due Diligence, which assesses the effectiveness of marketing in terms of strategy and shareholder value. The final section of this chapter therefore puts Marketing Due Diligence in the context of these other approaches.

Marketing Due Diligence is different

Marketing Due Diligence is fundamentally different from all other methods of measuring marketing performance. The difference lies in the recognition that there are three distinct levels for measuring marketing effectiveness, as outlined below. Marketing Due Diligence, unlike other measures of marketing performance, measures specifically at the most fundamental strategic level rather than the tactical or promotional level.

Three distinct levels for measuring marketing effectiveness

When one of the authors was Marketing Director of a fast-moving consumer goods (FMCG) company, some 30 years ago, there were many well tried and tested models for measuring the effectiveness of marketing promotional expenditure. Indeed, some of these were quite sophisticated and included mathematical models for promotional campaigns, for advertising threshold and wear-out levels and the like. Readers seeking to know more about these might look at Lilien, Kotler and Moorthy's (1992) 800-page tome of dense mathematical models of marketing (i.e. promotional) effectiveness.

Indeed, it would be surprising if marketing as a discipline did not have its own quantitative models, given the massive promotional and other expenditure of FMCG companies. Over time, these models have been transferred to business-to-business and service companies, with the result that, today, any organization spending substantial sums of shareholders' money on promotion should be ashamed of themselves if those responsible could not account for the effectiveness of such expenditure.

But, at this level, accountability can only be measured in terms of the kinds of effects that promotional expenditure can achieve, such as awareness or attitude change, which can be attributed more or less directly to promotional activity.

But to assert that such expenditure can be measured directly in terms of sales or profits is the height of idiocy, when there are so many other variables that affect sales, such as product efficacy, packaging, price, the sales force, competitors and countless other variables that, like advertising, have an intermediate impact on sales and profits.

So, the problem with marketing accountability has never been how to measure the effectiveness of promotional expenditure; this we have had for many years. No, the problem occurs because marketing isn't just a promotional activity. In world-class organizations the customer is at the centre of the business model. And marketing as a discipline is responsible for defining and understanding markets, for segmenting these markets, for developing value propositions to meet the researched needs of the customers in the segments, for getting buy-in from all those in the organization responsible for delivering this value, for playing marketing's own part in delivering this value and for monitoring whether the promised value is being delivered.

Indeed, this definition of marketing as a function for strategy development as well as for tactical sales delivery, when represented as a map, can be used to clarify the whole problem of how to measure marketing effectiveness.

From this map (Figure 1.11), it can be seen that there are three levels of measurement, or metrics, each of which requires different methods and contributes different things to our understanding and measurement of marketing effectiveness.

Level 1 is the level at which Marketing Due Diligence operates. It is the most fundamental of the three levels, because this is what determines whether the marketing strategies for the longer term (usually three to five years) destroy or create shareholder value added. As Sean Kelly agrees:

> 'The customer is simply the fulcrum of the business and everything from production to supply chain, to finance, risk management, personnel management and product development, all adapt to and converge on the business value proposition that is projected to the customer.'
>
> (Kelly, S., *Customer Intelligence – From Data to Dialogue*, 2005)

Thus, corporate assets and their associated competences are only relevant if customer markets value them sufficiently highly that they lead to sustainable competitive advantage and hence shareholder value added. This is the justification for evaluating the strategic plan for what is to be sold, to whom and with what projected effect on profits, since this is the route to establishing whether shareholder value will be created or destroyed.

Level 3 is the level of micro-promotional measurement that is most commonly referred to as marketing effectiveness although, as argued above, it is really only concerned with the narrow and tactical linkages between promotional spend and the direct outcomes of that spend, such as awareness or trial.

Level 2 is another level of measuring marketing effectiveness that sits between Marketing Due Diligence and promotional effectiveness. It considers the complete range of tactical marketing activity (not just promotion) and assesses its impact on the competitive strength of the overall value proposition in the target segment. Hence it is narrower in scope than Marketing Due Diligence, but broader than promotional effectiveness, as shown in Table 1.7.

The understanding of how we assess different levels of marketing effectiveness also requires that we destroy once and for all one of the great myths of such measurement – marketing return on investment. To use such terms is to accept the implicit assumption that marketing expenditure can be simply and directly linked to sales and profits. The inaccuracy of such an assumption is neatly summed up in a *Harvard Business Review* article:

> 'Measuring marketing performance isn't like measuring factory output – a fact that many non-marketing executives don't grasp. In the controlled environment of a manufacturing plant, it's simple to account for what goes in one end and what comes out the other and then determine productivity. But the output of marketing can be measured only long after it has left the plant.'
>
> (McGovern G. J. et al., *Harvard Business Review*, November 2004)

Table 1.7 Scope and outputs of different levels of marketing effectiveness

Level of marketing effectiveness	Areas considered	Outputs
Level 1 Marketing Due Diligence	The marketing strategy (i.e. the choice of target customers and value propositions)	An objective assessment of whether or not the marketing strategy will create or destroy shareholder value, together with the identification of how the strategy may be improved
Level 2 Marketing effectiveness	The marketing tactics (i.e. the full range of products, pricing, promotion and channels) employed for each segment identified and targeted by the marketing strategy	The likelihood of the marketing tactics creating the necessary competitive advantage in each segment
Level 3 Promotional effectiveness	The marketing communications activity (i.e. advertising, sales team, etc.) employed to communicate with each target segment	The effectiveness of the marketing communications activity in achieving marketing communications objectives such as awareness, recall etc.

As we have discussed earlier in this chapter, CEOs need a way of holding marketing accountable, despite the obvious complexity of the process. At the lowest level of promotional effectiveness, tools for this have existed for decades. They can, however, only tell us about the effectiveness of promotional activity, which is far removed from understanding the effectiveness of the entire marketing process. It is perfectly possible to communicate effectively with the right customers and still fail to improve sales or profit. At the next level of assessing the degree to which the whole mix of tactics creates advantage, existing and new tools allow us to predict and measure the degree to which that mix creates customer preference and hence sales and profits. It is, however, perfectly possible to create sales and profits whilst destroying shareholder value.

What CEOs and the board need is a way of measuring the risk associated with a marketing strategy and hence its likely shareholder value creation. That is the aim of Marketing Due Diligence.

Chapter 2
A process of Marketing Due Diligence

Fast track

Despite what many non-marketers think, marketing is much more than just promotion. It is much more, even, than designing and delivering the 'marketing mix' of promotion, product, pricing, place (distribution), process, people and physical evidence. As discussed at the end of Chapter 1, methods for measuring the effectiveness of these more obvious marketing activities have been in place for years. Whilst these tactical measures have their place, they tell us little about the effectiveness of the marketing strategy, that part of the marketing process that concerns itself with understanding the market and deciding what parts of it to focus upon and with what value propositions. It is with this aspect of marketing that the Marketing Due Diligence process concerns itself.

Marketing, in this broad strategic sense, is closely correlated to shareholder value. It is the choice of which customer segments to focus upon and what to offer them that lies at the root of sustainable competitive advantage. Good choices create customer preference which, in turn, creates better return on investment. Looked at through the lens of business risk, as investors do, strong strategy reduces the risk associated with a promised return. To investors, it is the risk-adjusted rate of return that matters, and managing risk is as important as managing returns, sometimes more so.

The Marketing Due Diligence process involves both diagnostic and therapeutic stages. The first evaluates business risk and assesses whether the plan creates or destroys shareholder value. The second, building on the outcomes of the first, adapts the business plan to improve its risk profile and enhance shareholder value creation.

Marketing Due Diligence begins with explicating the strategy, which is often implicit and unclear even to those who need to implement it. This explication results in a clear definition of which customers are to be served and what products, services and overall value proposition are to be offered to them. This explicit strategy is then assessed for market risk, share risk and profit risk.

Market risk arises from the possibility that the market may not be as large as hoped for in the business plan. It is, to a large degree, a function of the novelty of the business plan. Strategies involving new customers and/or new products are more likely to have high market risk than those involving existing products and customers.

Share risk arises from the possibility that the plan may not deliver the hoped for market share. It is the corollary of the competitive strength of the strategy. Share risk is reduced when homogeneous segments are targeted with specifically tailored value propositions which leverage strengths, negate weaknesses, avoid direct competition and anticipate future trends.

Profit risk arises from the possibility that the plan may not deliver the intended profits. It is a function of the competitor reaction engendered by the plan and of the aggressiveness of cost assumptions.

Significant levels of market, share or profit risk, or some combination of the three, suggest that the returns delivered by the plan are likely to be less than promised. The final stage of shareholder value creation is therefore to calculate whether this risk-moderated return represents the creation or destruction of shareholder value. This involves calculating the full value of the assets put at risk, including intangibles. Only if the likely return is greater than the cost of this capital is shareholder value created. In addition to shareholder value creation or destruction, a third possible outcome of this diagnostic phase is that the plan is insufficiently thought out to enable a judgement to be made about its value-creating potential.

The Marketing Due Diligence therapeutic process uses the tools of strategic marketing management to manage and reduce the risk associated with the strategy. Using the results of the diagnostic stage to direct efforts, it suggests improvements to the marketing strategy. Hence the implications of using Marketing Due Diligence are to improve the marketing strategy in terms of its ability to create shareholder value.

What is marketing?

As Chapter 1 describes, both boards and investors need a better method of assessing the probability of business plans creating shareholder value. The financial due diligence process, for all its rigour and detail, only really considers the tangible aspects of a company's valuation. Current, fashionable methods of valuing intangibles, such as brand valuation techniques, are fundamentally flawed. They assess the value of the intangible in terms of what it might cost to replace, or against a hypothetical parallel company without that asset. However, these approaches do not allow for a fundamental truth in asset valuation: value flows from how the asset is utilized, not simply what it costs to make or replace. As a result, those current methods of valuing intangibles are necessary but not sufficient. What is really needed, to complement financial due diligence and to give boards and investors what they need, is a way of assessing the effectiveness with which assets and resources are applied to the market. Such a process could be accurately described as a process of Marketing Due Diligence. Executed correctly, with rigour and using well-founded methods, such a process will predict accurately the likelihood of a business plan delivering the shareholder value it promises.

For some, giving a process for evaluating business plans and shareholder value creation the name Marketing Due Diligence might seem incongruous. To many, the term 'marketing' is synonymous with its highly visible aspects of advertising, sales promotion and other activities that are more accurately termed marketing operations. If one holds this limited view of what marketing is, one can be forgiven for thinking that 'Marketing Due Diligence assesses the probability of creating shareholder value' is exaggerating the importance of marketing.

However, as outlined in Chapter 1, the wider and more accurate definition of marketing is that marketing has both strategic activities (understanding the markets, defining the target segments and the value propositions) and operational activities (delivering and monitoring value). These activities form a continuous process of marketing which draws on and contributes to the company's asset base, as shown in Figure 1.10 in Chapter 1. This continuous cycle of activity is the management process known correctly as marketing. It is the assessment of this process and its connection with shareholder value that is properly and accurately called Marketing Due Diligence.

What is the connection between marketing and shareholder value?

At the risk of being simplistic, the connection between marketing (in the broad strategic and not just marketing operations sense) and shareholder value is quite simple. Despite this, the number of companies that fail to understand the link is such that it bears a simple illustration here. In most commercial organizations, shareholders or other providers of funds (banks, venture capitalists, etc.) provide money with which to create assets. These assets, whether plant and buildings, patents, brands or something else, are then utilized in the market to create goods and services for a group of potential customers. The sale of these goods and services creates revenues which, once costs are subtracted, become profits or returns on the shareholders' original investment. The shareholders hope that this return is greater than that which might have been obtained by investing the same money in another investment of similar risk. If the investor suspects that the return will not be superior to the alternatives of similar risk, he or she is, within some practical constraints, at liberty to invest elsewhere. The aggregate decision of many investors determines the price of the company's shares. In this simplified world of capital economics, therefore, shareholder value, the combination of share price and dividends, is directly linked to the risk-adjusted rate of return achieved by the company. In the simple, and hypothetical, case of there being one company in each market and one type of customer in each market, shareholder value is simply a function of the operational efficiency with which the company uses its shareholders' funds.

In the real world, however, there are competitors and not all customers are the same. In real markets, being efficient is not enough. As Michael Porter famously said, operational efficiency is usually a necessary but insufficient condition for creating shareholder value and so strategic effectiveness becomes important. The importance of marketing strategy arises from the fact that, in anything but the most embryonic or regulated of markets, there are competitors and different types of customers. Together, the activity of competitors and the heterogeneity of the market mean that companies have to make decisions about how to focus their (that is, their shareholders') resources. Even the biggest and richest company does not have the resources to meet the needs of all customer types perfectly and profitably. If they attempt to do so, competitors who have focused on one part of the market have a local superiority of resources that allows them to create a stronger, more compelling and more attractive value offer to the customer. In a free market, customers choose whichever supplier provides the best value to them. For some customers, 'best value' might mean superior technical performance, for others high service levels, for others low cost. Whatever the customers' definition of value, it takes resources to create superior value to that being offered by the competition.

So, the critical implication of competitor activity and market heterogeneity is that companies must choose which customers to focus on. Think, for example, of the way in which business-type hotels, motel chains and small country hotels offer not just different value propositions, but also target different types of customer. Nor is marketing strategy simply a case of picking the most attractive market segment. Different companies have different distinctive capabilities, which may determine the best choice of segment. Consider, for instance, the different capabilities of Mercedes, Toyota and Ferrari, and what that implies for their choice of target customers and what value proposition to provide.

In most cases, the choice of which segments to target and what to offer them is a difficult one, requiring an understanding of the market opportunities and threats as well as the company's strengths and weaknesses. A poor choice leads to an inferior or merely adequate proposition to the customer and the concomitant lack of customer preference. Alternatively, making and implementing the right choice of target segments and value propositions results in customer preference and sustainable competitive advantage. Higher returns (from higher share, higher margin or both) follow from this customer preference and lead to superior shareholder value. As companies like Tesco, Dell and BMW have found, it is marketing strategy which drives shareholder value, even as operational efficiency and technical ability underpin it. This is the logic summarized in Figure 2.1.

This strong and direct connection between marketing strategy decisions and shareholder value lies at the root of Marketing Due Diligence. Half a century of research reveals

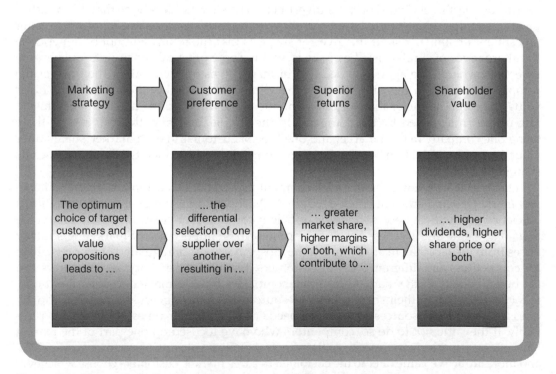

Figure 2.1 From marketing strategy to shareholder value

a remarkably clear correlation between certain characteristics of a marketing strategy and the shareholder value that flows from it. The lessons of this research, which transcends fads and bubbles, can be applied in two ways: first to find weaknesses in the strategy and then to cure those weaknesses. As described more fully in Part 2 of this book, Marketing Due Diligence is first a diagnostic process, resulting in an objective assessment of the shareholder value creation likely from a business plan. As with any good diagnostic process, however, it then becomes useful as a therapeutic aid, as described in Part 3 of this book, correcting those problems identified in the diagnostic phase.

Before describing the Marketing Due Diligence diagnostic and therapeutic processes in detail, however, this chapter gives an overview of the concepts underlying it. Chapter 3 then goes on to describe the implications of implementing Marketing Due Diligence.

What is the Marketing Due Diligence diagnostic process?

Before we consider what Marketing Due Diligence is, it is worthwhile considering at what level in the organization it is applied. Strategy (that is, resource allocation) decisions are made at all levels. At corporate level, these decisions involve which businesses to be in. At lower levels, smaller scale decisions are made about, for instance, single products in a certain country. Between these two extremes lies the Strategic Business Unit (SBU), a unit of the firm that is usually defined as having three distinct characteristics:

● It is fairly independent in its activities, which do not interact much with those of the rest of the firm
● It deals with a relatively self-contained market
● It is able to address the market on its own, without much direct support from the rest of the company.

Typical examples of an SBU include the therapy area of a pharmaceutical company, the PC division of an IT hardware company or the B2B (business-to-business) division of a telecoms company. SBUs should not be confused with the functional division of a firm, such as manufacturing or R&D, which could not meet the three criteria listed above.

It is at this SBU level that Marketing Due Diligence is applied. At organizational levels higher than the SBU (for instance, with the board of a multiple SBU business) Marketing Due Diligence can assess shareholder value creation by aggregating the results of each SBU. Below SBU level, the strategy decisions at product, channel or country level aggregate to determine the Marketing Due Diligence of the SBU. For the rest of this chapter, and indeed for the rest of the book, the descriptions of Marketing Due Diligence therefore refer to processes and analysis carried out at SBU level, rather than corporate or functional levels.

Marketing Due Diligence is a sophisticated process. It is not easily reduced to simple mnemonics and acronyms, a fact that reflects the complexity of the strategy/shareholder value linkage. However, the process can be understood by considering each layer of this complexity one step at a time. The first of these layers is to consider Marketing Due Diligence as consisting of a three-stage process, as shown in Figure 2.2. Stage One makes the marketing strategy explicit and so provides the input into Stage Two. In this second

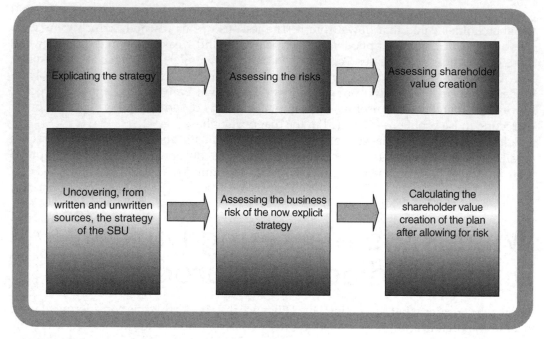

Figure 2.2 The outline process of Marketing Due Diligence

stage, the risks associated with the marketing strategy are thoroughly examined. In Stage Three, the risk evaluation is used to calculate whether or not the marketing strategy will create shareholder value.

Explicating the strategy

The first step of Marketing Due Diligence may seem superfluous. It is a reasonable, if ultimately false, assumption that the strategy of an SBU is laid out in its business plan. Certainly, the length and complexity of the typical annual planning cycle, together with the size of the resultant document, suggests that all that is needed here is to read the plan. In practice, this is not the case. Although all business plans contain the basic outline of the strategy, use of Marketing Due Diligence reveals that, in practice, most plans do not provide a full picture of the strategy.

The important detail of the strategy, which reveals its inherent risk, is more often held in a labyrinth of unwritten or informal forms. Sometimes these are easily accessible, such as supporting marketing research reports or product design documents. Often, however, they are held in the heads of the executives as implicit and unspoken strategy decisions that have important ramifications for the probability of the plan working. Obviously, to avoid a superficial and incorrect assessment, it is necessary to surface all of the strategy before assessing the risk. In doing so, however, we also realize one of the very important benefits of the Marketing Due Diligence process, which is additional to assessing shareholder value creation. In the act of explicating the strategy, the management team identifies the gaps, inconsistencies and errors that can result from even the most rigorous strategic planning process. This is a very valuable outcome of the process that occurs even before the risk assessment is begun.

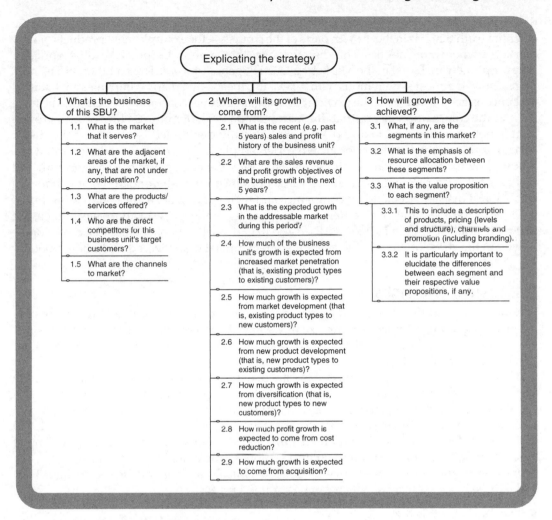

Figure 2.3   Questions to explicate the strategy

Uncovering the unwritten, often implicit, elements of the strategy requires that a structured set of questions are answered. In simple terms, these are:

- What is the business of this SBU?
- Where will its growth come from?
- How will it achieve that growth?

Usually, only a partial answer to these questions will emerge from a careful consideration of the written plan. To uncover the implicit strategy, a detailed set of questions, derived from the three basic questions, are needed. These are summarized in Figure 2.3, although an effective explication of the strategy may require some detailed and intelligent variations and extensions around these questions.

These questions, in addition to being a useful tool for explicating the strategy, reveal a fundamental aspect of the Marketing Due Diligence process. That is, the process looks especially hard at the growth elements of the strategy. Experienced managers will see in the questions their basis in the work of Igor Ansoff and his famous matrix. The focus on growth reflects the essential truth that it is in the growth parts of the strategy – for example, new products or new markets – where most risk lies. This discovery was the foremost lesson of Ansoff's work and is appropriately included in the Marketing Due Diligence process. The fact that, in business plans, 'new' is almost synonymous with 'risky' also means that many companies are habitual and unconscious risk takers. The expectations of shareholders constantly to outgrow the market and the competition means that, for many companies, submitting a low-or-zero growth plan is not an option, and taking risks is inadvertently demanded by investors. Let us be clear that this is not a criticism of growth-oriented plans, or a recommendation in favour of low growth, non-innovative, strategies. However, the correlation between growth and risk and between risk and shareholder value does mean that shareholders are making an implicit but insistent demand on companies and their boards: we want you to grow, but at the lowest risk possible. Such a demand requires that managers do all they can to ensure that their strategies minimize risk, as discussed in Part 3 of this book. Before that can be done, however, the risks inherent in the current strategy must be uncovered and understood.

Assessing the risks

Having explicated the strategy and made clear what the SBU is about, where it is looking for growth and how it intends to realize it, we have to assess objectively the business risk inherent in the strategy. Only then can we make a rigorous assessment of the shareholder value created by the plan.

At first sight, assessing the risks associated with any SBU's business plan seems an impossible task. If we think for a moment what could go wrong, then an endless risk of frightening possibilities opens up. There are innumerable things that could go wrong and all of them look unquantifiable and, therefore, practically useless. However, a more detached look at why some plans work and others fail enables a more practicable understanding of business risk, based on the fundamental assertions made in all business plans.

In essence, and at the highest level of detail, all business plans say the same thing. They make three basic assertions, which can be summed up as:

● The market is this big
● We're going to take this share of the market
● That share will make this much profit.

Each of these assertions carries a level of risk that it may be wrong. The market may not be as big as asserted, the plan may not deliver the share anticipated and the share may not deliver the profit. Each of the three assertions may fall short of its promise. Business risk is the combined risk of these three things, which can therefore be said to have three components:

● Market risk – the risk that the market may not be as big as promised in the plan
● Share risk – the risk that the strategy may not deliver the share promised in the plan
● Profit risk – the risk that the strategy may not deliver the margins promised in the plan.

It is worthwhile here to reflect for a moment on this three-part structure of business risk, because it is fundamental to the concept of Marketing Due Diligence. As simplistic as it appears, this structure captures all of the hundreds of possible reasons a business plan can fail to deliver its promises. Fickle customers, aggressive competition and flawed forecasts are all addressed within the three components of business risk. Thinking of risk assessment in these terms shifts the problem from one of complexity (have we counted all the risks?) to one of rigour (have we accurately assessed each of the three risks?). This problem of rigour is all the more challenging due to one of the practical requirements for Marketing Due Diligence. It is not enough to simply assess with rigour; it must be done using information that is practically accessible to the organization rather than requiring lots of new and difficult-to-access data. It is this challenge that is addressed in turn, in the following paragraphs, for each of the components of business risk.

Assessing market risk

If market risk is the probability that the market will not be as large as the business plan promises it to be, assessment of it depends on asking questions that inform an objective judgement of that probability. The research that underpins this book revealed that market risk was accurately quantified if five sub-components were assessed and combined into an aggregate value for market risk. These five sub-component risks are described in Table 2.1.

The five sub-components shown in Table 2.1 describe the contributing factors to market risk. How each of these is assessed and how they are combined into market risk is described in Chapter 4. For now, however, it is sufficient to understand what each of the sub-component risks represents and why they are an effective diagnostic for market risk. Each of the sub-components represents a set of assumptions that are built, implicitly or explicitly, into any strategy and business plan. Assumptions, to the extent that they are not completely tested, are sources of risk because they may prove ill-founded and erroneous. Together, the five sub-components represent all of the significant assumptions made and risks taken regarding market size. There will be, in some cases, overlap between the categories. This means not only that the five sub-components cannot simply be added, but also that no important assumptions or risks will be missed. Equally, the risk impact of each sub-assumption is not equally weighted and varies from case to case. These complicating factors mean, on one hand, that some qualitative judgement is needed but, on the other hand, that the assessment is comprehensive. The methodology described in Chapter 4 is designed to

Table 2.1 Sub-components of market risk

Sub-component of market risk	Explanation
Product category risk	This is the risk that the entire product category may be smaller than planned. It is higher if the product category is novel and lower if the product category is well established.
Market existence risk	This is the risk that the target segment may be smaller than planned. It is higher if it is a new segment and lower if the segment is well established.
Sales volumes risk	This is the risk that sales volumes will be lower than planned. It is higher if sales volumes are 'guessed' with little supporting evidence and lower if the sales volumes are well supported by evidence such as market research.
Forecast risk	This is the risk that the market will grow less quickly than planned. It is higher if forecast market growth exceeds historical trends and lower if it is in line with or below historical trends.
Pricing risk	This is the risk that the price levels in the market will be lower than planned. It is higher if pricing assumptions are optimistic and lower if they are conservative.

counter any error or bias in the qualitative judgement both by providing a graduated scale for each sub-component risk and by the cancelling out of errors in multiple judgements.

Assessing market risk accurately, therefore, requires careful questioning of the written and unwritten business plan, using the five-sub-component framework in Table 2.1 with rigorous graduated scales, as described in Chapter 4. However, as a general rule of thumb, we can observe that new products and new markets, poorly researched and aggressively forecast on price and volume, constitute high market risk. Existing products and mature markets, with extensive market research and conservative forecasts, have inherently less market risk. As discussed later in this chapter, our market risk assessment can be used to moderate the market size assertions in the business plan. The next task is to consider how great a share of that moderated market the strategy might win.

Assessing share risk

Whilst market risk is a function of both market choice and strategy design, share risk flows solely from the strategic decisions on which the plan is based. In short, share risk is the corollary of strategy strength. A strong strategy has a high probability of delivering the planned share, whilst a weak strategy has a high probability of failing to meet its promises. The challenge, therefore, is to understand what constitutes a strong strategy compared to a weak one. More particularly, a useful process must be able to make an objective judgement of strategy strength (and therefore share risk) independent of the SBU's market context. As with market risk, this appears initially to be an impossible task. How can one judge the strength of a strategy without a mountain of market-specific detail and without making lots of error-prone value judgements?

As with market risk, the research foundations of this book considered the issue of strategy strength and share risk. Again, a pattern of consistent factors emerged which clearly differentiated strong strategies from weak, risky strategies. This pattern revealed that the choice of target markets and value propositions can be objectively assessed against five criteria, again representing five sub-components of share risk. These are summarized in Table 2.2.

Whilst the detail of assessing and combining the sub-components of share risk are described later in this book, it is important at this stage to grasp what these different risks represent. Instead of assumptions leading to risk, as with market risk, these five factors represent error or wastage in allocation of resources so that the plan has an increased chance of failure. In short, a plan which targets a tightly defined segment, all of whom want the same thing, is more effective than one in which the target is a broader and necessarily heterogeneous group (e.g. ABC1 males or 'blue-chip companies'). Similarly, plans work when the customer is offered a tailored value proposition and fail with a 'one size fits all' approach. The rare exception to this rule is a situation in which one supplier has a quasi-monopolistic position, in which customers have little choice.

In the situations we more commonly face, then, the best plans understand and use internal strengths and weaknesses, and align them to market opportunities and threats. The worst plans ignore or neglect such 'SWOT alignment'. Low-risk strategies sidestep the competition and anticipate market changes. High-risk strategies go head-on and plan for yesterday's market. Although, as described later, there are other, minor factors contributing to share risk, these five factors are a functionally complete tool by which to assess whether or not the strategy will deliver the promised share.

As with assessing market risk, the sub-components of share risk overlap to some degree and vary in relative weighting between cases. Hence some judgement is still necessary in the assessment. However, the graduated scales for each sub-component and cancelling

Table 2.2 Sub-components of share risk

Sub-component of share risk	Explanation
Target market risk	This is the risk that the strategy will work only in a part, not all, of its target market. It is higher if the target market is defined in terms of heterogeneous customer classifications and is lower if it is defined in terms of homogeneous needs-based segments.
Proposition risk	This is the risk that the offer to the market will fail to appeal to some or all of the target market. It is higher if all the market is offered the same thing and lower if the proposition delivered to each segment is segment specific.
SWOT (Strengths, Weaknesses, Opportunities, Threats) risk	This is the risk that the strategy will fail because it does not leverage the company's strengths to market opportunities or guard its weaknesses against market threats. It is higher if the strategy ignores the firm's strengths and weaknesses and lower if the strengths and weaknesses of the organization are correctly assessed and leveraged by the strategy.
Uniqueness risk	This is the risk that the strategy will fail because it goes 'head-on' with the competition. It is higher if the choice of target market and value proposition are very similar to the competition and lower if they are very different.
Future risk	This is the risk that the strategy will fail because the market's needs have changed or will change in the time from strategy conception to execution. It is higher if the strategy ignores market trends and lower if it assesses and allows for them.

out effects of multiple errors mean that share risk can be judged accurately and comprehensively. An objectively moderated view of the probable share can then be combined with the expected market size to calculate the likely future revenue of the SBU. The next task is to see if that revenue will deliver the planned profit.

Assessing profit risk

Market risk flows from the strategic decision to allocate resources to a market and assumptions about that market. Share risk flows from strategic decisions about which customers within that market to target and what to offer them. Profit risk, however, arises from assumptions about the implementation of the strategy in the chosen market. In particular, profit risk arises from assumptions about competitor response and from planned versus actual costs and prices. Again, it initially presents as an insuperable task. How can we possibly predict, with any accuracy, what will happen during implementation, how the market will move and what the competition will do? Again, however, this seemingly impossible task is simplified and made practical by considering the implementation failures and successes of good and bad plans. By looking at the detail of why some strategies deliver their promised margins and others do not, we can discern five sub-components of profit risk. These can form the basis of a comprehensive and rigorous assessment of profit risk and are summarized in Table 2.3.

Table 2.3 Sub-components of profit risk

Sub-component of profit risk	Explanation
Profit pool risk	This is the risk that profit will be less than planned because of competitors' reaction to the strategy caused by a combination of the strategy and the market conditions. It is higher if the profit pool is static or shrinking and lower if the targeted profit pool is high and growing.
Profit sources risk	This is the risk that profit will be less than planned because of competitors' reaction to the strategy. It is higher if the profit growth comes at the expense of competitors, and lower if the profit growth comes only from growth in the profit pool.
Competitor impact risk	This is the risk that profit will be less than planned because of a single competitor reacting to the strategy. It is higher if the profit impact on competitors is concentrated on one powerful competitor and that impact threatens the competitor's survival. It is lower if the profit impact is relatively small, distributed across a number of competitors and has a non-survival threatening impact on each.
Internal gross margin risk	This is the risk that the internal gross margins will be lower than planned because the core costs of manufacturing the product or providing the service are higher than anticipated. It is higher if the internal gross margin assumptions are optimistic relative to current similar products and lower if they are relatively conservative.
Other costs risk	This is the risk that net margins will be lower than planned because other costs are higher than anticipated. It is higher if assumptions regarding other costs, including marketing support, are less than current costs and lower if those assumptions are more than current costs.

As with market risk, the sub-components of profit risk represent the risks that flow from the various assumptions built into the plan. Profit is threatened when assumptions about costs prove too optimistic, ignoring experience with other similar products, or those about prices prove naive, assuming benign and passive competitors.

As before, the five sub-components do overlap to some extent and their relative contribution to overall profit risk is different in different cases. However, the deconstruction of profit risk into the five sources allows a much better judgement of risk than if profit risk were assessed as a single entity. As a rule of thumb, implementation risk is lower when the profit pool in the market is large and growing quickly, when the strategy has little impact on competitors, and when assumptions about costs are realistic and supported by other similar activity. The risk of not delivering the promised margins is high when the total profit available in the market is small and shrinking, the strategy impacts heavily on a single powerful competitor and assumptions about costs are overly optimistic.

The assessment of business risk inherent in the strategy, as described above, is a complex and sophisticated part of the overall Marketing Due Diligence process. This is entirely appropriate and any simple approach to a subject as complex as the business risk of an SBU will inevitably be naive and misleading. In the Marketing Due Diligence risk assessment stage, a single, monolithic judgement about the chances of the plan succeeding is broken down into three separate judgements which are much more amenable to objective evaluation. These three are then further broken down into five sub-component risks, each of which can be measured on a graduated scale using objective and accessible data. The detail of this is described in Chapters 4–6, but for now it is sufficient to understand the final output of the risk assessment stage. Once market, share and profit risk assessments are completed, the result is a quantitative assessment, albeit based on careful, semi-qualitative judgements of each risk. It is these quantified judgements which form a well-founded basis for the third and final stage of the Marketing Due Diligence process, that of assessing shareholder value creation.

Assessing shareholder value creation

The notional SBU we have addressed so far has, in the course of its business plan, promised a certain turnover and a certain return on sales. Those returns imply a certain level of shareholder value created, dependent on the capital employed to create those sales. In the traditional capital market model, investors discount this value according to the probability of the promises being delivered. The investors' judgement is based on a number of factors, such as the macroeconomic environment, the health of the sector and historical performance. Each of these factors suffers from being both a lag indicator (that is, it indicates past, not necessarily future, performance) and a general indicator (that is, not being specific to the strategy of the SBU in question). The over- or undervaluation of many, if not most, companies is an indicator of the imperfect nature of this traditional approach to risk assessment. Such an imperfect, judgemental and weakly based method of valuing companies is unsatisfactory for both sides of the capital market. Boards complain that investors fail to appreciate the strategy and consequently undervalue the company. Investors accuse boards of over-promising and imperfect disclosure of key indicators and therefore discount share price valuations to protect themselves.

The Marketing Due Diligence process addresses both the lag indicator and generalization criticisms of traditional methods. It is fundamentally different from the traditional model, in that it considers the specifics of the company's strategy (not sector or macroeconomic effects) and the implications of that strategy for the creation of shareholder value in the future, rather than extrapolating the past.

The assessment of shareholder value creation in Marketing Due Diligence begins by allowing for sensitivity of the plan to business risk. Some strategies are more sensitive to risk than others and sensitivity to the three different components of business risk varies according to the internal and external context.

Strategies are sensitive to market risk (that is, they are vulnerable to poor assumptions about market size) if they involve fast growth and high market share. When the SBU's objectives have a large growth component (that is, a lot of the planned-for return is new business) and they already have a large market share, a smaller than predicted market will have a large impact on returns. Conversely, a business plan with a low growth component and which involves going from a very small share to only a slightly larger one is less sensitive to misjudgement about the size of the market. Simply put, a company trying to move from $2 million to $2.2 million in a multibillion dollar market is little affected by even a significant error in its estimate of market size. A company trying to move from $40 million to $50 million in an $80 million market is much more sensitive to market risk. This sensitivity to market risk is illustrated in Figure 2.4.

Strategies are sensitive to share risk (that is, they are vulnerable to weaknesses in their strategy) if they involve fast growth in the face of strong competition. Similar to market risk sensitivity, when the SBU's objectives have a large growth component in the face of

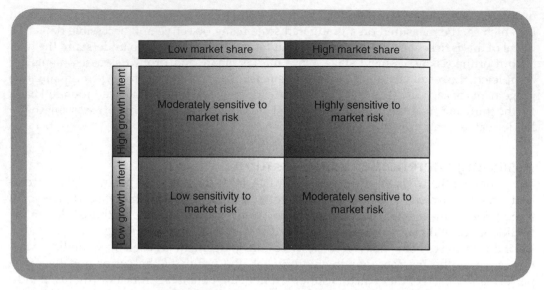

Figure 2.4 Sensitivity to market risk varies with growth intent and share position

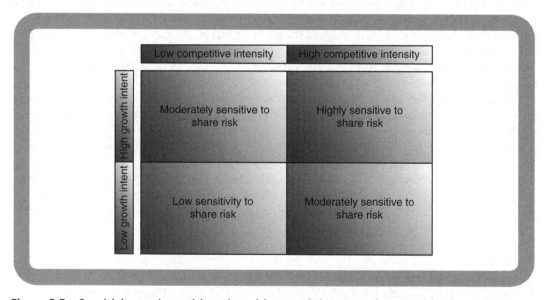

Figure 2.5 Sensitivity to share risk varies with growth intent and competitive intensity

large and effective competitors, a weak strategy will have a large impact on returns. Conversely, a business plan with a low growth component and which involves competing with small or weak competitors is less sensitive to a weak strategy. Simply put, a company trying to take a little share from much smaller and weaker competitors is less sensitive to weaknesses in its strategy. By contrast, a small, new entrant trying to make significant inroads into a market dominated by a strong incumbent is highly vulnerable to share risk. This sensitivity to share risk is shown in Figure 2.5.

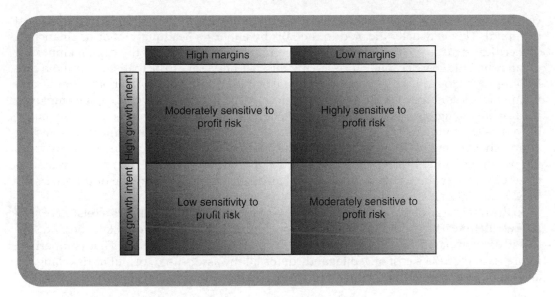

Figure 2.6   Sensitivity to profit risk varies with growth intent and margin

Strategies are sensitive to profit risk (that is, they are vulnerable to poor assumptions about price and cost) if they involve fast growth and operate on low margins. When the SBU's objectives have a large growth component and planned margins are low, a lower than planned margin will have a large impact on returns. Conversely, a business plan with a low growth component and which involves very high margins is less sensitive to a weak strategy. Simply put, an SBU trying to grow slowly and with 80% margins is less sensitive to a small fluctuation in its costs or prices. By contrast, an SBU planning to grow quickly with margins of less than 10% is very susceptible to even small fluctuations in costs, prices or both. This sensitivity to profit risk is shown in Figure 2.6.

Using these differing sensitivities to the various components of business risk, the Marketing Due Diligence process then considers the market size, market share and profit assertions in the plan and moderates them in the light of the assessed risk and sensitivity. Hence market size is adjusted or confirmed depending on the level of market risk, share for share risk and profit for profit risk. This adjustment is not a simplistic, linear, change in line with the value of the risk assessment and the sensitivity. Typically, small levels of risk result in little or no adjustment. At the other extreme, very large levels of risk mean that the strategy is so unsound that, frankly, the probability of achieving the growth component of the plan is unknowable, rather than simply low. More usually, moderate levels of risk imply significant changes in the growth assertions. In any case, the non-growth, historical trend of the business is largely unaffected by the risk.

Obviously, the adjustments are cumulative. An adjusted profit assertion is built on an adjusted share, which is built on an adjusted market size. Taken together, the end result is a revised profit figure for the returns reasonably expected from the plan. This figure represents the original assertion reduced, confirmed or, rarely, increased after allowing for the risk associated with the plan.

The next step in assessing whether or not the SBU's strategy delivers shareholder value is to compare the revised or confirmed profit figure with that which would represent the cost of capital. Marketing Due Diligence does not attempt to suggest an appropriate cost of capital. This is usually dictated to the SBU by either its headquarters or its financiers. The critical issue is whether the profit figure represents a return on the capital employed greater than the cost of capital. In assessing this, it is necessary to be realistic about the capital employed to realize the profits. In particular, it is important to count both tangible and intangible assets employed. It is easy, for instance, to make a high return on capital employed if valuable intangibles such as brands or intellectual property are ignored and only tangible assets are counted. This is typically the case when an SBU uses an umbrella branding approach. In doing so, it 'uses' the asset of the brand which has been created by many years of investment. If the strategy fails, that brand value, or part of it, is at risk. Accurate assessment of return on investment should count all assets employed, tangible or otherwise, as they are all 'at risk' in the investment.

So the final stage of this diagnostic phase of Marketing Due Diligence is a relatively simple calculation. The profit figure, adjusted or confirmed in the light of risk levels and sensitivity, is compared to what is necessary to create shareholder value. That comparison figure uses the SBU's cost of capital and counts all the assets used, or put at risk, tangible and otherwise. This simple comparison results in one of two conclusions:

● The profit generated by the SBU's business plan, when assessed for and adjusted for all three areas of business risk, exceeds the cost of capital. The strategy is likely to create shareholder value.

● The profit generated by the SBU's business plan, when assessed for and adjusted for all three areas of business risk, falls short of the cost of capital. The strategy is unlikely to create shareholder value.

Whichever of these statements is appropriate is the output of the diagnostic phase of the Marketing Due Diligence process.

There is a third outcome of the process that is actually more common than either the positive or negative results. This is the result when one or more of the 15 tests applied during Marketing Due Diligence cannot be answered. It is not uncommon for SBUs not to know (that is, not to have considered) issues such as the existence of segments, SWOT alignment or the impact on competitors. In those circumstances, the only possible statement is that, on the basis of what is known from the written and unwritten strategy, the shareholder value creation of the SBU cannot be verified. To a large degree, this common result is worse than a negative result, in that it demands not just improvements in the strategy but a more thorough understanding of the SBU's strategic position.

As useful as these statements of Marketing Due Diligence (positive, negative or unknown) are, they represent only the first practical outputs of the diagnostic stage of the process. Just as important, and arguably more valuable, is the way that the results of the diagnostic process inform the second, therapeutic part of Marketing Due Diligence. This is discussed in the next section.

What is the Marketing Due Diligence therapeutic process?

Marketing Due Diligence is an appropriate name for the process described in this book for two reasons. Firstly, it relates to marketing, albeit in its broader definition rather than in its purely marketing operations sense. Secondly, it does reflect the diligence that is due if we are to manage large amounts of other people's money, as directors of both public and private companies inevitably do. These two characteristics are in marked contrast to other processes that seek to address marketing effectiveness or shareholder value creation. In its scope (strategy, not just operations) and rigour (specific and future oriented, not generalized lag indicators), Marketing Due Diligence is a much more challenging test of a business plan than other approaches. This rigour of this challenge means that few firms emerge from the process without revealing some weakness in the plan. Commonly, the diagnostic phase of the process reveals either a higher than desired risk or, perhaps worse, a totally unconsidered set of risks, from one, two or all three of the sources of business risk. However, as is ideal in a diagnostic process, Marketing Due Diligence does not just identify those risks but, in the detail of the sub-components, provides clear guidance about how to quantify and reduce those risks. More detail about the therapeutic stage of Marketing Due Diligence is provided in Chapters 7–9 but, for now, it is sufficient merely to grasp the principles.

Market risk arises primarily from the strategic decision to attack a certain market. As already discussed, high market risk is usually the consequence of launching new products or services, entering new markets or both. Such a strategy is obviously more risky than staying in the existing market, but is often the inevitable corollary of seeking growth when already in a dominant position in a mature market. Given this inevitability of increased market risk, the challenge is to ensure that it is minimized. The most common way to reduce market risk is to gather more information about the market and thereby reduce the number of risk-creating assumptions. The detail of the Marketing Due Diligence diagnostics enables managers to focus their information gathering on that which best reduces risk, an important factor given the costs in time and money of gathering market data. Typical steps to reduce the different sources of market risk are summarized in Table 2.4.

As already discussed, share risk arises primarily from weaknesses in those strategic decisions about which customers to focus upon in a particular market and what value

Table 2.4 Typical steps to reduce market risk

Source of increased market risk	Typical steps to reduce that risk
Product category risk	This can be reduced by targeting another, more established product category within the market or by making good use of whatever data does exist about this product category.
Market existence risk	This can be reduced by targeting another, more established segment within the market or by making good use of whatever data does exist about the use of other products by the same segment.
Sales volumes risk	This can be reduced by either reducing the targeted sales volumes or if the sales volume targets are well supported by relevant and valid market research data.
Forecast risk	This can be reduced by either reducing the forecast increase to at or below historical levels or by gathering relevant and valid market research data to support the forecast.
Pricing risk	This can be reduced by either reducing the planned pricing levels or by gathering relevant and valid market research data to support the forecast.

Table 2.5 Typical steps to reduce share risk

Source of increased share risk	Typical steps to reduce that risk
Target market risk	This can be reduced by research to elucidate the needs-based segmentation of the market and portfolio management techniques such as directional policy matrix to enable better targeting.
Proposition risk	This is reduced by use of the segmentation and targeting decisions to better inform and design an extended value proposition, typically summarized as the 7Ps (product, pricing, promotion, place, process, people and physical evidence).
SWOT (Strengths, Weaknesses, Opportunities, Threats) risk	This is reduced by careful analysis of internal strengths and weaknesses and external threats and opportunities using a range of strategic management tools and techniques. The outputs of these techniques are then aligned using SWOT analysis.
Uniqueness risk	This is reduced by targeting different segments and offering different value propositions, compared to the competition. Usefully, this often flows as a side-effect of correct segmentation, proposition design and SWOT alignment.
Future risk	This is reduced by identifying relevant macroenvironmental factors and drawing out their implications for the SBU. This is typically done using a technique such as SLEPT analysis.

proposition to offer them. In other words, weaknesses in the marketing strategy-making process make it less likely that the strategy will achieve its planned share of the market, especially in the face of intense competition. The fact that most markets are increasing in their competitive intensity means that the challenge is to optimize strategy strength and therefore reduce share risk. From the detailed consideration of successful and unsuccessful marketing strategies, it is clear that the essence of reduced share risk is effective segmentation, targeting and positioning. The detail of the Marketing Due Diligence diagnostics enables managers to identify weaknesses in how they have attempted these critical marketing tasks and thereby directs their corrective action. Typical steps to reduce the different sources of share risk are summarized in Table 2.5.

The third area of business risk, profit risk, derives from assumptions about costs, prices and competitive response. In practice, profit risk is increased by over-optimism and naivety, sometimes compounded by political pressures during the plan approval process. The difficulty of making accurate assumptions about margins and competitor reactions makes it all the more necessary to minimize profit risk and is not an excuse to neglect the task. Fortunately, a study of how successful and unsuccessful marketing strategy implementations contrast with each other guides the steps needed to reduce profit risk. The detail of the Marketing Due Diligence diagnostics enables managers to identify when cost estimates are optimistic, price estimates are naive and competitive response likely to be strong. This leads to the typical steps to reduce the different sources of profit risk summarized in Table 2.6.

Hence, as summarized in these three tables, the therapeutic stage of Marketing Due Diligence flows as a natural consequence of the diagnostic process. The outcome is a strategy and business plan for the SBU that is stronger and much more likely to succeed than prior to the detailed examination of the strategy.

Table 2.6 Typical steps to reduce profit risk

Source of increased profit risk	Typical steps to reduce that risk
Profit pool risk	This can be better understood by assessing the total profit pool in the market and its trends. It can only be reduced by changing the target market to one which has a larger and growing profit pool.
Profit sources risk	This can be better understood by assessing in some detail sources of profit growth. It can be reduced by changing the detail of the strategy implementation to increase the proportion of the profit that comes from growth in the profit pool and reduce that which comes at the expense of competitors.
Competitor impact risk	This can be better understood by assessing in some detail the impact of the strategy on competitors. It can be reduced by changing the detail of the strategy implementation to spread the competitive impact across competitors and towards smaller, less powerful rivals.
Internal gross margin risk	This can be better understood by realistic assessment of the core costs of the product or service, including comparison with similar lines. It can be reduced by increasing the cost estimates in line with that assessment.
Other costs risk	This can be better understood by realistic assessment of the other costs of the product or service, including selling costs. It can be reduced by increasing the cost estimates in line with that assessment.

Implications of the Marketing Due Diligence process

At a fundamental level, Marketing Due Diligence is very simple. Whilst it will never be possible to eliminate business risk entirely, it is possible to reduce it to a practical minimum. In doing so, what risk remains is identified, located and, most importantly, understood. To achieve this, the process does not take a naive, simplistic approach. Instead, it uses the results of many years of research in which business successes and failures are examined. Just like looking at the black box of many crashed aircraft, this allows us first to group the reasons for failure, then to suggest ways to avoid it. In that sense, Marketing Due Diligence can be considered as analogous to pre-flight checks, with the same implications for the reliability and success of the business plan.

When, in time, Marketing Due Diligence becomes a routine process for assessing the strategic decisions of company directors, the flaws it detects and the challenges it throws up may be fewer and more routine. In the meantime, however, application of Marketing Due Diligence will have many important implications for the board. These are discussed in Chapter 3.

Chapter 3
The implications of implementing Marketing Due Diligence

Fast track

The key objective of the Marketing Due Diligence process is to link marketing strategies directly to the creation or destruction of shareholder value. This requires an assessment of the particular risks associated with any proposed marketing strategy, as risk and the corresponding required rate of return are directly linked.

Unfortunately the normal financial focus of marketing strategies and plans is on predicting outcomes, not assessing the associated risks. These potential financial outcomes are often presented as single-point, apparent certainties rather than being expressed as a range of the possible outcomes that may result, given the volatility of future business environments.

Where risk is taken into consideration, this is normally done by altering the discount rate that is applied to the predicted future cash flows; thus, higher risk strategies have a higher discount rate applied to all these cash flows. This can give a false result particularly, as is the case for many marketing strategies, where the strategy depends on the successful completion of a sequence of individually somewhat risky activities, such as are involved in the development and launch of a new product or the entry into a new market.

The Marketing Due Diligence process looks at the specific risks associated with each element of the marketing strategy, so that individual probability assessments of success/failure and the consequent impact on financial outcomes are identified. This enables these predicted financial outcomes to be directly adjusted, where necessary, in the light of identified risks. The level of any adjustment that is required clearly depends on how the forecasts were originally prepared. Thus, plans that include extremely optimistic stretch targets ('best case' plans) will normally need more adjustment than more conservative plans that already allow for expected risks and consequent volatility in financial returns ('most likely' plans).

In order to produce a shareholder value 'figure' from the Marketing Due Diligence diagnostic process, this probability adjusted set of expected future cash flows is then compared to the financial return required by the business. This is done by assessing the true capital tied up in implementing the proposed marketing strategy. The true capital includes the critically important, and often highly valuable, intangible marketing assets as well as the more obvious tangible assets of the business.

As the specific risks of the proposed marketing strategy have already been taken into account in the diagnostic review, the return required on this capital employed can be calculated by reference to the company's normal cost of capital. In other words, there is no need arbitrarily to increase the required rate of return to try to take account of the complex myriad of risk factors.

There can be one additional adjustment to the predicted financial return if the proposed marketing strategy places any existing assets at risk. This concept of 'capital at risk' is used to highlight strategies that leverage off existing marketing assets, such as umbrella branding. Often, this is done to reduce the required marketing expenditure, but the expected financial returns do not normally include the potentially offsetting decrease in value of the existing asset, if the strategy is not completely successful. This adjustment is made as part of the full Marketing Due Diligence review.

Even if the existing marketing planning information is not sufficient to enable a numerical value to be calculated, the Marketing Due Diligence diagnostic process will still highlight the key risk areas of any proposed strategy and show up the specific deficiencies in the current marketing plan. In many cases these deficiencies can be remedied by applying the therapeutic process within Marketing Due Diligence, which reviews and improves the marketing planning process.

The application of Marketing Due Diligence clearly has significant implications for both internal and external stakeholders in any business. The rigorous review of proposed marketing strategies should be a key element in any sound corporate governance process. Marketing Due Diligence provides a methodology to do this consistently across even a diversified group and through time. Indeed, the knowledge that all marketing plans and strategies will be subjected to this type of analysis will rapidly improve the quality of the processes used internally within the marketing function.

Thus, the critical resource allocation decisions at board level should be based on much better and more validly comparative information. Knowing this should provide great reassurance to external analysts and shareholders, as they can be more confident that future marketing strategies will be shareholder value enhancing.

The linkage to shareholder value

The most common financial objective of modern commercial corporations is the sustainable creation of shareholder value. This can only be achieved by providing shareholders with a total return, from capital growth and dividend yield, that exceeds their risk-adjusted required rate of return for this particular investment, as was discussed in Chapter 1. However, for most companies, the current share price already reflects some expected future growth in profits. Thus, these current investors and, even more particularly, potential future shareholders are trying to assess whether the proposed business strategies of the company will produce sufficient growth in sales revenues and profits, both to support the current share price and existing dividend payments, and to drive the capital growth that they want to see in the future. At the same time, these external stakeholders also need a method of assessing the risks associated with these proposed strategies as, obviously, the associated risks have a direct link to their required rate of return.

As already stated, in today's highly competitive environment, the major sources of share-holder value creation are the intangible marketing assets of the business, such as brands, customer relationships and channels of distribution (the 80% of the company's value that does not appear on the traditional balance sheet). Consequently, the critical future marketing strategies of a company, which indicate how these assets are to be developed, maintained and exploited, should be subjected to a rigorous review process. Unfortunately, not only is such focused forward-looking information still normally absent from the externally available data produced by companies, but also, even more worryingly, there is often not even a rigorous internal evaluation of the shareholder value impact of such proposed marketing strategies. Yet these same companies would undoubtedly have formally constituted, board-level audit committees that are responsible for reviewing all the major business risks that they face. Also, they would all conduct comprehensive financial due diligence processes on any major acquisitions or strategic investments.

Indeed, in recent years, the financial appraisal processes applied to major strategic investments have become increasingly sophisticated. The normal discounted cash flow techniques are now supplemented by the use of probability assessments, simulation techniques and even real option analysis. The one major area that has most commonly been excluded from this approach has been the marketing strategy of the business. Obviously, the objective of the Marketing Due Diligence process is to address this significant deficiency, but there are several significant implications of applying such a rigorous evaluation process to most existing marketing strategies.

The risk and return relationship

As set out in Chapter 2, the Marketing Due Diligence process subjects any proposed marketing strategy to a structured, sequential process that will indicate the probability of such a marketing strategy leading to increased shareholder value. The whole basis of shareholder value is the direct linking of the level of risk to the level of financial return that is required. Indeed, as shown in Figure 3.1, the causality relationship is that the 'perceived risk profile of the investment' drives the 'level of return required by investors in this particular investment'.

The two axes are deliberately labelled 'perceived risk' and 'required return': the return required by investors is driven by the risks they perceive in the investment. If risk perceptions are so important to the creation of shareholder value, by delivering total returns that exceed this risk-adjusted required rate of return, there is clearly a need for a definition of risk from the perspective of any investor. Risk is created by volatility in future expected returns. In Figure 3.1, a minimum positive required rate of return is shown where the risk/return line cuts the vertical axis. This minimum required rate of return carries a zero-risk perception, which means guaranteed, certain future returns. For investors in stable economies this normally means government guaranteed borrowings (e.g. US Treasury Bills, UK Government Gilts, European Central Bank Debt). At the time of writing, the returns on these investments are low, but they are still seen as risk free due to their lack of volatility; the interest on our US Treasury Bill may be low, but we are certain of what we will get and when it will arrive.

Logically, therefore, a normal, rational, risk-averse investor requires an increase in the expected future return from any more risky investment in order to compensate for any potential volatility. Thus, the cause and effect relationship is as shown diagrammatically

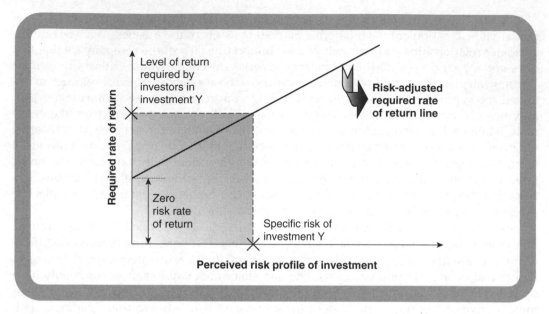

Figure 3.1   Risk-adjusted required rate of return

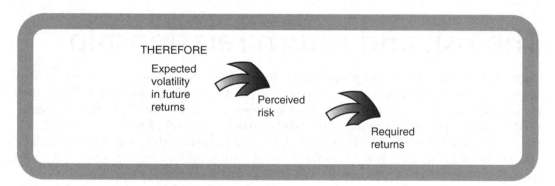

Figure 3.2   Risk and return

in Figure 3.2; any expected volatility in future returns creates an increased perceived risk profile in investors that increases their required rate of return.

Of course, investors know in advance of making their investment in most government-backed debt investments (Gilts, Treasury Bonds, National Savings Certificates, etc.) exactly what their return will be (i.e. the interest rate payable is stated on the debt offering). This is clearly not the case with most equity (i.e. stocks and shares in companies) investments, and this lack of certainty increases risk perceptions and hence required rates of return. Further, if the historical track record of a company's shares shows significant volatility in share prices and even dividend payments, investors will require much higher returns from the company, as they will extrapolate this past performance as their best guide to the future performance of the company's shares.

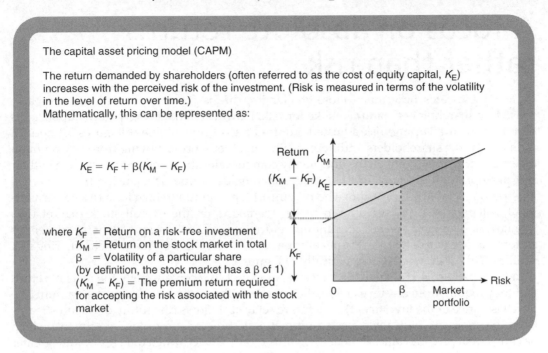

The capital asset pricing model (CAPM)

The return demanded by shareholders (often referred to as the cost of equity capital, K_E) increases with the perceived risk of the investment. (Risk is measured in terms of the volatility in the level of return over time.)
Mathematically, this can be represented as:

$$K_E = K_F + \beta(K_M - K_F)$$

where K_F = Return on a risk-free investment
K_M = Return on the stock market in total
β = Volatility of a particular share
(by definition, the stock market has a β of 1)
$(K_M - K_F)$ = The premium return required for accepting the risk associated with the stock market

Figure 3.3   Risk and return – the financial markets formula

Table 3.1 Relative costs of capital (i.e. required rates of return)

Base assumptions
K_F = Return on a risk-free investment = 4% p.a.
$(K_M - K_F)$ = Equity market premium = 5% p.a.
Share A β = 1.5
Share B β = 0.8
Using CAPM, i.e. $K_E = K_F + \beta(K_M - K_F)$
For share A, K_E = 4% + 1.5(5%) = 11.5%
For share B, K_E = 4% + 0.8(5%) = 8%

Financial markets use various models to estimate the relative volatility of different industrial sectors and of the companies within each sector. The main formula is derived from the simple risk/return line and is known as the capital asset pricing model (CAPM). This is shown in Figure 3.3.

The CAPM derives the beta factor for each company by calculating the correlation of the company's historic volatility with that of the stock market as a whole. If the stock market rises or falls by 5% and share A moves by 7.5% but share B only moves by 4%, then share A is relatively more volatile than share B; arithmetically, share A has a beta factor of 1.5 while share B has a beta factor of only 0.8. This means that the required return (K_E) for share A will be significantly higher than for share B. A numerical illustration of this is given in Table 3.1.

A focus on absolute returns rather than risk

Table 3.1 indicates how much more challenging life is for a highly volatile company, caused by shareholders' natural dislike for risk. However, what is even more important is that the upward sloping 'risk-adjusted required rate of return' line of Figures 3.1 and 3.3 is, in reality, the shareholders' indifference line. In other words, moving from any point on the line to any other point on the line merely compensates the investor for a change in their risk perception; it does not, of itself, create shareholder value. Thus, using the numerical illustration of Table 3.1, investors who require a 4% per annum return for a risk-free investment will require a 9% per annum return for taking on the overall stock market risk. Similarly, they regard an 11.5% per annum return from share A as equivalent to (i.e. neither better than nor worse than) an 8% per annum return from share B, due to their differing risk profiles. This is shown diagrammatically in Figure 3.4.

In financial terms, if shareholders receive, or expect to receive, exactly the level of return that they require from any investment, they have simply swapped a present capital sum (the purchase price of the investment) for a future set of cash flows (the future dividend streams from the company plus any expected ultimate sale proceeds from the investment) which have an equal present value. Shareholder value is only created when total returns are greater than the risk-adjusted required rate of return. Thus, a company can achieve growing profits over time without creating shareholder value, if the associated risk profile is also increasing. Hence we prefer the term 'super-profits' to describe shareholder value-enhancing levels of profit. A super-profit represents the excess rate of return over the required rate of return.

Unfortunately, the normal focus of marketing strategies and plans is on predicting absolute financial outcomes, rather than placing these expected outcomes in the context

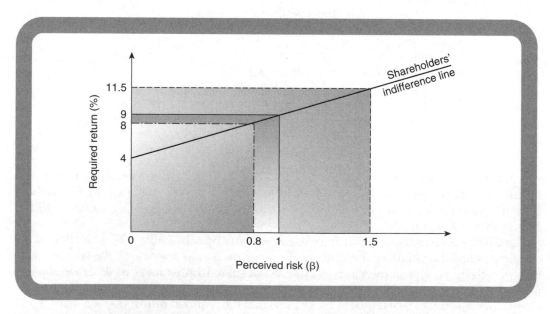

Figure 3.4   Risk-adjusted required rate of return as shareholders' indifference line

of the required rate of return. There is an implicit assumption in most marketing plans that the risk profile will be unchanged due to the implementation of new strategies, such as launching new products or entering new market segments. One of the key objectives of the Marketing Due Diligence process is to make these critical assumptions about the risk associated with proposed marketing strategies explicit, so that they can be analysed rigorously. Alternative new strategies can have significantly different impacts on risk, which will change their potential for creating shareholder value. This is shown diagrammatically in Figure 3.5.

Most marketing strategies are aimed at generating growth in sales revenues and profits but, as we discussed in Chapter 2, for many mature products and markets, such strategies increase the risk profile of the business; indeed, the word 'growth' can normally be taken to indicate a risk-increasing strategy. This does not automatically mean that these strategies cannot be shareholder value enhancing, but it does mean, as can be seen from directions A and B in Figure 3.5, that the return from the more risky strategy must increase proportionately more than does the risk profile of the company. (Remember that merely moving along the shareholders' indifference line does not create shareholder value; this is only achieved by moving to a position above the line.)

More interestingly, direction C in Figure 3.5 highlights another type of shareholder value-enhancing strategy that is often ignored in marketing plans. A reduction from the current risk profile of the business (diagrammatically shown as a move to the left) means that shareholder value can be created even if the rate of return is reduced slightly. This time, the reduction in return must be proportionately less than the reduction in the risk profile. Since risk is associated with volatility in returns, this means that marketing strategies that make the future returns more stable and predictable can be shareholder value

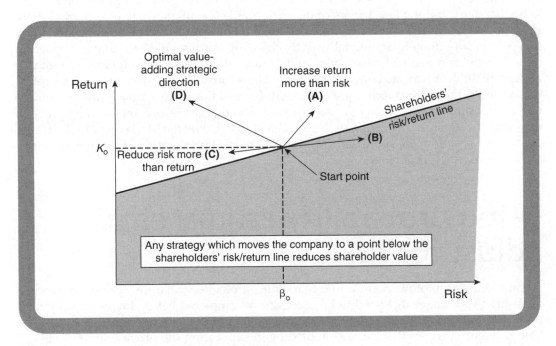

Figure 3.5 Shareholder value-adding strategies

enhancing, even if these less volatile future returns are slightly reduced. Thus, marketing strategies designed to increase customer loyalty through long-term discounts etc. can, if properly designed, be shareholder value enhancing, even though the discounts given actually reduce profit levels.

Obviously, the optimal marketing strategy seeks to increase returns while reducing the associated risk levels (i.e. the volatility of these increased returns), direction D of Figure 3.5. Any such strategy must leverage some already established, sustainable competitive advantages, or first seek to develop a new sustainable competitive advantage. As clearly stated in Chapter 1, the overall purpose and focus of strategic marketing is the identification and creation of such sustainable competitive advantages. This is why the detailed analysis of marketing strategies is the focus of the Marketing Due Diligence process.

However, as well as needing to put the predicted absolute financial outcomes of marketing strategies into an appropriate relative framework, there are other problems with the current methods of financially appraising marketing plans. Most financial outcomes of marketing strategies are presented as single values, e.g. the expected profits and cash flows for the next three or five years. These single-value outcomes are self-evidently calculated as some expected value from the wide range of potential outcomes that could be achieved if the plan is implemented. Different planning processes and organizational cultures mean that these single-point financial results can be more or less aggressive or optimistic; this is considered in depth later in this chapter. The potential range of outcomes is, of course, a good indicator of the volatility of the proposed marketing strategies and therefore of its associated risk profile. Therefore, the inputs to the Marketing Due Diligence analysis should incorporate the range of potential outcomes, before they have been subjected to any averaging or best estimate process.

Gaining an understanding of the distribution of potential financial outcomes (i.e. their range and relative probabilities) is critical to really appreciating the risk profile of the marketing strategy and the key drivers of that risk profile (i.e. market size risk, market share risk and/or profit risk). Where risk is considered in the appraisal of marketing strategies, this is normally done in an overall way by changing the discount rate that is applied to the predicted future cash flows. Thus, 'higher risk' strategies have a higher discount rate applied to all their expected future cash flows. Unfortunately, this turns the highly sophisticated financial analysis technique of discounted cash flow into a very blunt instrument that cannot differentiate among the vast array of risks that can impact on the value creation potential of alternative marketing strategies. Our objective with the Marketing Due Diligence process is to assist in the appraisal and control of marketing strategies, by using appropriately tailored analytical tools.

Using probability estimates to adjust for risk

A common feature of many proposed marketing strategies is that they consist of several, quite-high-risk stages that need to be successfully completed before the potentially high financial returns can be realized. This introduces another challenge into the Marketing Due Diligence process that can be handled by incorporating the probability estimates of success/failure into a phased assessment of the total strategy.

Figure 3.6 shows two potential investments with the same expected value but very different risk profiles, due to their dramatically different ranges of possible outcomes. Investment A is expected to have a value of 1000 or nothing, while B is only expected to vary between 80 and 120 at the extreme (i.e. very close to its expected value of 100). Indeed, 50% of the time, B should actually generate its expected value, while A cannot achieve its expected value of 100. Investment A will always have a high variance; 10% of the time it will over-perform, by 900, while 90% of the time it will under-perform by 100. It is clearly this volatility in possible outcomes that drives the assessment of the risk profile, but it should also indicate where the focus of management attention should be placed.

Many marketing planning teams would spend most of their time and effort trying to refine their assessment of the value of the successful outcome of investment A. Is it really 1000 or 900 or 1100? This is a waste of time for such an unlikely outcome; the high-risk investment has a small likelihood of delivering a very high return. Our focus should be on making it more likely that this high return will be achieved. As shown in Figure 3.7, if the probability of success could be increased from 10% to 20%, the expected value of the

	Investment A				Investment B		
Value of outcome	Probability of outcome	Expected value		Value of outcome	Probability of outcome	Expected value
1000	10%	100		80	25%	20
–	90%	–		100	50%	50
				120	25%	30
	100%	100			100%	100

Figure 3.6 Implementation issues – use of probability estimates

	Investment A				Investment B		
Value of outcome	Probability of outcome	Expected value		Value of outcome	Probability of outcome	Expected value
1000	20%	200		80	20%	16
–	80%	–		100	60%	60
				120	20%	24
	100%	200			100%	100

In Investment A, a 10% increase in the probability of success to 20% results in the doubling of the expected value of the element, although the remaining 80% probability of total loss means that this element still has a high-risk profile.

In Investment B, a 10% increase in the probability of the most likely outcome has no effect on the expected value of the investment.

Figure 3.7 Revising initial probability estimates

Years	1 Expected annual cash flow (£m)	2 Probability of success of previous stage	3 Cumulative probability factor [2 × previous year's 3]	4 Probability-adjusted expected annual cash flow 1 × 3 (£m)
1	(2)	100%	100%	(2)
2	(4)	50%	50%	(2)
3	(4)	60%	30%	(1.2)
4	(6)	70%	21%	(1.26)
5–15	11	80%	16.8%	1.85

Figure 3.8 Use of expected values in high-risk strategic investment decisions

investment is doubled; the remaining 80% probability of total loss still means that the investment has a high-risk profile. However, in the already low-risk investment B, increasing the probability of actually receiving 100 from 50% to 60% does nothing at all for the overall expected value. In low-risk investments, the focus of management should be on the assessment of the value of the outcomes rather than on refining still further their probability distributions.

This simple illustration highlights how the use of probability estimates can help, but it becomes much more powerful when there is a series of high-risk stages, as shown in Figure 3.8. In this highly simplified example of a real marketing strategy, the company identified a phased investment programme for the development and launch of a completely new product. In Year 1, some marketing research costing £2 million was to be undertaken. This would be reviewed at the end of the year and was assessed as having an initial probability of success of 50%; if it was unsuccessful, the rest of the investment would be cancelled. The next stage in Year 2 involved product feasibility testing and more marketing research, costing £4 million and with a probability of success of 60%. If, and only if, this worked, Year 3 involved pilot scale production and test marketing, resulting in a net cash outflow of another £4 million with a success expectation of 70%. Year 4 was the full international launch with consequent negative cash flows of £6 million, but a higher probability of success of 80% due to the successful outcomes of all the previous stages. Following a successful launch, the company expected to generate £11 million cash inflows per year (representing £10 million annual profit plus £1 million add-back of depreciation expense) for 11 years from Year 5 to Year 15.

The cash flow items shown in column 1 of Figure 3.8 represent the cash flows that will occur if each stage is successful; hence they are often referred to as 'success' cash flows. However, given the probabilities of success associated with each stage, it is relatively unlikely that the company will actually receive its £11 million per year in Years 5 to 15. Mathematically, the cumulative probability of success of each subsequent stage can be calculated by multiplying together the probabilities associated with all the prior stages; this is done in column 3 of Figure 3.8. This shows that it is only 16.8% likely that the ultimate international launch will be successful. Put another way, as is done in column 4 of Figure 3.8, the probability-adjusted expected cash inflow each year from Year 5 to Year 15 is not

Years	Probability factor-adjusted cash flows			Unadjusted cash flows		
	Expected annual cash flows (£m)	Discount factor @ 15% (i.e. company cost of capital)	Present value	Original annual cash flows (£m)	Discount factor @ 35%	Present value
1	(2)	0.870	(1.74)	(2)	0.741	(1.48)
2	(2)	0.756	(1.51)	(4)	0.549	(2.20)
3	(1.2)	0.658	(0.79)	(4)	0.406	(1.62)
4	(1.26)	0.572	(0.72)	(6)	0.301	(1.81)
5–15	1.85	2.992	5.53	11	0.828	9.11
	Net present value		+0.77	Net present value		+2.00

Figure 3.9 Comparison of net present value calculations

£11 million but only £1.85 million (i.e. £11 million multiplied by 0.168). Each of the earlier cash outflows has similarly been reduced by its appropriate cumulative probability of success, or individual risk factor.

Thus, this marketing strategy now has two very different looking cash flow projections and a decision is needed as to which one should be discounted to generate the net present value of the investment, column 1 or column 4 of Figure 3.8. Many companies would choose to discount the success assuming cash flows in column 1, although the Marketing Due Diligence process discounts the probability-adjusted cash flows of column 4. The key issue is that the discount rates used must be very different. The whole purpose of using the phased probability estimates is to identify and focus on the specific risks associated with each stage of the marketing strategy. Therefore, the probability-adjusted cash flows should be discounted at a significantly lower rate, and normally the company's cost of capital is reasonably appropriate. If the success cash flows are used, a much higher discount rate must be used to take account of the higher risk profile that is still included in these cash flows. As shown in Figure 3.9, a discount rate of 35% per year has a similar impact to applying the cumulative probability factors and then using a discount rate set at the level of the company's cost of capital. The problem with this method is that it means that a very high discount rate (i.e. 35%) is applied to all the projected cash flows, even though they obviously have very different risk profiles, ranging from the certainty of spending £2 million this year to the much less likely receipt of £11 million in Years 5 to 15.

Some companies have trouble with the idea of assessing probabilities of success (i.e. specific risk profiles) for specific elements of marketing strategies because they 'see the process as subjective'. Yet these same companies see nothing subjective in projecting cash flows many years into the future and then choosing a 'high' discount rate to reflect the overall risk associated with the strategy. The use of specific risk profiling for the key elements of the marketing strategy and using these risk assessments to adjust the expected cash flows directly puts the appropriate line managers back in control of the assessment of their strategies. In most companies, the choice of a risk-adjusted discount rate is solely under the control of the finance function. Even more importantly, this is how the external capital

Update on investment

The first investment stage (Year 1) has now been successfully completed on budget. No other estimates have been changed and the same probability factors have been applied to the expected remaining future cash flows.

Years	Annual cash flow (£m)	Probability of success of previous stage	Cumulative probability factor	Probability-adjusted expected annual cash flow
1	(4)	100%	100%	(4)
2	(4)	60%	60%	(2.4)
3	(6)	70%	42%	(2.52)
4–14	11	80%	33.6%	3.70

Figure 3.10 Increasing present values as success becomes more likely

	Probability factor-adjusted cash flows			Unadjusted cash flows		
Years	Expected annual cash flows (£m)	Discount factor @ 15%	Present value	Original annual cash flows (£m)	Discount factor @ 35%	Present value
1	(4)	0.870	(3.48)	(4)	0.741	(2.96)
2	(2.4)	0.756	(1.81)	(4)	0.549	(2.20)
3	(2.52)	0.658	(1.66)	(6)	0.406	(2.44)
4–14	3.70	3.441	12.73	11	1.118	12.30
	Net present value		+5.78	Net present value		+4.70

As the total risk associated with the investment has now reduced, the discount factor used on the gross unadjusted expected cash flows should be reduced; approximately 30% would generate a similar NPV as produced by the probability-adjusted cash flows.

Figure 3.11 Recomputing net present values

markets take account of specific risks. Hence any company that claims to have the objective of creating shareholder value should align its internal processes with those used by its shareholders.

Alignment with capital markets

As stated earlier in this chapter, investors in financial markets start by assessing the relative risk profile of an industry (its beta factor) and use this to calculate the required rate of return for that sector. This is then translated into a cost of capital for individual companies within this industry. Thus, companies do have different costs of capital and consequently different rates of discount will be applied to their expected future cash flows.

However, these different risk profiles show the degree to which these returns are correlated with the overall capital market, what is technically referred to as systematic risk. Therefore, beta factors only take into account general risk factors that will affect all or most companies. They do not take into account all the specific risks that are faced by a single company with its individual marketing strategy. The financial markets take these into account by adjusting the level of future cash flows that are discounted at the company's cost of capital rate.

Let us use an example to make this clearer. The total shareholders' returns from the cigarette industry in the USA have been highly volatile for many years, as share prices of such companies have oscillated due to news of impending litigation, results of specific court cases and, particularly, government-led action against the industry. Yet cigarette companies all have beta factors that are significantly below 1, i.e. these companies are less volatile than the overall stock market. This is because this litigation threat is seen as a specific, non-systematic risk of the tobacco industry that has no effect on other companies in the capital markets; therefore, it is not reflected in the beta factor calculations. However, its impact needs to be taken into account by investors in tobacco companies, as it clearly does have an effect on the returns available to them. This is done by adjusting the anticipated level of future cash flows, which are then discounted at this relatively low rate.

Thus, the UK-based cigarette group, BAT plc, had, for many years, a directly owned USA-based subsidiary, Brown & Williamson (B&W). This subsidiary was highly profitable and provided the group with a substantial proportion of the cash flow that was needed to pay the annual dividends to its external shareholders. However, in the forward projections of profits and cash flows that are so fundamental to determining the level of a company's share price, investment analysts and institutional investors did not include any future earnings streams from the USA due to the threat of litigation. Indeed, despite constant reassurances from the company, these external stakeholders were so concerned about the possibility of a carry-over of this litigation absorbing group assets and interests outside the USA that BAT's USA involvement had quite a significant further negative effect on the group's share price. As a consequence when, in 2004, BAT announced that it was merging its B&W shareholding into R J Reynolds USA tobacco business in exchange for a minority stake in the enlarged business, there was a substantial increase in the group's share price. This was despite the group losing direct managerial control over the USA business and its dividend policy.

Turning Marketing Due Diligence into a financial value

Adjusting marketing planning outcomes

Given the focus on aligning the Marketing Due Diligence process with the creation of shareholder value, it should come as no surprise that the Marketing Due Diligence diagnostic process adjusts the expected cash flows generated by proposed marketing strategies by using the probabilities assessed through the structured risk analysis process set out in Chapter 2. However, the level of the actual adjustment is not mechanistically prescribed because it has to take account of the way in which the marketing plans were originally established.

Different companies have very different planning philosophies, cultures and processes, and these will significantly impact the level of adjustment that is needed for any given level of strategy risk. Strategic management in most modern complex organizations is, of necessity, multi-tiered and the marketing strategy and planning processes need to be similarly structured. The detailed planning process at the individual strategic business unit level should be tailored to the specific needs of each such SBU and its particular competitive environment. However, most large groups have an overriding corporate philosophy and culture that has a strong influence on both the corporate goals and objectives that are established and also the marketing strategies that are implemented to try to achieve them.

At one extreme, the philosophy and culture can be described as 'conservative incrementalism', where businesses quite deliberately take a prudent approach to establishing their targets and objectives, as their corporate culture is that 'targets should be met or even slightly exceeded'. At the other extreme, targets can be set that are severely stretching and may only be achieved if everything goes really well. However, by aiming at such BHAGs (big, hairy, audacious goals) as these have now become known, the business may greatly exceed normal expectations, even if it falls a little short of the very aggressive, stated objective. Neither behaviour and resulting planning process is right or wrong, but their financial outcomes clearly require very different levels of adjustment following a Marketing Due Diligence diagnostic assessment.

In the very cautious planning environment, it is to be expected that the vast majority of objectives will actually be achieved. Hence the emphasis of the planning process should be on ensuring that these achievable objectives contain acceptable levels of economic return (i.e. that they will create shareholder value) and management stretch. The 'actual versus plan' variances for such a conservative plan are likely to be relatively small and will normally be, on balance, slightly positive as the culture is one of overachievement. This means that the expected financial outcomes included in the marketing plan will already include some level of risk adjustment, so that the outcomes represent the 'most likely' result or even slightly more conservative levels. In many such businesses, the overachievement of actual performance is created by consciously 'under-promising' during the planning process.

The much more aggressive 'let's go for it' style of planning will result in much more significant deviations from the highly stretched targets included in the plan, and most of these resulting variances will represent shortfalls against the planned performance. The financial outcomes included in these plans represent the successful achievement of the proposed strategies, more of a 'best case' result rather than a 'most likely' outcome. Clearly, once the Marketing Due Diligence diagnostic process has identified the key risk profiles of the marketing strategy, the relative level of any necessary adjustment to the planned outcomes needs to take account of the corporate style and philosophy under which the plans have been prepared.

Thus, the logic of the Marketing Due Diligence process is always to adjust the predicted financial outcomes where necessary. But the level of any such adjustment obviously takes into account how these plans were originally formulated.

Placing the adjusted financial return into context

This first stage of the Marketing Due Diligence diagnostic process, therefore, should result in an adjusted set of forecast sales revenues, profits and cash flows from the proposed marketing strategy. We now need to assess these adjusted expected cash flows as to whether they are shareholder value enhancing. This is done by putting them into the context of the capital employed in implementing the marketing strategy and the resulting required rate of return on this capital employed.

Not surprisingly, given the arguments set out in Chapters 1 and 2, the capital employed that we use for this computation is the genuine capital that is required in the business in order to implement this marketing strategy. In other words, it includes the value of the relevant intangible assets owned and used by the business and is not limited to the historically based, tangible asset-oriented balance sheets published by most companies.

Clearly, this involves the exercise of judgement in assessing the current value of such intangible assets, but this should be an integral part of the development of the proposed marketing strategy. Indeed, marketing expenditure should be split between development and maintenance activities rather than being categorized into the more normal, but much less relevant, categories such as 'above-the-line' media advertising and 'below-the-line' promotions. Development marketing expenditure is aimed at increasing the value of marketing assets such as brands, customer relationships and channels of distribution. It is, therefore, an investment that, if successful, will generate financial returns in subsequent years. As already stated, for most companies it is the return from these successful marketing investments that is the major source of sustainable shareholder value. Thus, a major element in producing a sound marketing strategy is assessing whether and, if so, how existing and/or new marketing assets can be further developed. These marketing investments also represent the main focus of the Marketing Due Diligence process as they are often quite-high-risk expenditures; if they are unsuccessful, the money spent is normally completely irrecoverable.

Maintenance marketing activities are designed to hold existing marketing assets at their current level, as it is very well established that all assets, but particularly intangible marketing assets, decline in value unless they are properly maintained. This means that the impact of maintenance marketing expenditure is normally seen in the relatively short term, while the financial return from developmental marketing investments may be several years in the future. Unfortunately, the normal accounting treatment for marketing expenditure does not classify even such long-term marketing activities as true financial investments, with all marketing expenditure being written off in the current year's profit and loss account. This means that it can be possible to improve the short-term financial performance of a business by cutting back on development marketing activities, even though this means that the marketing assets will never achieve their full potential. If development marketing budgets are reduced in an attempt to boost short-term profits, the long-term performance measures used within the business must highlight the risks that are being taken with the sustainability of the business.

However, it must also be remembered that marketing assets are developed in a competitive environment and the effectiveness of marketing expenditure is significantly affected by competitors' levels of spending. This is taken into account in the Marketing Due Diligence process, and is discussed in depth in Chapter 6.

Where the proposed marketing strategy is primarily aimed at increasing the value of an existing marketing asset or creating a completely new one, there may be little or no increased financial return during the three years or so for which detailed financial outcomes are predicted. The financial returns are expected even further into the future, but can be captured by increasing the value of the particular marketing asset at the end of the projection period. Clearly, the increased time delay between the expenditure of the marketing investment and the anticipated financial return is an indicator of increased risk, as the market may change or competitors may be able to respond effectively. This is again taken into account in the Marketing Due Diligence diagnostic process.

For publicly quoted companies, the assessment of the total value of their intangible assets is relatively easy. The gap between the company's stock market capitalization and the net tangible assets disclosed on the published balance sheet shows their shareholders' estimate of this value. This total value then needs to be analysed across the business so that the major elements are identified, but there are now a number of techniques in use for placing approximate values on marketing assets (e.g. brand valuation techniques, customer relationship valuations) that can be used as necessary.

Once an estimate of the capital employed in implementing the marketing strategy has been made, we can compute the required return on this investment by applying the appropriate risk-adjusted rate of return to this capital employed. Because the specific risks associated with the marketing strategy have been taken into account by adjusting the projected resulting cash flows, the appropriate rate of return will be close to the company's cost of capital. It may, of course, need some adjustment as this marketing strategy may be relevant to only a part of the total company, while the cost of capital can apply to the total portfolio of businesses comprising a group. Thus, the output of the Marketing Due Diligence diagnostic process is an adjusted cash flow forecast from which is deducted the required return on the investment involved. A resulting positive net cash flow indicates both that shareholder value should be created and the level of this shareholder value that should be created by implementing this marketing strategy.

Allowing for 'capital at risk'

Unfortunately, there is still one more adjustment that needs to be made to some marketing strategies. The previous section effectively charged a tax on the return generated by the marketing strategy for the use of the assets employed by the strategy, resulting in what accountants refer to as residual income. This charge represents the opportunity cost of tying up the company's capital, but it assumes that the capital will still exist at the end of the planning period. However, some marketing strategies may make it more likely that part of this capital could be lost if the marketing strategy is not completely successful. In other words, this capital is put 'at risk' by the marketing strategy.

There are many ways in which this can happen, but the most common is in an attempt to reduce the initial costs of implementing a new marketing strategy. This can often be done by leveraging on an existing marketing asset of the business, so that the upfront marketing development investment required is significantly reduced. Focusing initial sales of new products on existing loyal customers can reduce launch selling costs compared with finding completely new customers. However, if these new products do not match either the existing customers' expectations or existing product quality levels, the loyalty of these valuable current customers can be significantly eroded.

Probably the most common example of this leveraging type of strategy is the use of umbrella or corporate branding, where a new product is launched under the umbrella of an existing, well-known, successful brand. Obviously the objective is to create rapid awareness and trial of the new product without the need for massive marketing expenditure. As long as the new product is a very good fit with all the existing brand's attributes and target customers, this can be successful, but there can be a significant risk to the value of the current brand. There are many examples of companies launching brand extensions that

Table 3.2 Translating Marketing Due Diligence into a financial value

---

Shareholder value expected to be created by proposed marketing strategy

$$= \begin{matrix} \text{Probability-adjusted} \\ \text{cash flows} \\ \text{expected from} \\ \text{marketing strategy} \end{matrix} - \begin{matrix} \text{Value of capital} \\ \text{employed} \end{matrix} \times \begin{matrix} \text{Required rate} \\ \text{of return} \end{matrix} - \begin{matrix} \text{Potential loss} \\ \text{from capital} \\ \text{at risk} \end{matrix}$$

---

had negative impacts on their existing brand franchise; yet, often, this 'capital at risk' is not taken into account in the review of the marketing strategy.

This is clearly unfair, as the financial returns projected from this marketing strategy will include the 'benefit' of the cost savings achieved by placing this capital at risk. It is this anomaly that is addressed by this additional adjustment required in the Marketing Due Diligence process. It is only needed for those marketing strategies that seek to leverage on existing, indirectly associated marketing assets and, by doing so, run the risk of reducing their current value.

The mechanics of making the adjustment require an assessment both of the current value of the marketing asset that is being put at risk and of the potential proportionate reduction in this value that could result from its use in this strategy. In some cases, this could represent a total loss of its current value. The Marketing Due Diligence assessment process is then, as usual, to assign a risk weighting, i.e. a probability factor, to this loss in value and this adjusted loss in value is subtracted from the net expected return from the proposed marketing strategy.

This means that, as shown in Table 3.2, the output from the Marketing Due Diligence diagnostic process should be a numerical value representing the expected shareholder value to be created by any proposed marketing strategy. The computational process has been broken into segments quite deliberately, as some companies may find it difficult initially to do the second and third stages (i.e. assessing the return required on the actual capital tied up in the strategy and adjusting for the potential loss from the capital placed at risk by this strategy). Even so, making the Marketing Due Diligence required adjustments to the expected financial returns from the proposed marketing strategy will enable a much more rigorous review and appraisal to be undertaken, as is discussed in the next section.

The potential shareholder value creation (or destruction, obviously, if the final answer is a negative value) of the proposed marketing strategy should greatly enhance the resource allocation decision process within a company, but the Marketing Due Diligence process can add value even without a final numerical result.

Highlighting deficiencies and key risks

When we have applied the Marketing Due Diligence process to existing marketing strategies and plans, it has come as no great surprise to find that there are often gaps in the information supporting the resulting financial forecasts. (There have also been many instances of self-apparent inconsistencies between the marketing plans and these resulting financial outcomes.) In many cases, this lack of information has made it impossible to carry out a full Marketing Due Diligence appraisal of the marketing strategy in order to compute an adjusted financial outcome. However, the appraisal process has been of value to the company even in these cases, as a major benefit of the Marketing Due Diligence process is that it clearly highlights the specific deficiencies in the existing marketing plans.

Quite often, some, if not all, of these deficiencies are readily rectified as the required knowledge either already exists within the business, but has not been explicitly incorporated into the marketing plan, or can be easily obtained by management. However, if this is not the case, the therapeutic process within Marketing Due Diligence, which is discussed in detail in Part 3 of the book, has helped to remedy the identified deficiencies. This is done by improving the rigour of the marketing planning process that is used within the business. A logically structured and rigorously applied marketing planning process, which actually starts by identifying genuine market needs, removes the need for any dangerously false, but very common, implicit assumptions about 'new' opportunities for selling existing products or developing 'new products' for unspecified customers.

However, probably the major non-financial benefit of the Marketing Due Diligence diagnostic process is that it indicates the key risks associated with any proposed marketing strategy. This is achieved by demonstrating the relative impact of the individual risk assessments that are made during a Marketing Due Diligence appraisal. The management team is able to focus its attention on these critical areas of risk and uncertainty and thereby improve the marketing planning process in the future. Consequently, Marketing Due Diligence should be viewed as an ongoing process rather than a one-off review or audit. By concentrating planning resources and marketing research effort on the identified key areas, the business should be able to make better predictions. This does not mean that future marketing strategies will necessarily be less risky, but that the level of risk that is being undertaken is more fully appreciated and will be better controlled and monitored.

Implications for users

Hopefully, it should by now be clear that a Marketing Due Diligence process can add value to both internal and external shareholders in a business. For external stakeholders, such as existing and prospective shareholders, the knowledge that all proposed marketing strategies will be subjected to a rigorous and structured review should provide reassurance that the resulting critical resource allocation decisions are more likely to be shareholder value enhancing. Indeed, it could be that institutional investors and stock market analysts will require a Marketing Due Diligence process to be put in place as part of any sound corporate governance process. This makes even more sense for the other external financiers involved in non-publicly quoted companies, such as private equity funds and other corporate financiers. Such a process also has significant relevance to debt providers, particularly in highly leveraged companies.

The obvious linkages inside a company should be through the board of directors, who have ultimate responsibility for the corporate governance process operated across their organization. Instigating a Marketing Due Diligence process should seem like a great idea to any non-executive director who wants to be confident that future strategies and plans are being properly reviewed and controlled. With legislation around the world placing more and more emphasis on control procedures and corporate governance, with increasing potential penalties on individual directors, the need for an objective, recognized and well-structured review and approval process is also clear.

The Marketing Due Diligence process should be of interest to external auditors as they seek to validate the effectiveness of their clients' control procedures. However, as their responsibility is still focused on reporting on the actual financial performance of a business, Marketing Due Diligence is even more relevant to the internal audit functions of large, multi-business corporations. Due to the geographical spread and complexity of most of these modern companies, their boards of directors require reassurance that the information provided to them is as accurate and relevant as possible. This is particularly true for the critical, strategic investment decisions where, by definition, the financial justifications are based on forecasts of future expected outcomes.

Hence the main focus of most internal audit functions is already on business risk identification, assessment and control. Integrating the Marketing Due Diligence process into their existing business risk analysis routines would therefore greatly reinforce their ability to report back to the board level audit committee on the company's internal control processes.

However, this still casts Marketing Due Diligence in a post-plan preparation review role. Ideally, the Marketing Due Diligence process should be seen as a normal line management responsibility. In other words, no proposed marketing strategy will be considered by the top executive management team unless it has been subjected to a thorough Marketing Due Diligence process review. As stated in the book's title, this is how CEOs can hold their marketing directors to account and ensure that their marketing strategies do deliver shareholder value.

The initial implementation of this change in corporate culture may be achieved in some companies by getting internal audit departments to carry out Marketing Due Diligence reviews, while in others the finance function may have a role in vetting the expected financial outcomes of proposed marketing plans. Increasingly, however, companies have finance teams integrated within their marketing functions and these marketing finance managers are ideally placed to coordinate the implementation of a Marketing Due Diligence process. Their role can only be that of coordination, as the assessment of the risk level associated with each specific facet of any marketing strategy requires appropriate professional expertise and may necessitate marketing research to obtain additional information. Thus, as with much other value-adding marketing and financial information, such as competitor analysis or value chain analysis, the process must involve many different people across the organization.

Once the culture of subjecting all proposed marketing strategies to a rigorous, structured assessment process is accepted within the company, it becomes totally logical for marketing functions themselves to incorporate Marketing Due Diligence into their marketing strategy development process. If they still propose marketing plans that regularly fail the eventual Marketing Due Diligence process, their credibility will fall even lower within the organization. The parallel with the discounted cash flow evaluations of other major investment proposals is clear to see. Nowadays, almost nobody will propose a major investment decision to their board unless they know that it meets the prescribed financial criteria – except for marketing plans!

In this first part of the book we have set out the need for the Marketing Due Diligence process and what it is. This should also have demonstrated how it differs from the techniques that are currently in use. Part 2 considers each element of the Marketing Due Diligence diagnostic process in detail while, in Part 3, the way in which the therapeutic process can strengthen marketing planning processes is developed.

The Marketing Due Diligence Diagnostic Process

Chapter 4

Assessing market risk

Fast track

Despite the loose use of the terms by some, markets and products are not the same thing. Markets are groups of people with related needs; products are bundles of benefits that might meet those needs. Market risk arises when a company attempts to match one to the other.

Market risk is the risk that the market size will not be as large as hoped for by the plan, as a result of which the intended shareholder value would not be created. It is distinct from, but aggregates with, share risk and profit risk. In short, market risk arises when the market projections turn out to be wrong. This happens for a number of reasons: the targeted market is very new; the product category is very new; the product enters a new stage in its life cycle; or the uncertainty arising from this 'newness' is not compensated for by effective research and analysis.

Market risk is the cumulative risk of five component risks:

- *Product category risk.* This is the risk that the entire product category may be smaller than planned. It is higher if the product category is novel and lower if the product category is well established.
- *Market existence risk.* This is the risk that the target segment may be smaller than planned. It is higher if it is a new segment and lower if the segment is well established.
- *Sales volumes risk.* This is the risk that sales volumes will be lower than planned. It is higher if sales volumes are 'guessed' with little supporting evidence and lower if the sales volumes are well supported by evidence such as market research.
- *Forecast risk.* This is the risk that the market will grow less quickly than planned. It is higher if forecast market growth exceeds historical trends and lower if it is in line with or below historical trends.
- *Pricing risk.* This is the risk that the price levels in the market will be lower than planned. It is higher if pricing assumptions are optimistic and lower if they are conservative.

Two important, but often neglected and abused, techniques of strategic marketing planning are Ansoff's growth matrix and the product life cycle. Used correctly, these tools are critical to understanding, assessing and managing market risk. For all marketing strategies, but especially those that involve new markets or products, assessing market risk is a necessary step in creating shareholder value.

Some important background to what constitutes 'success'

Short-term success

We can recall from Chapter 2 that the first of the three major questions that have to be answered in the Marketing Due Diligence diagnostic process is:

> Does the market on which the forecasts and budgets are based exist and, if so, what are the risks associated with that market?

Before going deeper into this, however, let us recount the tale of a board session that took place some years ago, attended by 60 Managing Directors of a major construction company. Whilst this conference was held in France by way of a reward for the 65% increase in net profits, it was nonetheless intended to be a serious management development event, with marketing strategy as the main theme.

One of our authors had been asked to attend to discuss marketing strategy. However, it quickly became clear that, with such a significant profit increase under their belts, these Managing Directors were in no mood to countenance a Professor of Marketing discussing strategies for markets. Their success obviated the need, in their view, to worry about such things.

Given such learning obstinacy, the Marketing Professor selected the Managing Director with the highest increase in net profits – 185%!! – and asked him how he had achieved such impressive success. The answer was straightforward: 'We had a mild winter!'

Rather than rushing back to the office to begin research on a new book on 'Barometer Marketing', the Marketing Professor asked the Managing Director four further questions relating to his success:

1 Did the market grow last year and, if so, how much of your growth in profits came from market growth?
2 Did your company increase its market share last year and, if so, how much of your growth in profits came from growth in market share?
3 Did you increase your net prices last year and, if so, how much of your growth in profits came from net price increases?
4 Did you have any productivity increases last year and, if so, how much of your growth in profits came from productivity increases?

The Managing Director was unable to answer any of these questions. The remaining 59 MDs began to pay more attention, no doubt relieved to have been spared the embarrassment of being subjected to a similar depth of questioning.

The point of the story is simple. In those days of heady growth, virtually anyone in the construction industry could make lots of money just by dint of being in this industry at that time. No one really needed any intellectual thinking about what was happening, as endemic growth in a market where demand exceeded supply ensured commercial success for most players. So, the state of development of the market clearly has a major influence on any player's hopes for growth in sales and profits.

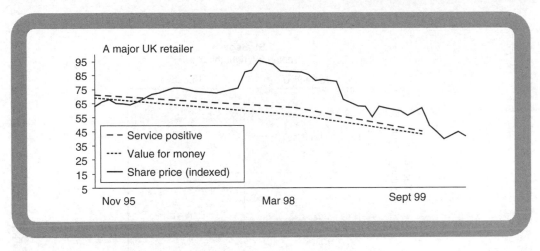

Figure 4.1 Share price vs competitive position

There is, however, a major problem for strategists hidden in market growth scenarios. The situation illustrated in Figure 4.1 typifies the kind of problem that gets hidden by short-term success.

It shows that, whilst the share price was growing steadily, the underlying competitive situation was deteriorating, as measured by their customers' perceptions of service. It didn't particularly matter as long as the market was growing but, as we shall see later in this chapter, markets have a habit of slowing down. At such times, customers exercise their choice and 'get their own back' on suppliers who have been treating them badly during good times for the supplier.

The retailer in this particular figure was one of the most famous retail companies in the world, but one, alas, that became arrogant as a result of its own success. Many years later, it is still struggling to get its tarnished reputation back, whilst its profits continue to slump.

Figure 4.1 also illustrates another crucial point. In Chapter 1 we highlighted the problem that most companies report backward-looking financial data, with little explanation about the underlying market forces that have shaped the financial results. What this means is that all manner of short-term, value-destroying decisions can be made in any fiscal period which may not result in a downturn in sales and profits for two or three years. The corollary is also true, in that investments in customer value-enhancing activities, such as improvements in customer service, product performance, channel changes, communications and the like, may not result in improved results in sales and profits for two or three years after the investment. This time delay encourages short-term managerial behaviour. The result? Strategy may deteriorate despite an improvement in tactics, so affecting the underlying competitiveness of the supplier. This is discussed next and illustrated in Figure 4.2.

By contrast, companies led by Chief Executives with a proactive orientation that stretches beyond the end of the current fiscal year have begun to show results visibly better than the old reactive companies with only a short-term vision.

Strategy and tactics

This brings us to the starting point in marketing planning – an understanding of the difference between strategy and tactics and their association with the relevant adjectives,

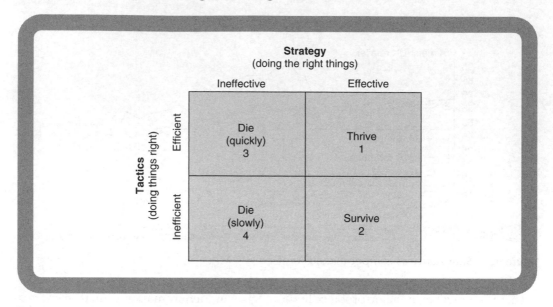

Figure 4.2 The impact of strategy and tactics on competitiveness

'effective' and 'efficient'. This is illustrated in Figure 4.2, which shows a matrix in which the horizontal axis represents strategy as a continuum from ineffective to effective. The vertical axis represents tactics on a continuum from inefficient to efficient. Those firms with both an effective strategy and efficient tactics (box 1) continue to thrive. Those with an effective strategy but inefficient tactics (box 2) merely survive. Those firms with an ineffective strategy appear to the left of the matrix. Often, companies end up with an ineffective strategy because they place too much emphasis on tactics and fail to address the underlying strategic issues surrounding changing market needs. Either way, such businesses are destined to die. The question is whether they will do so slowly or quickly, and organizations doing the wrong things more efficiently (box 3) are destined to die more quickly than their less efficient counterparts (box 4). It is a bit like encouraging an incompetent manager to work harder, thus doubling the amount of chaos and customer dissatisfaction he creates!

In other words, both sound strategy and efficient tactics are necessary to a successful business. Having only one of these is insufficient. And the only thing that can be said of having neither is that failure comes as a surprise and is not preceded by a period of worry and depression.

The strategic marketing plan

It is because the strategy is so important that Marketing Due Diligence is not concerned with tactical plans, but with an organization's strategy as manifested in strategic marketing plans for three years or beyond. It is only by testing strategies beyond the first fiscal year that it can be established whether they are likely to destroy or create shareholder value.

Market risk

Firstly, let us remind ourselves what is involved in market risk. From the overview of Marketing Due Diligence given in Chapter 2, we can summarize that market risk comprises the following sub-components:

- Product category risk, which is higher if the product category is novel and lower if the product category is well established
- Market existence risk, which is higher if it is a new segment and lower if the segment is well established
- Sales volume risk, which is higher if sales volumes are 'guessed' with little supporting evidence and lower if the sales volumes are well supported by evidence such as market research
- Forecast risk, which is higher if forecast market growth exceeds historical trends and lower if it is in line with or below historical trends
- Pricing risk, which is higher if pricing assumptions are optimistic and lower if they are conservative relative to current pricing levels.

We intend to take each of these five areas and explain how the risk associated with them can be quantified.

Before doing this, however, we ask the reader to bear with us whilst we provide some essential background information in order to justify the approach we have taken. We will do this as quickly and simply as practicable, but we do ask the reader to understand this logic before going into the detail of market risk.

The meaning of 'product' and 'market'

Commercial organizations all sell something to someone (for the purpose of this chapter, the word 'product' will also be taken to include service products).

The clue to what constitutes a product can be found in an examination of what it is that customers buy. Customers have needs and they buy products to satisfy them. At its simplest level, someone who needs a hole may buy a drill. But herein lies the problem of defining markets in terms of products, because if a better way of making a hole is invented, say a laser, demand for drills may fall. This fundamental truth explains so many commercial disasters. Some years ago, Gestetner got into serious difficulties because they thought they were in the duplicator market, when it was clear that other solutions to the duplication problem had become available. In the same way, IBM lost billions of dollars in the 1990s because of their deeply held belief that they were in the mainframe market.

Countless similar cases still do not appear to have convinced organizations that their market definitions shouldn't be made in product terms. Even when an industrial buyer purchases a piece of equipment, he or she is still buying a bundle of benefits which they perceive will solve a particular set of needs they have.

A product, then, can be perceived as a kind of bundle of benefits, as depicted in Figure 4.3. This illustrates that, in most cases, about 80% of the impact of a product comes not from the core product itself, but from the two outer circles, often referred to as the 'product surround'.

The importance of this point is clear from the intangible value of brand names. For example, most pantries contain brands like Kellogg's, Heinz and Mars, whilst merely putting the name 'Castrol GTX' on a can of oil gives it about 65% world market share.

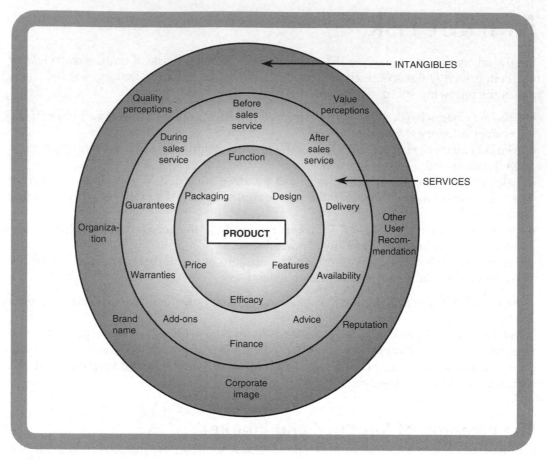

Figure 4.3   The product and product surround

Likewise with bearings, steel, processors and the like, names such as SKF, Alfa Laval and Intel endow their products with massive global market share.

The point we are making here is that what constitutes a product has to be closely entwined with the needs it is seeking to fulfil and it isn't just the core product that does this.

We can now turn to the more difficult issue of what constitutes a market, and it will be immediately apparent that a 'market' must be the aggregation of all those products that can satisfy a particular need. For example, a pension is a specific product that satisfies a need, but there are a number of other products that can also satisfy the same need.

So, what is a market?

The general rule for market definition is that it should be described in terms of a customer need, in a way which covers the aggregation of all the alternative products or services that customers regard as being capable of satisfying that same need. For example, we would regard the in-company caterer as only one option when it came to satisfying lunchtime hunger. This particular need could also be satisfied by external restaurants, public houses, fast-food specialists and sandwich bars. The emphasis in the definition, therefore, is clearly on the word 'need'.

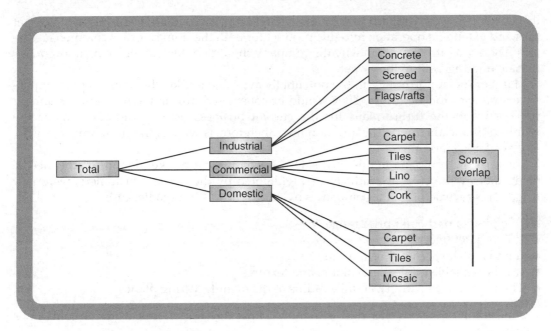

Figure 4.4 Total available market for floor covering (illustrative)

Aggregating currently available products and services is, however, simply an aid to arriving at the definition; it is important to recognize that new products, yet to be developed, could better satisfy the users' need. For example, the button manufacturer who believed their market was the 'button market' would have been very disappointed when zips and Velcro began to satisfy the need for fastenings! A needs-based definition for this company would have enabled the management to recognize the fickleness of current products, and to accept that one of their principal tasks was to seek out better ways of satisfying their market's needs and to evolve their product offer accordingly.

The following example may help in defining the market your business is in.

A company manufacturing nylon carpet for the commercial sector wanted to check that it had a realistic definition of the market it was in. The first step was to map out the total available market for all floor coverings (see Figure 4.4).

In practice, market definition is, to some degree, a matter of judgement. A sound judgement will be wide enough to include all relevant products and competitors, but not so wide as to include every possible product that is related to the business. As we saw with the button and Velcro example, a sound judgement requires both market knowledge and foresight. In this case, it would clearly be too broad to include in the company's market definition all types of floor coverings, such as those used in the industrial sector. The qualities required from such flooring cannot hope to be matched in a carpet made from any currently known type of fibre. Similarly, in both the commercial and domestic sectors, nylon carpet is not a competitor for the luxury end of the market. This luxury part of the market buys carpet made from natural fibres, particularly wool.

This leaves the non-luxury commercial and domestic sectors which, in total, represented the company's potential available market. It was potentially available because the company could, for example, produce nylon carpet for the domestic sector and extend its market this way. Similarly, the company could move into manufacturing nylon carpet tiles and extend its operation into this product for both the domestic and commercial sectors. There was also no reason why the company should not look at replacing lino, cork or mosaic flooring with nylon carpet.

Many of the opportunities in the potentially available market, however, represent possible strategies for the future. They would be considered during the marketing planning process when the future plans for the current business activity did not achieve the required financial targets. The question now, therefore, is what is the company's realistically available market?

To assist the company in this final stage of arriving at a market definition, the 'needs' being met by the current products, as highlighted by the current customers, were first listed. This revealed that the company's nylon carpet was bought because:

- It fell into a particular price range
- It was quiet underfoot
- It had a life expectancy of 15 years
- It was available in pleasant colours and textures
- The market was within a 60-mile radius of the manufacturing plant.

In addition to the obvious, this list removed lino, cork and mosaic from the company's available market.

Finally, the company looked at the applicability of its current distribution and selling methods to the potentially available market, ruling out those sections of the market which required different selling and distribution approaches. This meant that it was unrealistic to include the domestic sector in the market definition.

Products and manufacturers which met all the criteria were now listed, along with their end users. The company had now arrived at both a market definition and a current market size, while still keeping open the option of extending it, should the need arise.

This example also illustrates the need to arrive at a meaningful balance between a broad market definition and a manageable market definition. Too narrow a definition has the pitfall of restricting the range of new opportunities segmentation could open up for your business.

On the other hand, too broad a definition may make marketing planning meaningless. For example, the television broadcasting companies are in the 'entertainment' market, which also consists of theatres, cinemas and theme parks, to name but a few. This is a fairly broad definition. It may therefore be more manageable for the television broadcasters, when looking at segmenting their markets, to define their market as being the 'home entertainment' market. This could then be further refined into the pre-school, child, teenager, family or adult home entertainment market.

Another example is given in Table 4.1, this time an attempt to define markets in the financial services sector.

Whilst a degree of common sense is essential because, clearly, this isn't a science, the whole point is not to describe a market in terms only of a product, but in terms of customer needs.

To summarize, correct market definition is crucial for the purpose of:

- Share measurement
- Growth measurement
- The specification of target customers
- The recognition of relevant competitors
- The formulation of marketing objectives and strategies.

Table 4.1 Market definitions – financial services sector

Some market definitions (personal market)	
Market	*Need (on-line)*
Emergency cash ('rainy day')	Cash to cover an undesired and unexpected event (often the loss of/damage to property)
Future event planning	Schemes to protect and grow money which are for anticipated and unanticipated cash calling events (e.g. car replacement/ repairs, education, weddings, funerals, health care)
Asset purchase	Cash to buy assets they require (e.g. car purchase, house purchase, once-in-a-lifetime holiday)
Welfare contingency	The ability to maintain a desired standard of living (for self and/or dependants) in times of unplanned cessation of salary
Retirement income	The ability to maintain a desired standard of living (for self and/or dependants once the salary cheques have ceased)
Wealth care and building	The care and growth of assets (with various risk levels and liquidity levels)
Day-to-day money management	Ability to store and readily access cash for day-to-day requirements
Personal financial protection and security from motor vehicle incidents	Currently known as car insurance

Combining product and market

Here is a small exercise to illustrate what is at stake. As we have already discussed, there is often confusion about what constitutes a market for the purpose of strategy development. Unless such confusion is dispelled from the outset, the whole marketing edifice will be built on sand. However, it is often the case that what, on the surface, appears to be a relatively simple task can prove to be extremely testing. Consider the following example (illustrated in the product/market matrix in Figure 4.5), which vastly simplifies the problem.

XYZ Ltd. has five major products, A, B, C, D and E, which are sold to five different markets, as represented in Figure 4.5. Virtually all sales are achieved in the shaded areas.

Is this company's market:

1 The shaded areas?
2 The intersection of products A, B and C and markets 2, 3 and 4?
3 Products A, B and C for all markets?
4 Markets 2, 3 and 4 for all products?
5 The entire matrix?

The answer to this question is that it remains a matter of pragmatism and management judgement, as long as there is a sensible rationale to justify the choice.

Often, the way a market was selected in the first place can provide clues regarding how it can be defined. Generally, either consciously or intuitively, a screening process is used to eliminate unsuitable markets to arrive at those with potential. This screening process often works something like that shown in Figure 4.6.

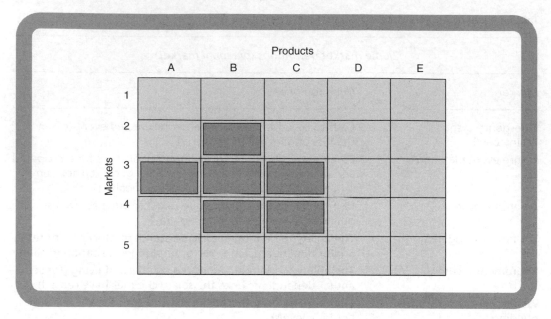

Figure 4.5 Product/market matrix

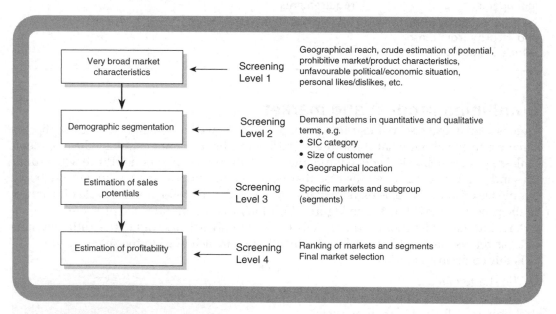

Figure 4.6 Market screening process

Product/market growth or decline

At this point, we can remind readers about the introduction to the diffusion of innovation curve described briefly in Chapter 1, as this is clearly related to the product/market life cycles, as indicated in Figure 4.7.

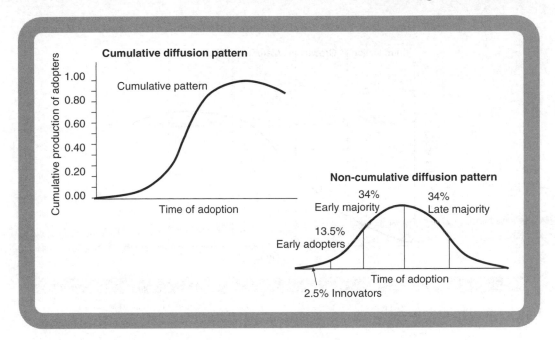

Figure 4.7 Generalized cumulative and non-cumulative diffusion patterns

There are many examples of entrepreneurs who set themselves up in business to manufacture, say, toys such as clackers or Rubik cubes, who make their fortune and who then just as quickly lose it when this fashion-conscious market changes to the next new fad. Such examples are merely the extreme manifestation of what is known as the product life cycle. This, too, is such a vital and fundamental concept that it is worth devoting some time to a discussion on the subject.

Historians of technology have observed that all technical functions grow exponentially until they come up against some natural limiting factor that causes growth to slow down and, eventually, to decline as one technology is replaced by another. There is universal agreement that the same phenomenon applies to products, so giving rise to the concept of the product life cycle, much written about in marketing literature during the past four decades.

The product life cycle postulates that if a new product is successful at the introductory stage (and many fail at this point) then, progressively, repeat purchase grows and spreads and the rate of sales growth increases. At this stage, competitors often enter the market and their additional promotional expenditure further expands the market. But no market is infinitely expandable and, gradually, the rate of growth slows as the product moves into its maturity stage. Eventually, a point is reached where there are too many firms in the market, price wars break out and some firms drop out of the market, until finally the market itself falls into decline. Figure 4.8 illustrates these apparently universal phenomena.

Nevertheless, while the product life cycle may well be a useful practical generalization, it can also be argued that particular product life cycles are determined more by the activities of the company than by any underlying 'law'.

For example, Baileys Liqueur, whilst exhibiting all the characteristics of the classic product life cycle, went on to new record sales heights following the appointment of a new

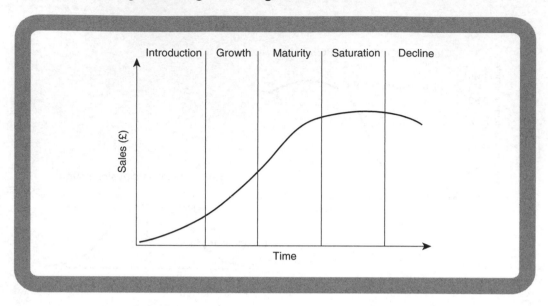

Figure 4.8 Product life cycle

brand manager. Likewise, Guinness went on to renewed growth following its positioning to appeal to a younger market.

Nevertheless, while these examples illustrate the dangers inherent in incorrect interpretation of life cycle analysis, even in this case sales will eventually mature.

From a management point of view, the product life cycle concept is useful, in that it focuses our attention on the likely future sales pattern if we take no corrective action. There are several courses of action open to us in our attempts to maintain the profitable sales of a product over its life cycle.

Figure 4.9 illustrates the actual courses taken by an American company in the management of one of its leading industrial market products. As sales growth began to slow down, the company initiated a programme of product range extensions and market development that successfully took the brand into additional stages of growth. At the same time the company was aggressively seeking new products and even considering potential areas for diversification.

Even more important are the implications of the product life cycle concept on every element of the marketing mix. Figure 4.10 gives some guide as to how the product has to change over its life cycle. In addition to this, however, every other element also has to change. For example, if a company rigidly adhered to a premium pricing policy at the mature stage of the product life cycle, when markets are often overcrowded and price wars begin, it could well lose market share. It could be regretted later on when the market has settled down, for it is often at this stage that products provide extremely profitable revenue for the company. It will become clear later in this chapter why market share is important.

The well-known 3 M Post-It note is a perfect illustration of the changes that have to take place over the life of a product (see Figure 4.10). At first we are concerned with getting distribution for the product in the most important channels, whereas during the growth phase we have to consider ways of reaching the new channels that want our product. All of these

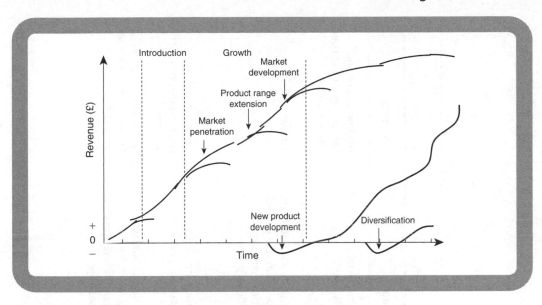

Figure 4.9 Product/market strategy and the product life cycle

Key characteristics	Unique	Product differentiation	Service differentiation	'Commodity'
Marketing message	Explain	Competitive	Brand values	Corporate
Sales	Pioneering	Relative benefits distribution support	Relationship based	Availability based
Distribution	Direct selling	Exclusive distribution	Mass distribution	80:20
Price	Very high	High	Medium	Low (consumer controlled)
Competitive intensity	None	Few	Many	Fewer, bigger international
Costs	Very high	Medium	Medium/low	Very low
Profit	Medium/high	High	Medium/high	Medium/low
Management style	Visionary	Strategic	Operational	Cost management

Figure 4.10 The product/market life cycle and market characteristics

points will become clearer in those chapters specifically concerned with the management of price, place and promotion.

Finally, Table 4.2 shows a checklist used by one major company to help it determine where its markets are in the life cycle and what strategies are appropriate.

Table 4.2 Appropriate strategies at different life cycle stages

Factor	Embryonic	Growth	Mature	Declining
		Maturity stage		
Growth rate	Normally much greater than GNP (on small base).	Sustained growth above GNP. New customers. New suppliers. Rate decelerates toward end of stage.	Approximately equals GNP.	Declining demand. Market shrinks as users' needs change.
Predictability of growth potential	Hard to define accurately. Small portion of demand being satisfied. Market forecasts differ widely.	Greater percentage of demand is met and upper limits of demand becoming clearer. Discontinuities, such as price reductions based on economies of scale, may occur.	Potentially well defined. Competition specialized to satisfy needs of specific segments.	Known and limited.
Product line proliferation	Specialized lines to meet needs of early customers.	Rapid expansion.	Proliferation slows or ceases.	Lines narrow as unprofitable products dropped.
Number of competitors	Unpredictable.	Reaches maximum. New entrants attracted by growth and high margins. Some consolidation begins towards end of stage.	Entrenched positions established. Further shakeout of marginal competitors.	New entrants unlikely. Competitors continue to decline.

Market share distribution	Unstable. Shares react unpredictably to entrepreneurial insights and timing.	Increasing stability. Typically, a few competitors emerging as strong.	Highly concentrated or fragmented as industry segments and/or is localized.
Customer stability	Trial usage with little customer loyalty.	Some loyalty. Repeat usage with many seeking alternative suppliers.	Extremely stable. Suppliers dwindle and customers less motivated to seek alternatives.
Ease of entry	Normally easy. No one dominates. Customers' expectations uncertain. If barriers exist, they are usually technology, capital or fear of the unknown.	More difficult. Market franchises and/or economies of scale may exist, yet new business is still available without directly confronting competition.	Difficult. Market leaders established. New business must be 'won' from others.
Technology	Plays an important role in matching product characteristics to market needs. Frequent product changes.	Product technology vital early, while process technology more important later in this stage.	Process and material substitution focus. Product requirements well known and relatively undemanding. May be a thrust to renew the industry via new technology.

Stable, with a few companies often controlling much of industry.

Well-developed buying patterns with customer loyalty. Competitors understand purchase dynamics and it is difficult for a new supplier to win over accounts.

Little or no incentive to enter.

Technological content is known, stable and accessible.

Product and market combined

Don't worry, we're nearly there! All that remains before explaining how market risk is assessed is to show how the two crucial issues of what is sold (the product) and to whom it is sold (the market) are combined as a basis for developing corporate strategy.

A firm's competitive situation can be simplified to two dimensions only – products and markets. To put it even more simply, Ansoff's framework is about what is sold (the 'product') and to whom it is sold (the 'market'). Within this framework Ansoff identifies four possible courses of action for the firm:

- Selling existing products to existing markets
- Extending existing products to new markets
- Developing new products for existing markets
- Developing new products for new markets.

The matrix in Figure 4.11 depicts these concepts.

It is clear that the range of possible marketing objectives is very wide, since there will be degrees of technological newness and degrees of market newness. Nevertheless, Ansoff's matrix provides a logical framework in which marketing objectives can be developed under each of the four main headings above. In other words, marketing objectives are about products and markets only.

Marketing objectives (i.e. what an organization wants to sell and to whom) are about each of the four main categories of the Ansoff matrix:

The only possible strategies to employ in matching sales and profit objectives are:

Market penetration (top left box):

- improve productivity
- share in whatever market growth there is going to be
- gain market share from competitors.

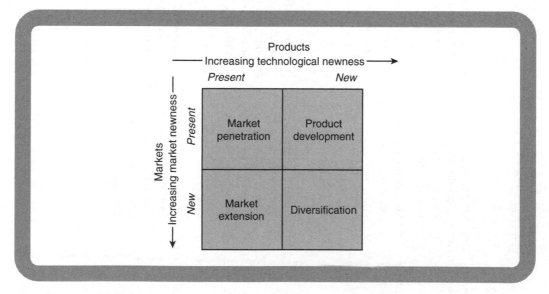

Figure 4.11 Ansoff's matrix

Product development (top right box):

● introduce new products for existing markets.

Market extension (bottom left box):

● take existing products to new markets.

Diversification (bottom right box):

● introduce new products to new markets.

If strategies for growth in each of the four boxes do not achieve the required sales and profit objectives, all that is left is the development of new strategies, usually via acquisition, joint ventures, licensing and so on.

As for growth options, it clearly makes sense to attempt to increase profits and cash flow using the least costly and the least risky strategy, venturing into new markets and product development only as necessary. If it can deliver the required returns, then market penetration, which uses the company's skills and knowledge of existing markets and customers, is preferable to the more risky options of transferring brand trust to new markets or developing new products. Similarly, the risk associated with *either* developing new products *or* extending into a new market is clearly less than attempting both simultaneously through diversification. The market audit should ensure that the method chosen to fill the gap is consistent with the company's capabilities and builds on its strengths.

For example, it would normally prove far less profitable for a dry goods grocery manufacturer to introduce frozen foods than to add another dry foods product. Likewise, if a product could be sold to existing channels using the existing sales force, this is far less risky than introducing a new product that requires new channels and new selling skills.

Exactly the same applies to the company's operations, distribution and people. Whatever new products are developed should be as consistent as possible with the company's known strengths and capabilities. Clearly, the use of existing operations capacity is generally preferable to new processes. Also, the amount of additional investment is important. Technical personnel are highly trained and specialist, and whether this competence can be transferred to a new field must be considered. A product requiring new raw materials may also require new handling and storage techniques, which may prove expensive.

The Ansoff matrix, of course, is not a simple four-box matrix, for it will be obvious that there are degrees of technological newness as well as degrees of market newness.

Figure 4.12 illustrates the point. It also demonstrates more easily why any movement should generally aim to keep a company as close as possible to its present position, rather than moving it to a totally unrelated position, except in the most unusual circumstances.

This brings us to a final point made regarding Ansoff's matrix, and that concerns the definition of the word 'new'. A new product could be new to the world or just new to a particular company. If the former is the case, the risk is obviously higher than in the latter case, but even here, if new products are at the very early stage of the life cycle, the company will still be learning how to make, sell and distribute them. In other words, it hasn't solved all the operational, scheduling, quality, design and technical problems in the same way it has for its established products.

Likewise, in considering whether a market is new or not, it could be new to the world or just new to the company – the former being much riskier than the latter. Even in the

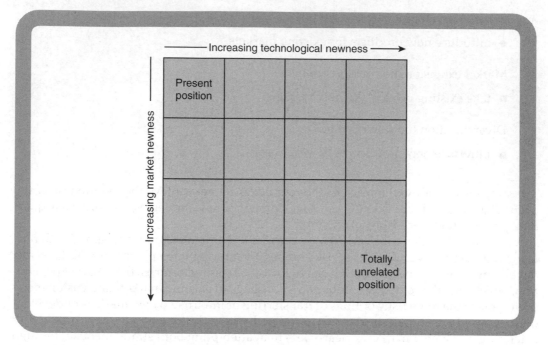

Figure 4.12 The risk implications of Ansoff's matrix

latter case, however, the question needs to be asked: 'How long does it take for a company's distinctive competence to become known in this market?' If this company has been involved in the market for a shorter length of time than is needed for its distinctive competencies to become known, then the market needs to be considered new and therefore riskier than an existing one.

Nevertheless, the product life cycle phenomenon will inevitably force companies to move along one or more of the Ansoff matrix axes if they are to continue to increase their sales and profits. A key question we need to ask, then, is how this important decision is to be taken, given the risks involved.

From the full list of possible methods involved in the process of gap analysis shown in Figure 4.13, we can see that there are options that an executive might take for every possible gap identified.

This figure illustrates the range of options available. If we use this tool in light of the lessons we learned from Ansoff's matrix about reduction of product and market risk, we should be able to make strategic growth choices that achieve the organization's objective to grow and respond to changes in the product life cycle, whilst keeping risk to a level commensurate with the growth and change actually required.

Market risk assessment

We can now turn our attention to the task of assessing the risks associated with markets. We recall from Chapter 2 that the sub-components of market risk are:

- Product category risk
- Segment existence risk

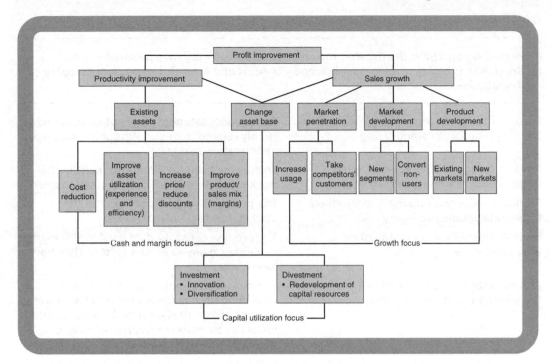

Figure 4.13   Analysis of options to improve profit

- Sales volumes risk
- Forecast risk
- Pricing risk.

As with any management science, however, it is not a black and white matter of a strategy being high or low risk. As convenient as this would be, in the real world, where most Marketing Directors need to operate, it is a matter of degrees, shades of grey if you like. We have therefore provided a graduated scale that shows where those different degrees of risk, from higher risk to lower risk, might actually sit. In the following sections, we provide a graduated scale for each sub-component of market risk to help with this assessment.

Product category risk

A graduated scale for the assessment of product category risk is shown in Table 4.3. In this table, we refer to our explanation above concerning what constituted a new product. iPod, for example, would have been categorized as a high risk, in that it constituted a new product category. An example of a low-risk product would have been *Red*, the woman's lifestyle magazine, in that the product category was already well established.

However, at the risk of becoming repetitive, as explained earlier in this chapter, this element of risk assessment really needs to be taken in the context of the next element of market risk assessment – segment existence.

Segment existence risk

A graduated scale for the assessment of segment existence risk is shown in Table 4.4.

Table 4.3 A graduated scale of product category risk

Product category risk is the risk that the entire product category may be smaller than planned. Risk is higher if the product category is novel and lower if the product category is well established.

Product category is very poorly established (very high product category risk)	The product category does not exist in this or closely related markets, although it may exist in unrelated markets.
Product category is poorly established (high product category risk)	The product category does not exist in this market but it does in closely related markets.
Product category is nominally established (moderate product category risk)	The product category does exist in this market, but few examples exist.
Product category is well established (low product category risk)	The product category does exist in this market and either many examples exist *or* they have a long history.
Product category is very well established (very low product category risk)	The product category does exist in this market; many examples exist *and* they have a long history, substantiated by a significant history or by market research, or sales of similar products.

Table 4.4 A graduated scale of segment existence risk

Segment existence risk is the risk that the target segment may be smaller than planned. Risk is higher if it is a new segment and lower if the segment is well established.

The existence of the segment is poorly substantiated (very high segment existence risk)	The existence of the segment is not demonstrated by either market research, sales of other products or sales of this product.
The existence of the segment is substantiated to some degree (high segment existence risk)	The existence of the segment is demonstrated only by either market research or sales of other products, but not by sales of this product.
The existence of the segment is nominally substantiated (moderate segment existence risk)	The existence of the segment is demonstrated only by both market research and sales of other products, but not by sales of this product.
The existence of the segment is well substantiated (low segment existence risk)	The existence of the segment is demonstrated by sales of this product, but it is relatively new and the stability of the segment is not substantiated by market research or sales of other products.
The existence of the segment is very well established (very low segment existence risk)	The existence of the segment is demonstrated by sales of this product and the stability of the segment is well documented.

Returning to the iPod example, although iPod was a high-risk product by dint of its newness, the market into which it was launched was certainly low risk, in that 'music on the move' as a segment was already well established by Walkmans and MP3 players.

Once again, however, we must refer to our explanations given above relating to newness in the context of markets, i.e. is the market entirely new or is it only new to the particular supplier? Many fabulous technological breakthroughs have been failures, because the need for them just didn't exist. The arch exponent of this phenomenon is Sir Clive Sinclair, whose C5 vehicle failed, in spite of its inherent attractiveness. Another example of a high-risk market is *Men's Health* magazine, in that the existence of a health-oriented new segment was not well proven in the men's magazine market.

As with product category, a certain amount of judgement is essential in assessing the risks associated with this product/market dimension. Nonetheless, the existence of a well-established, well-researched body of knowledge makes this a top priority, as many strategic plans make too many unfounded assumptions about these two critical drivers of commercial success.

It should be stressed that high-risk assessments on either product or segment existence mean that the strategy is in either the top right or the bottom left box of the Ansoff matrix. A high-risk assessment on both means that the strategy is in the bottom right box – i.e. the diversification box, the highest risk strategy that any organization could pursue.

Sales volumes risk and forecast risk

A graduated scale for the assessment of sales volumes risk is shown in Table 4.5. It is easier if this assessment is taken along with the next sub-component, forecast risk. A graduated scale for the assessment of forecast risk is shown in Table 4.6.

Table 4.5 A graduated scale of sales volumes risk

Sales volumes risk is the risk that sales volumes will be lower than planned. Risk is higher if sales volumes are 'guessed' and lower if the sales volumes are well supported by evidence such as market research.

The sales volumes are not supported by evidence (very high sales volumes risk)	The sales volumes are not supported by either past sales volumes, by sales volumes of a related product, or by market research.
The sales volumes are supported to a small degree (high sales volumes risk)	The sales volumes are supported only by market research or by sales of a similar product, but not by sales of this product.
The sales volumes are nominally supported by evidence (moderate sales volumes risk)	The sales volumes are supported by sales of this product, but there is little history.
The sales volumes are well supported by evidence (low sales volumes risk)	The sales volumes are supported by sales of this product and, although there is little history, market research or sales of other products support the sales volumes.
The sales volumes are very well supported by the evidence (very low sales volumes risk)	The sales volumes are supported by sales of this product, there is significant history and market research or sales of other products also support the sales volumes.

Table 4.6 A graduated scale of forecast risk

Forecast risk is the risk that the market will grow less quickly than planned. Risk is higher if forecast market growth exceeds historical trends and lower if it is in line with or below historical trends.

The forecast growth is not in line with historical trends (very high forecast risk)	The forecast growth is not supported by any historical trends or market research data.
The forecast growth is in line with historical trends to a small degree (high forecast risk)	The forecast growth is significantly greater than historical trends.
The forecast growth is nominally in line with historical trends (moderate forecast risk)	The forecast growth is the same as historical trends.
The forecast growth is well supported by historical trends (low forecast risk)	The forecast growth is significantly less than historical trends.
The forecast growth is very well supported by historical trends (very low forecast risk)	The forecast growth is zero, negative or much less than historical trends.

In Tables 4.5 and 4.6, we are referring on the one hand to evidence of historical volumes and on the other to forecast volumes.

It will already be clear to the reader that it is the product/market life cycle in relation to the diffusion of innovation curve that comes into play here. But, in order to make any kind of assessment, it is first necessary to establish what constitutes the 'market' referred to. For example, as stated earlier, there is clearly a market for pensions, but there are many other financial products that can satisfy the same need, so the only way to determine the future for pensions is to draw a future market map for the total need set, positioning pensions in it in order to establish whether they are declining or growing.

This, however, is largely contextual. (Readers will be shown how to construct a future market map in Part 3 of this book, which deals with the therapeutic process as opposed to the diagnostic process.) The more immediate issue is to analyse what has actually happened in a market and to predict what is likely to happen.

Perhaps the best way to illustrate this is to give a real example of a strategic plan, which the authors were called on to assess. It concerned a computerized business system, which was being launched into a number of different sectors, including construction and motor distribution. The following relatively simple assessment was made of the construction sector, using the diffusion of innovation curve (see Figure 4.14).

We can see from this example that three independent estimates were made of the market size in order to establish the current position on the diffusion of innovation curve.

In contrast, the same organization was planning to launch the same system into the motor trade, using the same undifferentiated product at the same relatively high price. A similar elementary study to that given in Figure 4.14 would have indicated that this market was already well into the late majority phase, when price and product features become more important.

The point about this example is that the strategy outlined in the plan made no differentiation between either of these two markets and the risk was therefore high for both, but for completely different reasons.

1. Number of contracting firms (Department of Environment, Housing and Construction).	160,596
2. Number of firms employing 4–79 direct employees.	43,400
3. Exclude painters, plasterers, etc.	<u>6,100</u>
4. Conservative estimate of main target area.	<u>37,300</u> (1) or 23% of total
5. Using the Pareto (80/20 rule) likelihood that 20% will be main target area, i.e. 160,596 × 20%.	<u>32,000</u> (2)
6. Total number of firms in construction industry (Business Statistics Office).	217,785
7. Number of firms classified by turnover from £100,000 to £1,000,000 (£K) 100–249 (£K) 250–499 (£K) 500–999 (£K)	 26,698 10,651 <u>5,872</u> 43,221 (3)
8. Company's best estimate of size of target market.	37,300
9. Company's estimate of the number of micro-installations in this segment.	43,500 (9.4%)

(1) Plotting this on the diffusion of innovation curve shows:

(2) Penetration of innovators and early adopters has taken four years. Adoption rate will, however, accelerate. It will probably be complete within one year.

(3) One year balance of early adopters = 6.6% = 2462 firms = installed base of 5968. Sales objective = 360 installations plus present base of 400 = 760 = 12.7% market share.

Figure 4.14 Example: assessing market risk

Pricing risk

A graduated scale for the assessment of pricing risk is shown in Table 4.7.

Given the assessments that have preceded this, it can be appreciated that pricing assumption assessments are comparatively simple.

Any organization that assumes it can get growth in volume and growth in prices in a mature market is being wildly optimistic, and it is surprising how many organizations do this in their forecast, in spite of the evidence. Let us refer back to Figure 4.10 and the example of 3 M Post-It notes. With many alternatives to choose from in a mature market, you will not find 3 M expecting growth in volumes and prices!

Pricing theory itself is comparatively simple. For example, few would argue with the two extreme options outlined in Figure 4.15.

The ability to follow the route of the benign circle in the model depends, of course, on the stage of the market itself. But it also depends hugely on how differentiated and how

Table 4.7 A graduated scale of pricing risk

Pricing risk is the risk that the price levels in the market will be lower than planned. Risk is higher if pricing assumptions are optimistic and lower if they are conservative.

The pricing assumptions are very ambitious. (very high pricing risk)	The pricing assumptions represent significant real price increases on either historical trends, competitors or substitutes.
The pricing assumptions are ambitious. (high pricing risk)	The pricing assumptions represent small real price increases on either historical trends, competitors or substitutes.
The pricing assumptions are neutral. (moderate pricing risk)	The pricing assumptions are in line with historical trends, competitors or substitutes.
The pricing assumptions are conservative. (low pricing risk)	The pricing assumptions represent small real price decreases on either historical trends, competitors or substitutes.
The pricing assumptions are very conservative. (very low pricing risk)	The pricing assumptions represent significant real price decreases on either historical trends, competitors or substitutes.

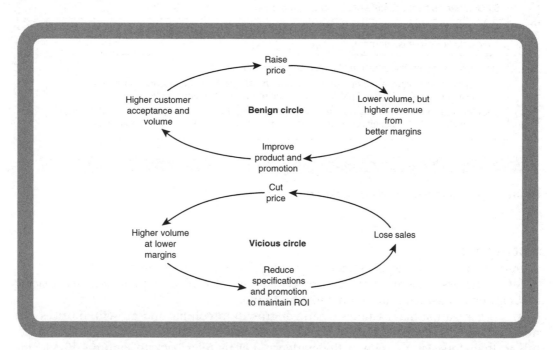

Figure 4.15 Pricing theory

well targeted the product is, as well as on how differentiated the total mix is. This is a concept that will be explained in detail in Chapter 5. It is also no accident that everything being assessed under market risk is also dependent on these same factors.

It is well known that price always has been and always will be the highest impact factor contributing to profitability. Take, for example, the simple example laid out in Table 4.8.

Table 4.8 Example: the impact of price on profit

	No discount	5% discount	10% discount
Unit price ($)	10.00	9.50	9.00
Unit profit ($)	2.00	1.50	1.00
Sales volume required to maintain profit	100	133.3	200

Table 4.9 Calculating the impact of price on profit

If you cut your price (%)	Gross margin							
	5%	10%	15%	20%	25%	30%	35%	40%
	You need to sell this much more to break even							
	%	%	%	%	%	%	%	%
1	25.0	11.1	7.1	5.3	4.2	3.4	2.9	2.6
2	66.6	25.0	15.4	11.1	8.7	7.1	6.1	5.3
3	150.0	42.0	25.0	17.6	13.6	11.1	9.4	8.1
4	400.0	66.6	36.4	25.0	19.0	15.4	12.6	11.1
5	–	100.0	50.0	33.3	25.0	20.0	16.7	14.3
6	–	150.0	66.7	42.9	31.6	25.0	20.7	17.6
7	–	233.3	87.5	53.8	38.9	30.4	25.0	21.2
8	–	400.0	114.3	66.7	47.1	36.4	29.6	25.0
9	–	1000.0	150.0	81.8	56.3	42.9	34.6	29.0
10	–	–	200.0	100.0	66.7	50.0	40.0	33.3
11	–	–	275.0	122.2	78.6	57.9	45.8	37.9
12	–	–	400.0	150.0	92.3	66.7	52.2	42.9
13	–	–	650.0	185.7	108.3	76.5	59.1	48.1
14	–	–	1400.0	233.3	127.3	87.5	66.7	53.8
15	–	–	–	300.0	150.0	100.0	75.0	60.0
16	–	–	–	400.0	177.8	114.3	84.2	66.7
17	–	–	–	566.7	212.5	130.8	94.4	73.9
18	–	–	–	900.0	257.1	150.0	105.9	81.8
19	–	–	–	1900.0	316.7	172.7	118.8	90.5
20	–	–	–	–	400.0	200.0	133.3	100.0
21	–	–	–	–	525.0	233.0	150.0	110.0
22	–	–	–	–	733.0	275.0	169.2	122.2
23	–	–	–	–	1115.0	328.6	191.7	135.3
24	–	–	–	–	2400.0	400.0	218.2	150.0
25	–	–	–	–	–	500.0	250.0	166.7

Example: your present gross margin is 25% and you cut your selling price 10%. Locate 10% in the left-hand column. Below, follow across to the column located 25%. You find you will need to sell 66.7% *more* units.

This example shows in simple, stark terms the additional volume that has to be sold for each 5% discount if the same profit level is to be retained. A more detailed calculation of the impact of price on profitability is shown in Table 4.9.

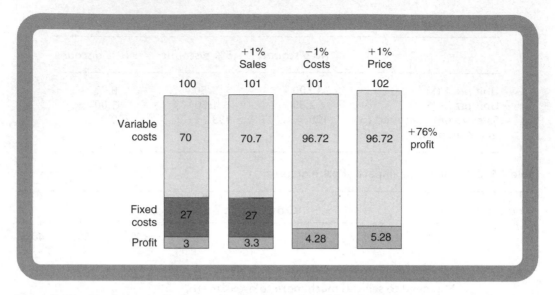

Figure 4.16 The impact of price on profit, compared with sales and costs

	Start point	Volume + 1%	Costs − 1%	Price + 1%
Volume @ $1	1000	1010	1000	1000
Turnover	1000	1010	1000	1010
Fixed costs	400	400	396	400
Variable costs	500	505	495	500
Profit	100	105	109	110
Profit increase (%)	0	5	9	10

Figure 4.17 The impact of price on profit, compared with sales and costs

Of course, as our readers may be quick to point out, an increase in sales volumes or reduction in costs will also have a positive impact on profit. However, as Figures 4.16 and 4.17 show, it is price that has the greatest impact of the three, with cost in second place and sales volume following in third place.

Given, then, that price is such a crucial determinant of profit, it will come as no surprise to hear that this last element of market risk assessment is one of the most important elements of Marketing Due Diligence and that, once again, much depends on the answers to the questions raised earlier about market growth.

Conclusion

Whilst we must stress that none of the above can be described as scientific, in the sense that there can never be an exact answer to any of the questions raised, there is, nonetheless, a logical process, underpinned by the long-established body of marketing knowledge, which can help determine the probabilities that the forecasts made in the strategic plan will occur as predicted.

In many cases of the plans reviewed by the authors, the following have proved to be the most frequent errors made:

1 Over-optimistic forecasts made for new product launches
2 Over-optimistic assumptions that the segment into which products are being launched exists
3 Over-optimistic forecasts for market growth, when all the evidence points to market maturity
4 Over-optimistic pricing assumptions in mature markets.

Errors (3) and (4) are most frequently made in relation to the first box of the Ansoff matrix, whilst (1) and (2) are most frequently made in respect of the remaining three boxes.

Finally, even in the case of a company making realistic market assessments, i.e. in cases where market risk is low, there follows the question of whether the strategy on which the forecast volumes and profits are based is sufficiently robust.

This is the crucial issue to be tackled in Chapter 5.

Chapter 5
Assessing share risk

Fast track

Share risk is the risk that the strategy will not create the degree of customer preference or competitive advantage that is needed to create the planned market share and hence fall short of creating shareholder value. It is distinct from, but aggregates with, market risk and profit risk. In short, share risk arises when what is offered to customers is not, in their eyes, valuable enough to them. This happens for a number of reasons: the wrong customers are targeted, they are offered the wrong things, or the strategy involves going head-on with a bigger, stronger competitor.

Share risk is the cumulative risk of five component risks:

- *Target market risk*. This is the risk that the value proposition will appeal only to a minority of the customers targeted; it is low when each target segment is homogeneous in its needs and high when each segment is heterogeneous in what it seeks.
- *Proposition risk*. This is the risk that the value proposition will not be quite right for any of the customers targeted; it is low when the strategy involves making specific offers to each target segment and high when the strategy involves a single offer to the whole of a segmented market.
- *SWOT risk*. This is the risk that the strategy does not make use of the company's strengths and does not compensate for its weaknesses; it is low when the targeting reflects the distinctive competencies of the company and high when it fails to understand them.
- *Uniqueness risk*. This is the risk that the strategy competes head-on with powerful rivals; it is low when the strategy involves targeting different customers and offering different value propositions and high when it offers the same thing to the same customers as do the competitors.
- *Future risk*. This is the risk that the strategy is designed for yesterday's market and not today's; it is low when the company understands the combined implications of the forces acting on the market and high when it ignores or neglects what is happening in the business environment.

For each of these sub-components of share risk, it is possible to make a rigorous assessment of risk level against a comparative scale. Each component has a different weighting according to the company and market context in which the strategy is to be implemented and the components can then be aggregated into an overall measurement of share risk. In addition, a number of other minor, but interesting, components of share risk can be assessed in a qualitative way to colour and inform the overall judgement.

Taken overall, a careful assessment of market share risk enables the strategist to do two things. Firstly, to adjust market share projections to allow for the strength of the marketing strategy. Secondly, to identify actions that will improve the strategy and the shareholder value creation potential of the business plan.

What do we mean by share risk?

As summarized in Chapter 2, the business risk inherent in any strategy arises from the three fundamental assertions made by the business plan: market risk flows from assertions about market size; share risk from assertions about what share will be won; and profit risk from assertions about costs, prices and margins. In this chapter, we consider the second of those three risks, share risk, the risk that the strategy will not deliver the share that it promises.

Share risk, the risk of not winning the hoped-for share of the market, arises from a fundamental truth: customers have a choice about where to place their business. It is worth remembering that this is not equally true in all markets. Some markets are 'imperfect' in the economists' sense of the term, meaning that customers cannot freely compare and switch between rival suppliers of a product or service. Such imperfections may arise from explicit regulation (the healthcare market, in many countries, is an example of this) or from implicit regulation (the legal profession, in many countries, maintains a subtle version of a closed shop). More often, the cost and difficulty of comparing and changing suppliers reduces the perfection of markets. The cliché that we are more likely to get divorced than change banks is an indicator of this. Despite these obvious imperfections in some markets, the truth remains that most markets are perfect enough (that is, customers have enough choice) to make a difference. There are now few markets in which the supplier side has so much power that they need not worry about customers expressing a preference and shifting their business. In addition, social trends, globalization and the information revolution mean that the trend is firmly in the direction of the customer.

In any reasonably free market, therefore, share risk is related to the probability of the customer expressing and acting upon a preference for a competitor. Such preferences have their roots in the customer seeking to satisfy his, her or (in the case of an organization) its needs. We may sometimes believe that customers behave irrationally, but in fact this is rare. Usually, customers act fairly rationally to meet their needs, even if their needs seem irrational to us. Just as customers' needs-addressing behaviour is generally rational, their needs are usually their own. Although some consumerists believe in a sort of conspiracy theory, that marketers twist and manipulate customers into thinking they need something they don't, any company that has tried to do this has failed in the long run. In other words, we create customer preference and reduce share risk by genuinely satisfying real customer needs better than the competition. We reduce customer preference and increase share risk by failing to meet those customer needs, relative to the competition, either completely or in part. Any reader who has decided not to return to a restaurant that gives poor service, or who has driven past one supermarket to get to another, has their own example of this. To the extent that we fail to meet customer needs, we contribute to business risk and, possibly, destroy shareholder value.

So much is obvious. The challenge lies in objectively assessing share risk. How we do this is described at length later in this chapter, but it is first necessary to be aware of the two most fundamental reasons why companies don't act on the obvious and satisfy customer needs. To put it bluntly, companies full of intelligent people act stupidly for two related reasons:

- *They are internally orientated*. They spend the large majority of their time considering internal processes and matters of efficiency. They spend much less time trying to understand the customer. As a result, companies often know much more about their product or service than about their customers. Competitive advantage then becomes defined in terms that the company can understand, measure and manipulate easily, rather than in terms that matter to the customer. The demonstration of this is given at most board meetings, where the metrics are mostly internal or, like sales and profits, so tenuously linked to customer preference as to be of little use.
- *They fail to understand customers*. Partly as a result of their internal orientation, companies often fail to understand the needs and wants that are driving customer behaviour. The most obvious manifestation of this is the obsession with features of the offering (e.g. price, design, functionality) and neglect of benefits (e.g. value, aesthetics, effectiveness). The second, but important, expression of failing to understand customers is the naive aggregation of their needs. Marketers often survey a class of customers (e.g. males aged 18–25, or IT companies of over 500 employees) and average their needs. This habit disguises the variation of needs within markets (i.e. segmentation) that is critical to understanding and creating customer preference.

These habits of internal focus and poor market understanding are deeply engrained in the majority of companies. They result in strategy weaknesses that are often invisible to the company itself. Such weakness of strategy leads to higher than desired share risk. Only careful, diligent assessment of the marketing strategy can reveal the weaknesses and inform corrective action. This is the subject of the next section.

Box 5.1   Share risk in the real world

The central concept underpinning share risk is the idea that there is some universal scale of how strong or good a marketing strategy is. Many managers have trouble grasping this point. Surely, they argue with some justification, the strength of a marketing strategy is entirely context dependent. What is good in one market is useless in another.

At a detailed level of tactics, these objections are well founded. A powerful '20% extra free' sales promotion might work brilliantly in some commoditized foods like potatoes or milk but backfire horribly in, say, a pharmaceutical market.

Even at a strategic level (the choice of target customers and what to offer them), there is no such thing as a panacea strategy. Going for the premium segment and offering them the clichéd 'Rolls Royce' product may be just the right thing to do for one player in

> one market and entirely the wrong thing to do in another market or even for another player in the same market.
>
> The point to grasp here is that all strong marketing strategies, whatever the target customers and the offer made to them, share common properties. Those common properties, as described in this chapter, can be used as a basis for assessing the likelihood that the strategy will deliver. In other words, the share risk.

How do we assess share risk?

If share risk arises from customer preference and strategy weakness, then our assessment of share risk begins with the analysis of our strategy towards customers – our marketing strategy. In Chapter 2 we defined marketing strategy as that set of management decisions about which customers to target and what propositions to offer them. It is the characteristics of that set of decisions that determine the probability of the strategy delivering the share it promises (i.e. the share risk). Readers may therefore find it useful, before reading further, to articulate the marketing strategy of their SBU in those terms. What is or are your target market(s)? What is or are the value proposition(s) you are making to it or them?

Given that we have a clear exposition of what our marketing strategy is, who we are targeting and what we are offering them, we can begin to test that strategy for share risk. We have already, in Chapter 2 (Table 2.2), introduced the idea that share risk is the aggregate of five sub-component risks. The next step is to apply some kind of graduated scale, to be able to make an objective judgement about the degree of risk stemming from each component in the case of any chosen marketing strategy. To do that, we need to have descriptions and examples of 'good' and 'bad' strategies, i.e. low- and high-risk strategies, for each of the five sub-components. Just such a graduated scale is the goal of the following paragraphs.

Assessing target market risk

Target market risk is the risk that the share will be less than expected because only some, not all, of the target market responds. It is in large part, therefore, a function of the heterogeneity or homogeneity of the target market. In other words, even an excellent value proposition is only excellent to those customers who share the same need for that proposition. Even a strong proposition, if it is targeted at a market which is heterogeneous in its needs, will cause only some of the customers to express a preference for it. That responsive fraction of the target therefore represents the upper limit on the possible market share.

A good, recent example of target markets with high share risk are those IT and telecoms companies who target the SOHO (small office, home office) segment. Their offer to that market assumes that everyone in it wants approximately the same thing. Even if true in a functional sense (e.g. limited networking, small volume printing) it is certainly not true in terms of their higher needs. Within the SOHO 'segment', there are technophobes and technophiles, design lovers and utilitarians, eco-warriors and the environmentally indifferent. A second example is those financial service firms who target 'high-net-worth individuals'. Within this group, who are homogeneous only in their financial worth, are the risk averse and risk takers, the hands-on and the delegators, the trusting and the cynical. In both

IT and financial services, the probability of achieving any given share must take account of this heterogeneity, which defines and limits the share available to any single value proposition.

By contrast, low-share-risk strategies are those which target relatively homogeneous segments. Usually, these are those which appeal to a very carefully defined set of emotional needs. *The Economist* magazine is a good example of this, with its focus on not just business people, but on those who see themselves as educated, knowledgeable and, frankly, different. Similarly, BMW's advertising strap line, 'The Ultimate Driving Machine', indicates their targeting on those who see driving as a pleasure and the car as an expression of their distinctive driving status. To both *The Economist* and BMW, demographics and other descriptors are less important than motivations and needs. To these companies, traditional descriptors are merely a proxy for the segment, not the segment itself.

Homogeneity and *distinctiveness* of the target markets are the two most telling characteristics of a strategy with low target market risk. They account for the first two letters of Kotler's acronym for a good segment: HDAV. The second half, *accessible* and *viable*, points towards the other two characteristics of a strategy with low target market risk. When target markets are hard to access or non-viable (that is, temporary or very small), the available market share is again constrained to something rather less than the nominal size of the market.

Taken together, these factors of target market risk allow us to assess it objectively against the criteria shown in Table 5.1.

It is useful at this point if readers refer back to their exposition of their own marketing strategy in terms of targets and propositions. Looking at the target or targets, where, on

Table 5.1 A graduated scale of target market risk

Target market risk is the risk that the strategy will work only in a part, not all, of its target market. Risk is higher if the target market is defined in terms of heterogeneous customer classification and lower if it is defined in terms of homogeneous, needs-based segments.

Target market is very poorly defined (very high target market risk)	The target market is defined no more clearly than by product category or channel.
Target market is poorly defined (high target market risk)	The target market is defined by product category and channel with some sub-targeting by descriptor (such as size, location, demographics).
Target market is nominally defined (moderate target market risk)	The target market is defined by product or channel and with descriptor sub-targets with local refinement at point of contact (such as sales team).
Target market is well defined (low target market risk)	The target market is centrally defined in terms of a set of distinctive needs that drive purchase and use behaviour. It can be partly characterized by measurable descriptors.
Target market is very well defined (very low target market risk)	The target market is defined in terms of a set of distinctive needs that drive purchase and use behaviour. It is well characterized by clear, measurable, descriptors which can be used to identify members of the segment.

the spectrum of target market risk, does your strategy fit? Later in this chapter we will return to how to use this assessment of target market risk, along with the other risk assessments, to assess shareholder value creation. For now though it is sufficient to draw out two lessons from the assessment of target market risk. Firstly, most strategies have a significant level of risk arising from their definition of targets. Secondly, this diagnosis is not only helpful in its own right, but already begins to hint at improvements in the strategy, as will be discussed in Part 3.

Box 5.2   Target market risk in the real world

When the Marketing Due Diligence diagnostic process is applied in practice, it frequently uncovers segments defined in terms of product or channel, or simplistic classifications like demographics. Understandably defensive, the responsible managers resort to two typical justifications.

Firstly, they argue that no segment of more than one customer is truly homogeneous. Every customer, they argue with good cause, is unique. This is true, of course, but it is a case of the best being the enemy of the good. What we are seeking to identify, in order to reduce target market risk, is a group of customers that are similar enough to behave in a similar way in this buying context. Product and other classifications rarely meet this criterion, whilst needs-based criteria usually do. The fact that a needs-based segment in, say, purchasing management books is not identical at a detailed level is no excuse for sticking with the old classifications. It's good enough that they behave similarly when offered a particular management book proposition.

The second defence is an appeal to practicality. We can't, to quote one of our case studies, open up the heads of each and every customer and look inside. We have to use the data we have, to approximate; this means using product, demographic or similar data. This is true, of course, but we must not forget that data is a means to an end. Once we have thought through and gained insight into real, needs-based segments, we can seek out data which is a good proxy for those needs. Career stage education and job role might be good data proxies for the management texts. Socio-demographics or residential location may not. We must be careful to avoid putting the cart (data) before the horse (needs-based segments).

Assessing proposition risk

Proposition risk is the risk that the share will be less than expected because the customer does not like the product, relative to the alternative. The alternative may not be a direct competitor, of course. Financial service companies selling critical illness cover compete not just against other insurance products, but also against those who 'self-insure' by covering their own risks. Proposition risk is a function of how well the value proposition meets the needs, rational and otherwise, of the target customer. We have already, in target market risk, allowed for that element of this risk that comes from targeting the wrong customers. Proposition risk arises when the strategy does not tailor the value proposition to the needs of even a good (i.e. HDAV) target. By contrast, proposition risk is lowered when a company tailors its propositions closely to the needs of the target segments.

In essence, proposition risk arises because of the internal–external orientation conflict inherent, to some extent, in all companies. Put simply, all companies would prefer to make one standardized value proposition designed to be easy and cheap to deliver. If only internal factors were important, the Henry Ford view would win out. On the other hand, every customer would like to see the product perfectly tailored to his or her needs. This is the classic conflict that is seen between operations and marketing in many companies. In most cases, this conflict results in some sort of compromise, in which tailoring to the needs of the target is sub-optimal. This is not a mistake, and is usually necessary, but its consequence is proposition risk. The benefits (usually lower costs) of standardization are balanced by the risks that a competitor might meet the targets' needs better and win them over. So, in principle at least, proposition risk is a simple idea.

Good examples of strategies with high proposition risk are those which therefore concentrate on operational efficiency, such as Asda (the UK subsidiary of Wal-Mart) and low-cost airlines like Ryanair and EasyJet. Compared to their 'premium' competitors, they sacrifice tailoring to the target for the sake of low cost and intend that low price will overcome the customers' preferences, as indeed it does in these relatively extreme cases. More informative are those companies who, due to the complexity of their offer, find it hard to tailor it at a realistic price. Such is the case in many pharmaceutical sectors but also, arguably, in some large professional service firms. In the former case, technical and regulatory constraints hinder tailoring. In the latter, the business model may depend on the delivery of a standardized service by relatively low-cost staff. The degree to which a company can realistically achieve proposition flexibility, therefore, is the degree to which it can reduce proposition risk. Of course, a relatively inflexible core proposition (e.g. the hardware or basic service) can be adapted to the needs of the segment by changing the extended parts of the offer. Car companies do this by adapting the expensive basics of a car into variants that are quite specific to certain segments. Look at the different, segment-specific propositions that Renault make using the core Megane offer. The rise of current account mortgages such as Royal Bank of Scotland's One account and Halifax's IF account seem to be due to their amenability to customers' fitting them to their own, varying needs. Similarly, in business logistics, for instance, Exel builds a complex tailored value proposition around the specific needs of its major customers, each of which is so large as to form a segment of one.

The great illusion we need to be aware of in proposition flexibility is that of the adaptation at point of delivery. Few companies, especially in technical markets, fail to claim that their proposition is tailored by the service at the point of delivery. For example, the sales person will construct a deal at the point of sale and adapt some elements of after-sales service. Whilst this does represent a small degree of proposition flexibility, it should not be mistaken for something greater than that. Such point-of-delivery customization is heavily constrained by the limited resources available at this point. True adaptation of the value proposition to the target almost always requires central coordination.

The degree to which a value proposition's core and extended elements are tailored to the needs of the target markets, as opposed to standardized across them, allows us to assess proposition risk objectively against the criteria shown in Table 5.2.

Again, it is useful at this point if readers refer back to their exposition of their own marketing strategy in terms of targets and propositions. Looking at the value propositions, where on the spectrum of proposition risk does your strategy fit? This diagnostic result will be aggregated with other risk levels to assess Marketing Due Diligence and it will also form the basis of improving the strategy.

Table 5.2 A graduated scale of proposition risk

Proposition risk is the risk that the offer to the market will fail to appeal to some or all of the target market. Risk is higher if all the market is offered the same thing and lower if the proposition delivered to each segment is segment specific.

The proposition is not target specific (very high proposition risk)	All of the components of the proposition are fixed, with no significant variation between the propositions offered to different targets.
The proposition is target specific to a small degree (high proposition risk)	The non-core components of the proposition are adapted to the needs of the targets at point of delivery.
The proposition is nominally target specific (moderate proposition risk)	The non-core components of the proposition are adapted to the needs of the targets at the point of delivery, together with product or service mix variations.
The proposition is target specific to a significant degree (low proposition risk)	The non-core components of the proposition are adapted to the needs of the targets in a centrally coordinated manner, as are product or service mix variations.
The proposition is totally target specific (very low proposition risk)	All of the components of the proposition are adapted to the targets' needs, with significant variation between the propositions offered to different targets.

Box 5.3   Proposition risk in the real world

When the Marketing Due Diligence diagnostic process uncovers significant proposition risk, it often evokes a frustrated response from managers. Proposition risk can only be managed by proposition flexibility, and managers feel constrained by technical, financial and sometimes political constraints. How, they ask in a rhetorical tone, can this be done in practice? The pragmatic answer is that there are no quick, easy answers, but there are often quick, partially effective answers and slow, costly, but powerful answers.

In the short term, adapting a value proposition with a more or less fixed core, such as an existing mature product or service, can only be done by tweaking the extended and augmented part of the value proposition to fit the needs of the different target segments. Thus, packaging, naming, pricing, channels and superficial design features can be changed to reflect the segments needs, even if only partially.

In the longer term, it may be that the core proposition may need to be re-engineered, complete with re-branding. The better match to segment needs thus achieved is inevitably reflected in the cost and time to do this.

Sadly, even this pragmatic answer often fails to satisfy managers who seek quick and easy, sustained competitive advantage. To those managers, we can only point out that such an advantage is an oxymoron.

Assessing SWOT risk

SWOT (strengths, weaknesses, opportunities, threats) risk is the risk that the share will be less than expected because the company fails to align its strengths with the market opportunities and to manage its weaknesses in the face of market threats. It is, therefore, a function of relative strength in the marketplace not in absolute terms, but at the point of execution of the strategy. So, if a company selects a strategy (remember, choice of targets and propositions) in which its strengths can be leveraged and its weaknesses are less relevant, then it will have a greater relative strength in the market than if it picks a strategy where those things are not so. With good SWOT alignment, it may even be possible to achieve a greater relative strength in the target markets than much larger competitors. So the degree to which a company's choice of target market and value proposition uses its strengths and manages its weaknesses is the degree to which SWOT risk is reduced.

An example of good SWOT alignment, and therefore low SWOT risk, is the BMW 'Ultimate Driving Machine' strategy, already mentioned. This strategy uses BMW's brand, engineering and design strengths. It also minimizes the importance of their relatively high cost base by selecting a less price-sensitive target market. With a completely different strategy, EasyJet uses its low-cost-base strength and negates its weaknesses of secondary airport bases and customer service levels, which are relatively unimportant to its chosen, price-sensitive customer segment.

By contrast, the frozen food chain Iceland completely ignored the concept of SWOT alignment when it attempted to reposition itself. Long established and quite successful at offering low-cost frozen food to a relatively price-sensitive target, Iceland attempted to respond to the competitive pressures resulting from the consolidation of the UK retail food market. It identified that, coincidentally, it had quite a strong record concerning the avoidance of food additives and genetically modified food. It attempted to leverage this by targeting a relatively upmarket 'green' segment of customers who sought to avoid additives, etc. The attempt failed horribly and the company has now reverted to something close to its former strategy. Simply put, this 'strength' was not of interest to its existing customers and other facets of the proposition (especially its store design, location and brand) meant that it was unable to access those customers who might have wanted additive-free, more 'wholesome' food.

Poor SWOT alignment, and hence high SWOT risk, comes most often from failing to really understand the company's strengths and weaknesses. In particular, it arises from mistakenly believing that strength is something we are competent at, instead of appreciating that strength is something we are better at than the competition. Differentiating between real and illusory strengths and weaknesses is aided by tools discussed in Part 3 of this book.

This understanding of SWOT risk allows us to assess it objectively against the criteria shown in Table 5.3.

As with target market risk and proposition risk, understanding SWOT risk is aided if readers consider where on this spectrum their own strategy might sit. The result both informs the Marketing Due Diligence assessment and any necessary corrective action.

Box 5.4   SWOT alignment risk in the real world

Assessing SWOT alignment risk in practice is an aspect of Marketing Due Diligence that is especially susceptible to the human failing of subjectivity. Not only do managers struggle to identify their real and distinctive strengths and weaknesses, but they also find it hard to accept any results of objective analysis. We see them subjectively filtering and selecting data to reduce cognitive dissonance between what they feel and what the data suggests. There is rarely enough hard data to overcome such entrenched opinions.

In practice, two fundamentals of SWOT alignment must be used to aid the understanding of our strengths and weaknesses and hence how well our strategy is SWOT aligned.

Firstly, strengths and weaknesses are *relative to the competition*. Accepting that our customer service, or technical performance, or some other aspect of what we offer the customer is weak is not the same as saying the offer (or worse, the company) is bad. It simply means that we are not as good as the competition in the irrational, subjective, eyes of the customer. The same applies to perceived strengths too, of course.

Secondly, let the market be your evidence. Current business will inevitably reveal success with certain customers or in certain contexts, and will, of course, reveal similar examples of relative failure. This evidence is important, because it is not our judgement. If we have failed to win technically-oriented customers but done well with technophobes seeking ease of use, what does that tell us, objectively, about our relative ease of use in the eyes of the customer?

In practice, of course, it is only the very rare management teams that can combine in-depth market knowledge with objectivity. For mere mortals, judicious use of consultants provides the latter.

Table 5.3 A graduated scale of SWOT risk

SWOT risk is the risk that the strategy will fail because it does not leverage the company's strengths to market opportunities or guard its weaknesses against market threats. Risk is higher if the strategy ignores the firm's strengths and weaknesses, lower if the strengths and weaknesses of the organization are correctly assessed and leveraged by the strategy.

The strategy is not SWOT aligned (very high SWOT risk)	The choice of targets and propositions fails to use organizational strengths or minimize organizational weaknesses, which are, in any case, not understood.
The strategy is SWOT aligned to a small degree (high SWOT risk)	The organizational strengths and weaknesses are self-perceived, not objectively assessed and tested. These are not leveraged or minimized by the choice of targets and propositions.
The strategy is nominally SWOT aligned (moderate SWOT risk)	The choice of targets and propositions coincidentally reflects the self-perceived strengths and weaknesses of the organization.
The strategy is SWOT aligned to a significant degree (low SWOT risk)	The choice of targets and propositions both leverages strengths and negates or minimizes weaknesses, but those strengths and weaknesses are self-perceived and not objectively assessed or tested.
The strategy is fully SWOT aligned (very low SWOT risk)	The strengths and weaknesses of the organization have been objectively assessed, tested and the choice of targets and propositions both leverages strengths and negates or minimizes weaknesses.

Assessing uniqueness risk

If your assessments of target market risk, proposition risk and SWOT risk have all suggested that your strategy is strong and that you are heading for a low share risk overall, then you will be unusual compared to many of the companies studied for our research. Furthermore, there may still be a significant chance of your strategy not delivering the share it promises for one or both of two reasons. The first of these is uniqueness risk.

Uniqueness risk can arise despite selecting a homogeneous target and addressing it with a specific proposition, even if that strategy is perfectly SWOT aligned. This is because the target and proposition chosen may be very similar to that of a large and powerful competitor. Even if the competitor you are going head-on with is less powerful than you, it will still limit the share available, compared to a strategy which effectively sidesteps competition by choosing a different target market and value proposition.

Strategy uniqueness is difficult to achieve, especially in mature markets, but even a limited degree of strategy uniqueness is preferable and lower risk than going head-on with the competition. Those companies that do achieve some degree of strategy uniqueness seem to do this by one or more of three approaches:

- *Core product uniqueness.* This is more common in technologically-based product markets, especially those at an embryonic stage, in which the intellectual property is more novel and easily defendable. An example is Olympus's use of Osyris electronic tagging technology for patient management in hospitals. The core proposition is unique and, because of patents and technology, hard to copy.
- *Extended product uniqueness.* This is more common in mature markets and in services where core product uniqueness is more difficult to sustain. It involves creating proposition uniqueness by the innovative development of the extended product, including service and related activities. An example of this is the way in which Jungheinrich is attempting to differentiate itself in the market for forklift trucks. With decreasing differences between the trucks themselves, the way in which the trucks are provided and maintained has become their point of strategy uniqueness, protected by organizational competencies rather than intellectual property rights.
- *Target definition uniqueness.* This is found in the most mature of markets, where both core and extended product uniqueness have been eroded by competitors. It involves creating and using a better understanding of segmentation within the traditional market definition, and using that to devise unique targeting and propositions. An example of this is NatWest, a UK retail bank that seems to have identified a need for 'traditional' banking service. The corresponding real segment, emerging as a reaction to competitors' cost-cutting and rationalization, has become their target and they have changed their proposition to reflect that. In this case, strategy uniqueness in both targeting and proposition is protected by proprietary market knowledge, management skills and the brand.

This understanding of uniqueness risk allows us to assess it objectively against the criteria shown in Table 5.4.

Uniqueness risk is difficult for managers to judge objectively. Often, the minutiae of product or service differences appear larger, close up, than they seem to customers. In one enlightening research interview, a respondent initially claimed a unique strategy but, on giving the matter more thought, said: 'In reality, we offer basically the same thing to the same people in the same way.' Many readers of this section may think the same way.

As with the other components of share risk, it is worth considering the level of uniqueness risk associated with your SBU's choice of targets and value propositions explicated

Table 5.4 A graduated scale of uniqueness risk

Uniqueness risk is the risk that the strategy will fail because it goes 'head-on' with the competition. Risk is higher if the choice of target market and value proposition are very similar to the competition, lower if they are very different.

The strategy is not unique to any significant degree (very high uniqueness risk)	The choice of target and proposition does not differ in any significant way from that of the major competitors.
The strategy is unique to a small degree (high uniqueness risk)	The choice of target or proposition, but not both, differs to a small degree from that of the major competitors.
The strategy is nominally unique (moderate uniqueness risk)	The choice of both target and proposition differs to a small degree from that of the major competitors.
The strategy is unique to a significant degree (low uniqueness risk)	The choice of target or proposition, but not both, differs significantly from that of the major competitors.
The strategy is unique (very low uniqueness risk)	The choice of both target and proposition differs significantly from that of the major competitors.

earlier in this chapter. The result will contribute later to the assessment of share risk and thence overall business risk and shareholder value creation. In addition, as with the other diagnostic tests, it will help inform therapeutic steps to reduce risk and improve shareholder value creation.

Box 5.5   Uniqueness risk in the real world

In the sort of mature markets in which share risk is the key challenge, low uniqueness risk can seem like an ivory tower myth to practising managers. In the absence of an entirely new group of customers and/or an amazing and unlikely technical innovation, all the main players are bound to fight over the same ground.

This is understandable, but risks becoming a self-fulfilling prophesy. 'What we can conceive we can achieve' may be a cliché of self-help books, but it has some truth as regards marketing strategy. The challenge for practising managers is to avoid two traps that lead to high uniqueness risk.

Firstly, letting convention determine how you see the market. In most markets, the way the market is described varies little between the plans of the major players. Categories, channels and other data are organized in a similar way. This seems to be due partly to the purchasing of the same market research data and partly to the incestuous recruitment patterns that lead to a homogenized industry culture. Only by breaking out of this comfortable but constraining paradigm can companies avoid their view of the market leading them to compete head-on.

Secondly, thinking in product terms. In all markets, but especially in ones with a high technical content such as IT, financial services or engineering, a technical skill set and qualifications are needed just to understand the language of the market. Given a team with similar educational and career backgrounds and similar teams in similar markets, it's not surprising that they all think of the market in terms of products, and come to similar conclusions with resulting high uniqueness risk.

As with other areas of strategy risk, uniqueness risk is an area where it takes an exceptional combination of closeness to the market and perspective to avoid falling into these two traps.

Assessing future risk

Even when target market, proposition, SWOT and uniqueness risks are all considered and addressed, there remains a component of share risk that can significantly reduce the probability of a strategy delivering the share that is expected of it. This is because even a strategy that addresses today's market can fail if the market changes in important and relevant ways over the course of the plan.

Unlike, perhaps, some of the other sources of share risk, future risk is not hard to understand. It arises when the market conditions change in such a way that some or all of target market, proposition, SWOT or uniqueness risks increase because of changes in one of three areas:

- *Customer changes*. These are changes in the nature of real segments in the market and the distribution of customers between them. An example of this in the UK clothing market is the large 'middle market' segment, upon which Marks & Spencer depended, and the fragmentation of it, to which the company subsequently failed to respond.
- *Competitive changes*. These are changes in the targeting and proposition decisions made by competitors, but also the indirect competitive forces such as new entrants, substitutes, or even suppliers and customers. An example of a new entrant competitive change is the entry of major retailers into financial services, a market previously dominated by generalist retail banks.
- *Channel changes*. These are changes in the existence and capabilities of channels by which the proposition is communicated and/or delivered to the targets. The obvious example here is the impact of web-based channels on many markets, from books to housing to packaging, all of which have seen a degree of disintermediation and re-intermediation.

Collectively, these three areas are the microenvironment in which the strategy operates. The microenvironment, however, does not change at a whim. It is driven by the wider, more distant macroenvironment in which the firm operates. Future risk is therefore a function of how well the strategy considers the macroenvironmental forces acting on the market and anticipates the resultant change in the microenvironment. This involves, as discussed later in the book, being cognizant of social, legal, economic, political, technological and other forces that drive all markets, and being able to draw out their implications for customer, channel and competitor changes.

Contrasting examples of high and low future risk strategies are represented by Kodak and GKN. The former, despite seeing the advent of digital technology well in advance, failed to draw out the implications for new entrants and, as a result, lost its commanding market position in the imaging market. By contrast, GKN intelligently anticipated the consolidation

Table 5.5 A graduated scale of future risk

Future risk is the risk that the strategy will fail because the market's needs have changed or will change in the time from strategy conception to execution. Risk is higher if the strategy ignores market trends and lower if it assesses and allows for them.

The strategy does not anticipate market change (very high future risk)	The implications of changes in the external macroenvironment and microenvironment are not identified or allowed for to any significant degree in the choice of target and proposition.
The strategy anticipates market change to a small degree (high future risk)	The implications of changes in the external macro-environment or microenvironment, but not both, are partly identified and allowed for to a small degree in the choice of target and proposition.
The strategy nominally anticipates market change (moderate future risk)	The implications of changes in both the external macroenvironment and microenvironment are partly identified and allowed for to a small degree in the choice of target and proposition.
The strategy anticipates market change to a significant degree (low future risk)	The implications of changes in both the external macroenvironment and microenvironment are fully identified but allowed for only to a limited extent in the choice of target and proposition.
The strategy fully anticipates market change (very low future risk)	The implications of changes in both the external macroenvironment and microenvironment are fully identified and have been fully allowed for in the choice of target and proposition.

of the car components market and the subsequent change in customer needs. They moved early to develop a proposition well suited to the consolidated market, including logistics management and shared design.

This understanding of future risk allows us to assess it objectively against the criteria shown in Table 5.5.

This last component of share is both hard to measure and critical to evaluate. As will be discussed later, it is especially important in turbulent markets. Again, making even a rough qualitative assessment of your own strategy is a useful way to embed the idea of future risk. As with the other components of share risk, future risk informs the Marketing Due Diligence assessment and suggests ways to improve shareholder value creation.

Box 5.6   Future risk in the real world

Of all the components of share risk uncovered in the Marketing Due Diligence diagnostic process, future risk is the one that seems most alien to the mindset of practising managers. Rightly, they point to the trends they are either going with or, they believe, creating. However, these trends are almost always small-scale trends in the 'near environment' of customers, channels and competitors. What managers often fail to grasp is that such trends are secondary, driven and created by larger and longer-term trends in the 'far environment' of SLEPT factors. In making that mistake, managers can condemn themselves to failure to predict trends in the market and misattributing such trends to themselves or the competition. In reality, it helps to hold on to two truths which, whilst not universal, are sufficiently general to be useful.

Firstly, any one player in the market is rarely strong enough to change that market. Even when they appear to do so, by creating a new business model or technology for instance, they are usually simply going with the grain of trends created by much larger forces in the far environment. It follows that it is useful to anticipate the consequences of these forces.

Secondly, whilst predictions about the future are always wrong in detail, rigour can get them right enough to be useful. We don't need to predict exactly when and how the demographic bulge of 'baby boomers' will create a demand for fashionable clothing amongst pensioners, simply to know that it will, and at about 60–70 years after their birth. Often, the desire to be detailed and precise relegates the importance of such 'blue sky' thinking and reduces companies to reacting to trends when they percolate through into the near environment.

Recognition of where market change originates and the acceptance of limited accuracy is, therefore, needed to reduce future risk in practice.

Assessing other sources of share risk

The five components of share risk described at length above represent the vast majority of threats to the business plan delivering the share it promises. No assessment of share risk is complete unless it includes those five types of risk. However, our research also indicated four secondary sources of share risk that are worth consideration, even if not to the extent of a full assessment.

Synergy risk

Share risk is reduced when the strategy creates either external or internal synergy, or both. The former occurs when two or more different target/proposition sets interact positively in the marketplace, the latter when they have some positive influence on each other inside the organization.

External synergy is often seen in technical markets and, superficially very different, fashion markets. In both these cases, small segments that lead market opinion can be difficult to penetrate and unprofitable, especially if they are 'promiscuous' and switch brand frequently. Despite this, companies target them because of the influence they have on other, more intrinsically valuable segments. The influence of one segment on another is not always in this innovator-to-follower direction. Staying with the example of the car market, Mercedes seems to have unlocked a source of external synergy with the A-Class. Small and inexpensive, by Mercedes standards, the A-Class seems to be targeted at a 'second car segment' of those families who currently drive a large Mercedes as a first car. The communication of the brand values from, for instance, spouse to spouse, seems to have helped Mercedes penetrate the competitive second car market when its costs and expensive reputation might otherwise have hindered it. The converse of external synergy is possible too, of course. Some have argued that the difficulty of Rover in maintaining a premium brand reputation was related to its 'stretching' the brand as far as the Metro, a small, inexpensive super-mini. In this case, the cheaper segment interacted negatively with the more upmarket segments targeted with larger Rovers.

Just as external synergy arises in the marketplace, internal synergy happens inside the company. Internal synergy arises from the fact that propositions can be made either better or more cheaply together than they can apart. Typically, examples of this are companies which can effectively serve a segment by adaptation of a proposition originally aimed at another segment. The conversion of civilian airliners into military transports is one simple illustration of this. Perhaps more impressive, as mentioned earlier, is the way in which Renault has attacked several disparate segments of the car market with propositions that are all based on the same basic design (the Megane). By sharing development, manufacturing, procurement and service assets across segments, Renault gains economies of scale. This amounts to greater efficiency than if they had attacked segments that could not share these resources.

Of course, Renault is not alone in doing this and the car market is not unique in this approach. Nor is internal synergy always the domain of manufacturing firms. Spinning off knowledge and expertise into several segments is the business model of many service and retail companies, and is another example of internal synergy. Tesco's supply chain management, developed for its big stores, has been a big factor in its penetration of the smaller, convenience store market. Whichever internal asset is employed, internal synergy attributable to shared resources is usually more common than external synergy attributable to interacting targets. Arguably, internal synergy is the least valuable in that its benefits are limited to the finite cost savings possible, whereas external synergy offers, usually, much larger market opportunities.

Whether internal or external, however, synergy effectively increases the resources applied to a target market without placing more resources at risk. If realized, it therefore reduces the risk that the plan may not deliver the promised share.

Tactical direction risk

Share risk is reduced when strategies make obvious the tactics that must flow from them. The primary mechanism for this is the way in which tactically unequivocal strategies reduce the risk of the implemented strategy 'drifting' and differing from the intended strategy. However, there also appears to be a secondary mechanism at work here, in which tactically explicit strategies reduce the time and effort taken to communicate internally.

It is important not to confuse tactical direction with some kind of centralized, controlling bureaucracy. The key point to appreciate is that the implementation of strategies involves making very many small detailed decisions about the components of the marketing mix (pricing, promotion, distribution, product, people, processes and physical evidence). At best, each of these small decisions takes time and therefore money. At worst, they represent opportunities for the strategy to drift off course. In the best strategies, the choice of target and proposition makes these tactical decisions 'no-brainers' and therefore faster, cheaper and less likely to drift.

For instance, Apple's strategy in the PC market involved targeting segments characterized by individuality and a degree of iconoclasm. Accordingly, its broad marketing mix decisions included a high-spec but stylish product, premium pricing, some channel specialization and so on. At the detailed implementation level, invisible to outside observers, this greatly restricted many management choices, kept the strategy focused and made implementation faster and more efficient. By contrast, a medical device company that targets 'cardiologists', a heterogeneous group, leaves huge margin for tactical discretion and hence both internal discussion and strategy drift. This is why a strategy that makes obvious what needs to be done reduces the risks of that strategy drifting off course. Coincidentally, this also reduces the 'internal transaction costs' – that is, the time spent internally communicating and negotiating implementation. By both means, strategies that give a high degree of tactical direction reduce share risk.

Proportionality to objectives risk

Share risk is reduced when the strategy is proportional to the objectives and increased when it is not. Whilst this may seem obvious, objectives are often imposed on SBUs and strategies are sometimes developed in isolation from objectives. There are two ways in which the strategy and the objectives can be proportionate or disproportionate to each other:

- *Target to objective proportionality*. In low-risk strategies, the total size of the target segment or segments is significantly larger than the revenue objective. This may seem obvious, but some marketing objectives, set on a 'last year plus' basis or driven by abstract financial goals, are way beyond the total size of the target. Whilst large, even dominant, share is a reasonable goal, a revenue objective that is larger than the target market size is clearly naive. Closely related to this, profit level objectives need to be proportionate to the pricing and costs attainable in the target segment. This may also seem obvious, but our research revealed numerous cases of strategies in which pricing was set for a premium segment and costs for an economy segment, in seeming ignorance of the internal contradictions in this approach.
- *Proposition to objective proportionality*. In low-risk strategies, the relative strength of the proposition is proportionate to the degree of change in share sought. Where the objective requires a large growth in share, or maintenance against a well-resourced competitor, the proposition must be significantly stronger than that of the major competitors, or else compensated for by promotional and other resources. By contrast, higher risk marketing strategies expect large shifts in share or substantial price premiums, even though the proposition is not significantly stronger than that of the competition. Again, this may seem obvious, but the habit of companies to focus on the minor advantages of their proposition often leads them to lose perspective and see their offer as much stronger than it really is.

Resource adequacy risk

Share risk is reduced when the resources made available to execute the strategy are adequate and increased when they are inadequate. Clearly, the mechanism at work here is that the implemented proposition is rather weaker than the intended one due to insufficient resources.

Adequate resourcing is not always the case. As with proportionality to marketing objectives, marketing strategies are often resourced simplistically, using internal reference points such as last year's budgets. In some cases, this leads to a situation in which the resource allocated to a strategy is completely inadequate to allow its implementation, no matter how intelligently it is used. There are two dimensions along which the overall allocation of resource to marketing strategy may be tested:

- *Proportional to the target*. The resource required to implement a marketing strategy is related to the target segment or segments in two ways. Firstly, larger volume segments require more resources to support promotion, distribution, service and other volume-related aspects of the proposition. Secondly, the nature of the segment may dictate larger resources if it is difficult to access or requires especially expensive contact, such as a technical sales team. Strong strategies are those that are resourced in relation to the volume of target customers and the costliness of accessing and communicating with them.

● *Proportional to the proposition.* The resource required to implement a marketing strategy is related to the proposition or propositions in two ways. Firstly, consider the nature of its differentiation from the competition. Simply differentiated propositions (such as price-based differentiation or those based on clearly novel technology) generally require fewer resources to support them than propositions differentiated in a complex way, such as by many small product differences or intangible service differences. Secondly, consider the extent of the proposition's difference from the competition. Closely related propositions requiring little change in customer habits, and with low 'switching' costs, require fewer resources to support them than propositions which require the customer to change behaviour significantly.

A strong example of appropriate resourcing was that of AstraZeneca's launch of Nexium™ into the market for ulcer drugs. Faced with many large competitors, a premium price and less than desired clinical differentiation from competitors, AstraZeneca supported the product with huge resources, including 2000 sales representatives in the USA alone. Frustratingly for authors, examples of poorly resourced marketing strategies are hard to find, since they tend to sink without trace.

Aggregating and applying share risk

The descriptions, examples and tables given in the preceding section provide the basis for assessing the level of risk for any given SBU strategy for each of the components of share risk. Even a superficial assessment of their own strategy against the graduated scales in Tables 5.1–5.5 often provides useful insight to managers. However, our goal is to assess the shareholder value creation of a plan objectively and quantitatively, and that requires the development of these scales into a reproducible management process. Such a process involves six steps. The bulk of the process described below is for the simplest of strategies, one in which one target market is addressed with one value proposition. As explained in the final step, however, the same principles can then be used to address more complex, multiple-target strategies.

Step 1: Explicate the marketing strategy

Clearly, no marketing strategy can be tested for share risk without first being made explicit. Whilst this may seem trivial, it is a necessary point to make. For many companies, marketing strategy is developed in a largely unconscious way, building incrementally on to previous strategies with small-scale decisions about allocating resources to certain markets and products. In such cases, the marketing strategy is rarely stated explicitly. Even when it is, it is not always an accurate representation of reality. In the research for this book, the initially stated marketing strategy was, on reflection, revised and refined into a more precise statement of who was being offered what. Typically, such refinement moves from product and broad market to extended offer and specific segment. A good example of this was a regional brewery, who defined their strategy as 'cask ale to beer drinkers'. On probing, the value proposition included heritage and traditional values, and the market was actually a subgroup of beer drinkers defined in terms of not only their geography and consumption, but also their attitude to life.

So the first stage in the objective assessment of share risk is perhaps the easiest. Who is it you target in practice? What is it you offer them in fact? Readers are urged, if they have not done so yet, to write down the answer to those questions now. The answer should take the form of one or more target markets and, for each, a statement of the value proposition to that group of customers.

Step 2: Assess the explicated strategy against the sub-components of share risk

Armed with an explicit statement of marketing strategy in terms of target markets and their respective value propositions, the task of assessing the share risk can now begin.

For each of the five sub-component risks, place the explicit strategy accurately and objectively on the graduated scales set out in Tables 5.1–5.5. In some cases, the risk level will be obvious, in some less so. In all cases, the accuracy and usefulness of the result is improved by using external and valid data to test the judgement. These will vary for each sub-component risk, as shown in Table 5.6.

Using the explicit statement of marketing strategy and Tables 5.1–5.5 as guides, together with all information practically available, enables us to make five judgements. For each sub-component, an assessment from very high risk to very low risk can be made. It is those five judgements that will be used in the next step. Although they remain, to some extent, subjective and only semi-quantified, they are already much better than the intuitive judgements made about share risk by most companies. To the extent that they are made with the aid of external data, tested and discussed by the board of directors and facilitated by an external and knowledgeable person, they represent the best – that is, the most diligent – judgement we can make. Further quantification might make us feel better, but also risks spurious results arising from falsely quantifying that which is essentially qualitative.

Step 3: Aggregate the sub-components into an overall assessment of share risk

At the simplest level, share risk is the additive of the five sub-components. A first approximation can therefore be made by looking at the raw outputs of Step 2. If we have, for example, two moderate risks, one high risk and two very high, we can make a first guess that our share risk is in the area of high risk.

To refine this first estimate, we need to consider the weighting of the five different sub-components and the influence of the secondary but not insignificant risks like synergy and resourcing.

Weighting the share risk sub-components

The five sub-components of share risk are all important factors, but there are some second-order factors to consider in combining them. In short, different market or organizational contexts make some of the factors matter less or more. These are summarized in Table 5.7.

Table 5.6 Evidence sources to support share risk assessment

Sub-component of share risk	The question to ask	Typical evidence sources
Target market risk	Is the target a homogeneous segment?	• Qualitative market research into needs-based segmentation • Quantitative market research about channels of distribution and needs-based segmentation • Tacit market knowledge about variation in needs between customers
Proposition risk	Is the proposition tailored to the target?	• Qualitative and quantitative market research about benefits sought by the customer • Comparison of this proposition to the 'ideal' for this target • Qualitative and quantitative market research about the customers' perceptions of the product • Market share data and trends • Comparison of this proposition to others offered to other targets
SWOT (Strengths, Weaknesses, Opportunities, Threats) risk	What are our real strengths and do we use them? What are our real weaknesses and do we manage them?	• Qualitative and quantitative market research about benefits sought by the customer, translated into what competencies are needed to deliver those benefits • Customer perception data • Benchmarking data versus significant competitors in this target market • Result of value chain analysis and testing
Uniqueness risk	How different is our marketing strategy from that of the competitors?	• Comparison of our targeting activity with that of other companies in the sector • Comparison of our value proposition with that of other companies in the sector • Customer perception of the targets and propositions of all companies in the sector
Future risk	Will target market, proposition, SWOT and uniqueness risk change over the period of the plan?	• Information about trends in the macroenvironment for the business (e.g. social, legal, economic, political and technological) • Information or inferences about how the macroenvironment might impact the microenvironment (e.g. customers, competitors and channels) • Testing of target market, proposition, SWOT and uniqueness risk in the context of the inferred

Table 5.7 Weightings of share risk sub-components

Sub-component of share risk	Factors influencing weighting
Target market risk	Target market risk is especially important if the market is mature and segmented and if your resource position is relatively disadvantageous compared to the competition. It is less significant if the market is embryonic and your resource position is relatively advantageous compared to the competition.
Proposition risk	Proposition risk is important if you operate in a market in which your competitors have taken up clear positions (e.g. low-cost option, technically superior option and high-service option). This factor is less important if you operate in a market in which all of the competitors are offering similar levels of performance, price and quality.
SWOT (Strengths, Weaknesses, Opportunities, Threats) risk	SWOT risk is important if the strengths and weaknesses of your organization differ markedly from those of the competition. It is less important if they are relatively similar to those of the competition.
Uniqueness risk	Uniqueness risk is important if the resources of your organization are significantly smaller than those of your main competitors. It is less important if you have a preponderance of resources compared to them.
Future risk	Future risk is important if the market is experiencing significant change or if it is very susceptible to macroenvironmental forces (e.g. regulation). It is less significant if the market is stable or isolated from such forces.

Of course, if circumstances are such that all five factors seem equally weighted, then a simple average of the assessments is sufficient.

Allowing for secondary factors

The secondary factors of synergy, tactical direction, proportionality to objective and resource adequacy usually act to moderate the impact of the five primary sub-components of share risk. Hence, if those five conclude that the risk is borderline between two levels, the secondary factors will tip the balance.

However, the secondary factors also act as a checklist for any anomalous quirks in the risk profile of the strategy. For instance, if internal synergy between a new proposition and an existing one was very large, such that the costs and asset risk of the new proposition were negligible, then this might impact on the whole share risk. Similarly, if the resources made available to a new strategy were clearly far short of what was needed, this would increase share risk whatever the other factors. Such extreme examples are anomalous, but the consideration of the secondary share risk factors enables them to be identified and a better overall assessment made.

By the end of Step 3, therefore, the assessment of share risk has moved from having a set of objectively supported assessments of the sub-components to an overall assessment of share risk which balances all these contributing factors. We can now assert with confidence that the share risk associated with this strategy is very high, high, moderate, low or very low. This assessment is used in Step 5 to moderate the share assertions of the business plan.

Step 4: Identify the growth component of the strategy

An important premise of Marketing Due Diligence is that risk is associated with growth. That is not to say that the core business is immune to weaknesses in the strategy, but to recognize that core business has a certain momentum and that new business is much more susceptible to risk. Hence it is the growth component of the market share that is moderated by the share risk and not the core business.

Identifying the growth component of market share is not straightforward. At a superficial level, an SBU business plan which promises growth from 10% to 15% market share has a growth component of 5% or 50% of the total. However, some allowance must be made for historical trend. If the share growth promised is only a little above historical trend, and there are no considerations suggesting a change in that, then the growth component is only that element above the historical trend. If, however, the growth in share is much higher than the historical trend, or if there are good reasons to expect the trend to decline (such as the entry of new competitors or a significant change in competitor strategy or effort), then the growth component is larger.

Clearly, there is some degree of judgement needed here. The growth component can be thought of as the difference between promised share and what might be expected if we did nothing. Most business plans assert a significant growth in share over the life of the plan, either in real terms or in the context of historical trends. This growth component is what is considered and moderated in Step 5.

Step 5: Moderate the growth component of the strategy to allow for risk

Step 2 of this process for aggregating and applying share risk led to an assessment of the different risks that make up share risk. In Step 3 these were aggregated into an overall level of share risk. In Step 5, this aggregate level of share risk will be used to moderate the growth in the market share identified in Step 4.

Although the scale of share risk appears linear, from very low to very high, there is no evidence to suggest that the relationship between share risk and likely share growth achieved is a simple linear one. In other words, reducing the share growth in fixed increments according to the level of share risk is too simplistic and not supported by our findings. We need to make a more thoughtful judgement.

At the extremes of share risk, that judgement is easier. Very low levels of share risk across all factors suggest that the promised share is likely to be realized. The market share assertions in the business plan can be left unaltered. In even more unusual cases, a 'perfect' strategy might imply too conservative a judgement of share risk and an upward moderation of the market share promises. This is very unusual, however, as shareholder pressures rarely allow boards of directors to be unduly cautious.

Very high levels of risk, on the other hand, do not imply simply a large reduction in the likely share growth. As risk grows, the likely outcome becomes not only worse, but also more unpredictable. Typically, such cases stem from very poor target market definition and product-led, untailored, value propositions. Further, the strategy goes head-on with competitors and fails either to use strengths or allow for market changes. In such cases, the conclusion is that we can have very little firm idea about the likely share growth, only that it is unlikely to be positive.

It is at the intermediate levels of share risk when a careful judgement of likely market share growth must be made. These risk levels suggest some moderation of the business plan promises, typically in the region of 10–30% of the planned growth. Exactly how much the promised share growth is moderated depends on exactly how high the level of risk is, and is necessarily judgemental. The newly moderated market share is, however, much more substantiated than the previous, untested, iteration. It can now be incorporated into the overall Marketing Due Diligence assessment.

Step 6: Allow for complex strategies

Steps 1–5 describe a process for first assessing and then aggregating the various components of market risk. This aggregated share risk was then applied to moderate the growth component of the market share promised by the business plan. This process is appropriate for the simplest marketing strategies, in which growth is intended to be won via the application of a single value proposition to a single target market. In reality, however, the business plan usually promises growth as the result of more complex strategies in which more than one target market is addressed simultaneously.

In this more complex and more common case, the process described in Steps 1–5 is carried out separately on the share growth attributed to each component of the strategy. For every proposition/target market combination planned, the share risk is assessed, aggregated and applied to moderate the promised share growth. These separate calculations are then combined to create a new, more substantiated promise of market share growth. Obviously, therefore, high share risk for components of the marketing strategy that are intended to contribute a lot to share growth will be more significant than the share risk of lesser contributing strategy components.

Steps 1–6 are summarized in Figure 5.1.

The outcomes of share risk assessment

The ideal outcome of the share risk assessment process described in this chapter is a number. It is the market share the business plan is most likely to deliver, which is made up of two elements. Typically, for mature businesses at least, the largest component of the market share is that which might be called the core market share – that which is implied by historical trends, after allowing for important influences on share such as new competitors. The remaining, smaller but critical component of the planned market share is the growth component. Unless the share risk is very low, the growth component that emerges from application of share risk is likely to be less than that promised in the original plan. This is, of course, the natural outcome of identifying and allowing for the share risk associated with the strategy. The newly tested and moderated share promised then becomes one part of the Marketing Due Diligence calculation.

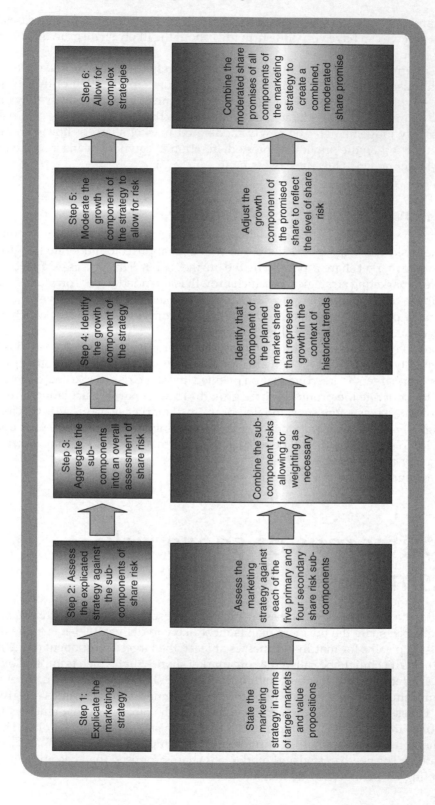

Figure 5.1 The process of aggregating and applying share risk

In many cases, however, the level of share risk is such that any amount of growth component is unsubstantiated by the share risk assessment. In these cases, some or all of the sub-components are so risky or so poorly understood by the company that promising any amount of share growth is utopianism rather than business planning. In this case, the moderated share which is used in the Marketing Due Diligence calculation is no more than that of the core market share suggested by historical trends and informed by known changes in the competitive environment.

In addition to these contributions to the Marketing Due Diligence calculation, however, the share risk assessment process, especially Step 2, inevitably reveals issues surrounding the marketing strategy, such as poor target definition, weak proposition design and failure to leverage strengths, avoid competition or predict future trends. These issues become the inputs of the Marketing Due Diligence therapeutic process described in Chapter 8.

Chapter 6
Assessing profit risk

It is still by no means certain that a marketing strategy will create shareholder value even if, when implemented, the strategy achieves the predicted market share of a market that generates the planned total sales revenue values. There are other risks that need to be assessed, and these are covered in the Marketing Due Diligence diagnostic process by the assessment of profit risk. Profit risk assessment considers the probability of creating the anticipated financial return from the predicted market share of the planned market value.

Not surprisingly, therefore, the profit risk is normally most important in relatively mature markets where established competitors, and other stakeholders in the total industry value chain, are often fighting to obtain a larger share of a static or even declining total profit pool.

As before, the total profit risk assessment has been subdivided into five elements, which are separately assessed in order to generate an overall view of the probability of achieving the planned level of profitability.

The first of these five elements, profit pool risk, assesses the probability that the future total profit pool will be less than planned. This risk is clearly higher if the existing profit pool is static or shrinking and lower if the targeted profit pool is high and growing. Another factor impacting on this risk is the relative proportion of this total available profit pool that the marketing strategy aims to take; the higher the proportion, the higher is the associated risk. The other major component of this risk assessment is the likelihood of significant changes within the total value chain that may impact on the potential profit attainable from the marketing plan.

The second element considers the profit sources risk assessment by looking specifically at whether overall competitors' reactions to the proposed marketing strategy are likely to reduce the profit below that planned. The profit sources risk is higher if the planned profit growth comes directly at the expense of competitors and lower if it comes from growth in the total profit pool. The highest level of this risk is therefore seeking to grow profits aggressively from a high existing base in a highly competitive market with a declining total profit pool and increasingly sophisticated customers.

However, many marketing strategies will have a disproportionate impact on one competitor, or a few specific competitors, while the remaining competition will be largely unaffected. The level of competitive response will therefore be determined by the scale of this impact on those most affected, and can be much greater than if the 'financial pain' is shared more widely across competitors.

Competitor impact risk consequently focuses specifically on the impact of the marketing plan on individual competitors, rather than considering them in total. This element evaluates the risk that profits will be less than planned because of a single competitor reacting aggressively to the marketing strategy. The competitor impact risk is higher if the profit impact on competitors is concentrated on one competitor and this impact threatens the competitor's survival.

The remaining components of profit risk examine the assumptions made regarding the internal cost structure of the business. Internal gross margin risk assesses the probability that gross margins will, in reality, be lower than planned. As the risks associated with forecasting selling prices will already have been assessed under the market value risk section, this component concentrates on the costs of manufacturing the product or providing the service. The risk is higher if the internal gross margin assumptions are optimistic relative to current similar products, or if the business has no previous experience or validated information on which to base its assumptions.

The other costs risk assesses the probability that net margins will be lower than planned because other costs are higher than anticipated. A commonly important component of these other costs is marketing support, and this is the most frequent cause of adverse profit impact, due to overspending against plan. Very often, the overspending is 'required' in order to achieve the targeted market share, but this still results in profit being lower than planned. This other costs risk is higher if assumptions regarding other costs, including marketing support, are optimistic, e.g. lower than current costs, or where the business has no previous experience in similar product areas.

Introduction

As discussed in Chapter 2, the Marketing Due Diligence diagnostic process breaks down the overall business risk associated with any proposed marketing strategy into manageable chunks that can be assessed using appropriately tailored techniques. The market risk and the share risk, which were considered in detail in Chapters 4 and 5 respectively, result from the strategic choices made by the business regarding which particular markets to focus on and how to gain the desired share of these targeted markets.

The third element of our Marketing Due Diligence diagnostic process is slightly different, in that it assesses the risks that follow from the implementation of the proposed marketing strategy. This profit risk component looks at the probability of delivering the planned profit, even if the business wins the anticipated market share from the predicted targeted market value. These first two stages of a marketing strategy will deliver sales volumes and sales revenues, but the creation of shareholder value is achieved by delivering 'greater than required financial returns', as was discussed in Part 1. Therefore, as shown diagrammatically in Figure 6.1, there is a need for a third element in our Marketing Due Diligence diagnostic process.

It is perhaps an indicator of the significant weaknesses in much marketing planning that our research has highlighted many marketing 'strategies' that stop at the level of 'targeted

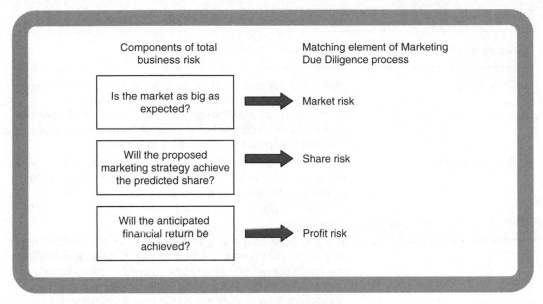

Figure 6.1 Matching the Marketing Due Diligence process to components of business risk

market share' or 'planned sales revenues'. As we will explain in detail in this chapter, a key element in assessing profit risk is predicting the reactions of competitors, customers and suppliers to the proposed marketing strategy. Yet many marketing plans predict significant growth in market shares and profits without any assessment of the potential responses from those affected. Also, many marketing strategies make extremely optimistic assumptions regarding the future improvements that can be achieved in the internal cost structures of the business. Thus, forecast gross margins are significantly above current levels, while all other indirect costs are predicted to decline substantially. In these same plans, the value offering to existing customers is to be improved, new products developed and launched, and new markets entered!

As with the market risk and share risk, the profit risk has been broken down into five sub-components in order to facilitate the structured analysis of the overall risk. These sub-components, which were introduced in Chapter 2 and are shown in Table 6.1, do overlap to some extent, but their relative importance differs in different competitive environments and with different types of strategy. The deconstruction of the total profit risk into these sub-component elements, therefore, enables a much better assessment of the overall profit risk than could be achieved without such subdivision.

Before starting to consider each sub-component in detail, it may be helpful to indicate when the profit risk is likely to be of major importance in the review of a marketing strategy. The market risk has already been seen to be of critical importance in 'new' environments, such as new products being launched into new markets. Once the market is established, this risk diminishes as the assessment of future market values becomes more accurate. Consequently, the share risk is normally most important in growing markets where a common objective is to try to grow faster than the total market, i.e. to grow market share. This risk is also critical for market share growth strategies in more mature markets, but there now starts to be some overlap with the profit risk component.

Table 6.1 Sub-components of profit risk

Sub-component of profit risk	Explanation
Profit pool risk	This is the risk that profit will be less than planned because of competitors' reaction to the strategy caused by a combination of the strategy and the market conditions. It is higher if the profit pool is static or shrinking and lower if the targeted profit pool is high and growing.
Profit sources risk	This is the risk that profit will be less than planned because of competitors' reaction to the strategy. It is higher if the profit growth comes at the expense of competitors and lower if the profit growth comes only from growth in the profit pool.
Competitor impact risk	This is the risk that profit will be less than planned because of a single competitor reacting to the strategy. It is higher if the profit impact on competitors is concentrated on one powerful competitor and that impact threatens the competitor's survival. It is lower if the profit impact is relatively small, distributed across a number of competitors and has a non-survival threatening impact on each.
Internal gross margin risk	This is the risk that the internal gross margins will be lower than planned because the core costs of manufacturing the product or providing the service are higher than anticipated. It is higher if the internal gross margin assumptions are optimistic relative to current similar products and lower if they are relatively conservative.
Other costs risk	This is the risk that net margins will be lower than planned because other costs are higher than anticipated. It is higher if assumptions regarding other costs, including marketing support, are less than current costs and lower if those assumptions are more than current costs.

Profit risk is critical when the main objective of the marketing strategy is to grow profit in stable or declining markets. Clearly, this may be done with or without increasing market share depending upon what is expected to happen to the total profit pool. However, in many such markets the total profit pool will itself be under severe pressure, and attempts to increase market share at the direct expense of well-established competitors will probably lead to severe competitive reactions in the marketplace. It is in these environments that a detailed analysis of the profit risk is particularly required.

Profit pool risk

The initial logic behind this first sub-component is very simple. Any marketing strategy has a higher probability of achieving its planned profit levels if the targeted profit pool

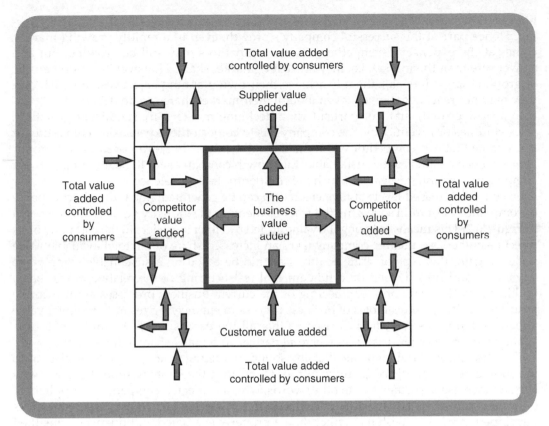

Figure 6.2   Game theory view of industry value chain

is both large and growing. This probability is further increased if the required share of this total profit pool is relatively small, as the likelihood of any significant response from other stakeholders in this profit pool is reduced. However, as is discussed below, there are some other issues that can lead to increasing risks, even if the profit pool is both large and still growing.

For this risk assessment, the profit pool under consideration is the total industry value chain of the targeted market. In other words, as shown in Figure 6.2, it includes the value gained by suppliers and intermediate customers, as well as by competitors. The emphasis on shareholder value creation in the Marketing Due Diligence process leads to a focus on the sources of the super-profits that generate this shareholder value. In fast-growing industries, the total value produced can itself be growing rapidly. More end users may be buying the good or service; existing users are buying more and may be willing to pay increased real prices for enhanced levels of benefits. It can be possible for all the participants in such an attractive market to generate shareholder value. This can be true, but is not normally the case, even in such high-growth markets.

The most logical marketing strategy in a growing market is to try to increase market share during this growth phase. Much empirical evidence highlights that the greatest shareholder value is produced by businesses with dominant market shares and that these high market shares are most economically developed while the market itself is still growing. Hence part of the successful company's growth, even in a rapidly growing market, comes at the expense of competitors. These competitors may still be growing, but at a slower rate than the market, i.e. they are losing market share. However, their slower rate of growth may still enable them to achieve their own planning objectives, in which case they may not react aggressively even though their market shares are in decline.

In a slow growth, static or particularly a declining market, any significant growth in sales volumes or revenues by one company has to come at the expense of a competitor. It is probable that this competitor will try to defend their existing levels of sales and profits. Hence if such a gain is to be sustainable, the growth company should be utilizing a strong competitive advantage, against which the competitor has no defence.

Of course, increased levels of financial return can be generated, not at the direct expense of competitors, but from squeezing the other elements in the industry value chain, as shown in Figure 6.2. This means reducing the value added by either suppliers to the company or its direct customers, so that the company takes an increased share of the total available value added. Again, this type of strategic thrust should be based on a sustainable competitive advantage and may depend on a fundamental restructuring of the relative power bases within the value chain or re-engineering of the current business processes applied in the industry. Really good examples of business process re-engineering result in the total value added by the industry being increased so that all the parties involved can benefit; once again, there are very few examples where *all* parties do actually share in these benefits.

This discussion should indicate that any sound marketing strategy should be clear as to the source of any predicted increase in profits. Further, the strategy should explain why such an increase is sustainable; in other words, why the affected competitors, suppliers or customers cannot do anything about it. Unless this process is carried out, the business has developed more of a 'wish list' rather than a properly evaluated and financially justified marketing strategy. In markets with large and growing total profit pools, it is much less likely that affected stakeholders will take aggressive actions in response to increased shares being taken by one player. They are all still doing quite well financially and have a strong vested interest in not destroying the currently attractive industry.

However, there are classic examples of some players very aggressively targeting other levels in the value chain with great success. The potential risk of this happening to any proposed strategy therefore needs to be evaluated.

There has been a dramatic shift in the relative power of supermarket retailers and their manufactured goods suppliers over the past 30 years or so. In the past, the large grocery product manufacturers, particularly those with strongly branded strategies, understood their target consumers and communicated directly with them regarding new product developments and even promotional activity on established lines. Their power meant that the supermarkets were merely a channel of distribution that needed to stock the brand leaders if they wanted these brand-loyal consumers to shop in their stores.

Of course, today this situation is very different. The development of very strong retailer brands and consolidation of the industry have resulted in a few leading supermarket retailers with immense power over their suppliers. Gaining distribution in these leading stores is now a critical success factor for grocery product manufacturers, as consumers are increasingly unlikely to go elsewhere to find a particular brand. This is leading to consolidation in the suppliers' industries (such as the merger between Procter & Gamble and Gillette, recently announced at the time of writing) as they seek to re-balance the power relationship with their customers. During this period, there has been an amazing reverse correlation between the growth in the profit margins of the most successful supermarket retailers and the relative decline in the profitability of many grocery product manufacturers.

An even clearer example of the leveraging of this increased power over the key element in a total value chain has been the move by supermarket retailers into industries that were previously dominated by huge multinationals (much bigger than even the largest supermarket at the time). The oil industry, like many others, was started by a few, very highly vertically integrated companies. Indeed, the 'oil' industry is still dominated by the major multinational or global players. (They used to be referred to as the 'seven sisters', but recent industry consolidation has sharply reduced the size of the family.) Over the years, they have faced increasing levels of competition in their 'upstream' operations (i.e. exploration and production) and some of the original oil majors have taken a strategic decision to curtail their direct involvement in some of their 'downstream' activities, e.g. by exiting from petrochemicals. However, these oil majors now face increasingly severe competition in the petrol retailing element of their downstream business.

This newer competition from supermarket retailers has been most successful in France and the UK, where retailers have gained very significant market shares in around 30 years. Supermarkets first sold petrol in the UK in 1974 and this move coincided with the opening of out-of-town superstores. Their existing overall marketing strategy was consistently applied, in that the petrol was retailer branded and sold at a discounted price, relative to the normal pricing of the oil majors. Indeed, initially the supermarkets gave back to consumers the total gross margin on petrol sales in vouchers that were redeemable in the newly opened superstores.

Thus, the supermarket retailers saw the product 'petrol' in a very different way to the oil majors. To the retailers, it was a commodity style product that was very price sensitive, but could be used to build up consumer loyalty both to the particular store location (most consumers do the majority of their grocery shopping in only one outlet) and to their fledgling retailer brands. At this stage, the actual profit generated by petrol sales was of secondary importance. They could take this view because their required investment in this new product category was minimal; their petrol stations were located in the car parks of their out-of-town superstores and only required around two additional staff per shift to operate, as they were utilizing the existing infrastructure.

The oil majors had invested consistently for years to build their corporate identities around their flagship petrol brands. Shell, for example, used their corporate logo on all their petrol stations around the world to stand for quality, reliability, applied technology and, most importantly, oil-based products. In other words, it was a product-based brand, while these new retailing-based competitors were using a customer-based brand that epitomized perfectly usable quality and value for money. The oil companies found it very difficult initially to accept that their high-technology end product was now seen by its final users as a standardized commodity.

By the early 1990s, supermarkets had, in total, taken a 20% market share and had around 600 petrol stations in the UK. This was a very small proportion of the 20,000 total, but this total was declining quite rapidly. Despite the supermarkets opening new sites, this was more than offset by the closures by the oil majors and, particularly, by the independent petrol station operators; thus, 600 sites closed in 1993 and 1000 in 1994.

In the mid 1990s, the supermarkets took their petrol retailing strategy into its next stage. This involved opening stand-alone petrol stations with small supermarkets attached, rather than the petrol station being attached to a major superstore. Tesco Express is the best example, being a 200-square-metre supermarket, selling a range of chilled and fresh goods located with a petrol station. In their published financial statements for 1996, Tesco highlighted the growing importance of petrol sales as a source of profitability; it was then contributing over 10% of the retailer's profits.

Not surprisingly, these developments forced the oil companies to review their own petrol retailing strategies and to acquire a much greater level of retailing expertise. Esso introduced its 'Price Watch' campaign in September 1995 that aims to make each Esso service station prices competitive against its local competition, including any supermarkets.

Shell focused on its on-site Select stores and has sought to develop them as convenience retail outlets. Select is now one of the top sandwich retailers in the UK. Shell has also invested heavily in customer loyalty technology with its SMART card concept; this has been given broader appeal by bringing in other companies. However, competition in this area increased when BP got involved in 'Nectar' collectibles with Barclaycard, Sainsbury's, Debenhams, etc.

BP has already redeveloped some of its sites with 'Express Shopping', providing hot foods and bakery products, with other oil companies bringing franchised fast-food facilities into their on-site outlets. Thus, all the oil majors are trying, in different ways, to become much more retail oriented in their service station operations, in an attempt to compete more effectively against the supermarkets. Part of this response is also to learn what works best so that it can be applied in an attempt to build entry barriers in those international markets where the supermarkets, or other new entrants, have not yet become the very serious threat they are in France and the UK.

More recently, the leading supermarkets have moved into other product categories through continuing to leverage on their retailer branding. Thus, they now have significant market shares in clothing, electrical products and other household goods. However, the most interesting moves are into financial services such as insurance and banking products, because these do not need to be sold through retail stores. Their competitive advantage is their loyal customer base rather than their retail network. Interestingly, this move and the technology revolution is accelerating the move of existing national retail banking networks from assets to liabilities.

Petrol retailing illustrates how changes in the value chain can dramatically affect the size of, and shares in, the total profit pool in a well-established, relatively mature industry. However, similarly dramatic changes can also take place in a fast-growing market. In the very early 1980s, the PC industry was starting and the dominant computer companies needed new suppliers for this very-high-growth potential product. This was particularly true for IBM which, although by far the largest and most profitable computer company in the world, was a late entrant into the PC market.

In an effort to get into this rapidly growing market as quickly as possible, IBM, unusually at the time, outsourced the operating system (to Microsoft) and the main processor chip (to Intel). It saw these items as necessary commodity inputs to a product that it would itself brand; thus, IBM would take the dominant share of the total value chain. It could also switch all its business to another supplier if it did not get the price it demanded!

In the following years, both Microsoft and Intel followed an aggressive consumer branding strategy in a very successful attempt to turn themselves from subservient commodity suppliers to dominant branded goods companies. Indeed, the key issues for most PC and laptop purchasers nowadays are that the machine supports Microsoft's latest version of Windows and contains an up-to-date Intel processor; the name on the outside of the box is largely irrelevant. Thus, the once dominant branded computer companies have been turned into the commodity suppliers, which now need the branded components. Their relative profitability and shares of the still growing total profit pool confirm the new balance of power.

Table 6.2 A graduated scale of profit pool risk

Profit pool risk is the risk that profit will be less than planned because of competitors' reaction to the strategy caused by a combination of the strategy and the market conditions. Risk is higher if the profit pool is static or shrinking and lower if the targeted profit pool is high and growing.

The profit risk is greatly increased by the profit pool conditions (very high profit pool risk)	The profit pool is eroding rapidly or is highly volatile, and a high share of this profit pool is required.
The profit risk is increased by the profit pool conditions (high profit pool risk)	The profit pool is eroding slowly but predictably, or is static and a high share of this profit pool is targeted.
The profit risk is neither increased nor decreased by the profit pool conditions (moderate profit pool risk)	The profit pool is static in real terms but is stable and the targeted share of this pool is modest.
The profit risk is reduced by the profit pool conditions (low profit pool risk)	The profit pool is either growing steadily or is very large in relation to the targeted profit objectives.
The profit risk is greatly reduced by the profit pool conditions (very low profit pool risk)	The profit pool is growing rapidly and is very large in relation to the profit objectives.

Thus, the profit risk can be significantly increased by potential changes in the structure of the industry value chain, particularly if the entry barriers into the business's present positioning are low. Where the business faces increasingly strong customers or suppliers, the profit pool risk can be high, even when the total profit pool is large and still growing. However, a static or shrinking profit pool indicates a higher risk, particularly if the value of the total profit is volatile. As discussed in Chapter 3, volatility in financial return indicates increased risk. A graduated scale of profit pool risk is summarized in Table 6.2.

Conversely, a low profit pool risk is often seen in a growing market, where the business and its current competitors together exercise a dominant position and there are complementary products to those that they sell. A complementary product is one that increases the total value of the package, such as DVD players and DVD films, computer hardware and software, etc. These products can enable customers and, in some cases, suppliers to improve their overall financial return by making relatively more money from the complementary products. Thus, they are unwilling to react aggressively, as the business increases its share of the total profit pool.

Profit sources risk

The next sub-component of profit risk requires an analysis of the sources of profit growth in terms of the impact on competitors. In the profit pool risk, the focus was on the other layers in the value chain, the overall level of the profit pool and its trend over time. It is quite

Table 6.3 A graduated scale of profit sources risk

Profit sources risk is the risk that profit will be less than planned because of competitors' reaction to the strategy. Risk is higher if the profit growth comes at the expense of competitors, lower if the profit growth comes only from growth in the profit pool.

The profit risk is greatly increased by the profit sources (very high profit sources risk)	All of the profit growth is planned to come from existing competitors.
The profit risk is increased by the profit sources (high profit sources risk)	Most of the profit growth is planned to come from existing competitors proportionately.
The profit risk is not significantly increased by the profit sources (moderate profit sources risk)	Some of the profit growth is planned to come from existing competitors and the rest from growth in the profit pool.
The profit risk is reduced by the profit sources (low profit sources risk)	Most of the profit growth is planned to come from growth in the profit pool.
The profit risk is greatly reduced by the profit sources (very low profit sources risk)	All of the profit growth is planned to come from growth in the profit pool.

normal for the sum of all the marketing strategies of the competitors in any market to be much greater than is available from the market, e.g. their individual targeted market shares add up to much more than 100%. Hence many companies have introduced game theory concepts to build on the dynamic interactions among themselves and against competitors. This is also the approach taken by the Marketing Due Diligence process, as is developed below.

The first requirement is to get a very clear definition of which 'competitors' are to be analysed. There is only one meaningful definition of competitors: your competitors are your customers' alternative suppliers. In other words, if your targeted customers do not buy from you, who else would they buy from, even if what they buy may not be exactly the same good or service as you are offering! This should not be a problem for any sound marketing strategy, as part of developing the target market and the method of attacking it should have identified the potential competition. However, many businesses still adopt an internal perspective to identifying competitors, based on the industry in which they operate, e.g. all other car manufacturers rather than those serving specific market segment needs. This often brings in too wide a spectrum of competitors.

Once the competition is properly defined, the profit sources risk can be assessed. As shown in Table 6.3, the marketing strategy has a higher probability of delivering its targeted profit if the source of profits growth is growth in the existing total profit pool. Consequently, a high level of profit sources risk is caused by a marketing strategy where all or most of the planned profit growth comes from existing competitors. Obviously, these sub-components are grouped together to produce a cumulative picture of the overall profit risk. Thus, a marketing strategy that tries to gain significant market share in a declining and volatile total profit pool with increasingly sophisticated customers would have a very high profit risk.

If existing competitors will lose out financially if the proposed marketing strategy is successful, there is a significantly greater probability that they will respond aggressively to try to regain their previous position. Unfortunately, in many cases these competitive reactions will actually result in the reduction in the total profit pool available to all competitors.

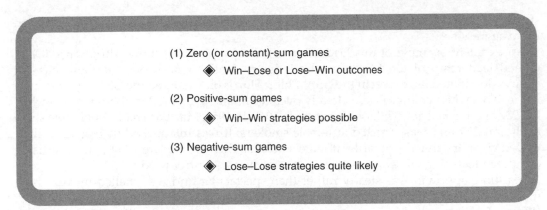

(1) Zero (or constant)-sum games
   ◆ Win–Lose or Lose–Win outcomes

(2) Positive-sum games
   ◆ Win–Win strategies possible

(3) Negative-sum games
   ◆ Lose–Lose strategies quite likely

Figure 6.3 Different types of games

This can be demonstrated using game theory. The basics of game theory are very easy to state, but its practical application can become very complicated. As in any competitive game (such as bridge or chess), developing a successful strategy is considerably assisted by predicting the future actions and reactions of the various players. In other words, you have to look forward to potential outcomes and then reason backwards to develop the most successful strategies. Most normal 'games' have a simple win–lose outcome (if I win then you lose, and vice versa); they can be described as zero-sum games. However, as shown in Figure 6.3, in business there are other types of game.

As we just mentioned, industries can degenerate into negative-sum games where all the players lose out. The total profit pool can disappear in an aggressive price war, started to try to regain lost market share. It is therefore important that the business assesses the risk of this type of response and result when developing its marketing strategy. Conversely, it is also possible for an industry to produce a positive-sum game, where all players in the market win, but not necessarily to the same extent. In a financially attractive market, it is possible for all competitors to create shareholder value although, as already stated, this is not that common. A win–win position is potentially more sustainable than a win–lose game, as no rational competitor should want to risk destroying the shareholder value that they are creating. This should still be true even if the win–win is 90:10 in one party's favour.

Thus, the strategic intent should be to avoid lose–lose situations completely but to move through win–lose games to sustainable win–win positions. As shown in Figure 6.4, if the industry remains as a zero-sum game, particularly one that the business is continually winning, there is a risk that it will regress to a lose–lose position. Losing competitors may become more willing to take greater and greater risks (i.e. implement increasingly aggressive strategies) due to their decreasing financial performance. It is still better, obviously, to be the winner in a zero-sum game, but the long-term sustainability of such a position must be considered.

Another key element of this business application of game theory is that it is the prime responsibility of the market leader to manage the total profit pool and the sustainability of the 'game' that is being played. If a competitor with a 10% market share seeks to increase the total value created by the industry, it is likely that 90% of any value created will go to its competitors. Unfortunately, in many industries, the leading competitor focuses exclusively on capturing even more of the existing value chain. This can still be true even when this strategy results in very competitive responses; the market leader simply becomes even more aggressive!

An excellent example of this leadership role is Philip Morris (now Altria) once it had gained leadership of the USA cigarette industry. Unlike Coca-Cola, Marlboro has not always dominated its market in the USA. Philip Morris only entered the USA cigarette market in 1934, when volumes were already over 100 billion per year. Marlboro was launched in 1937 and peaked at 2.3 billion cigarettes in 1945. In 1953, Marlboro had a negligible share of the market and was targeted at female smokers. It was relaunched in 1955 as a filter-tipped cigarette aimed primarily at male smokers. Then, in the late 1950s, an advertising campaign featuring wide open spaces and a cowboy was introduced!

Marlboro's growth was steady rather than spectacular and was fuelled by very high marketing support (i.e. brand development investment) in a still growing market. In 1983, Philip Morris became the largest USA-based cigarette company, selling 205 billion cigarettes out of a total of 597.5 billion, of which 120 billion were Marlboro. This was interesting because the market volume peaked in 1981 at 638 billion cigarettes, and then went into a slow but continual decline. Philip Morris had therefore taken market leadership while the market had been growing.

Once it had the leading position in the now mature market, its strategy changed and it looked to increase the profitability of the total market. Accordingly, as the price leader with the dominant brand, Philip Morris took retail selling prices up significantly faster than inflation. Through the 1980s, price rises averaged 7% per annum in real terms. Consequently, although total industry volumes were declining at 3% per annum, the total profit pool was still increasing – what should be a win–win game for all the players. Philip Morris's profits from the USA cigarette market increased dramatically, so that in 1992 it made $5.2 billion of operating income on sales revenues of $12 billion. However, the profits of most of its competitors also rose, but not to the same levels.

These increasing profit margins opened up new opportunities for competitors, and these are considered in the next section on competitor impact. However, other industries

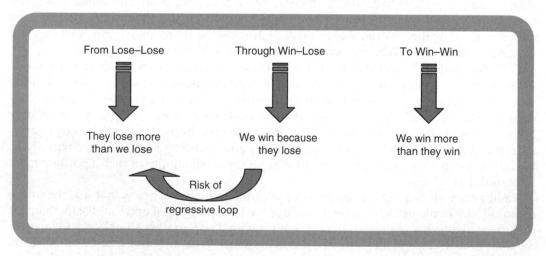

Figure 6.4   Strategic intent of different types of games

suffer from the lack of a dominant player that is able to manage the total value created by the industry. There are many examples of markets with four or five relatively evenly balanced competitors that quite regularly degenerate into value-destroying price wars. Such price wars are most unlikely to force any such competitors out of the market, and thus total profitability in the market is dramatically reduced. This position is often triggered because the total aspirations of all the competitors cannot be met, e.g. where five competitors all have objectives to achieve 25% market share.

Competitor impact risk

The third sub-component of profit risk is closely linked to the first two, in that it considers the impact of the proposed marketing strategy on specific competitors and assesses the risk of aggressive, value-destroying competitive reaction. The marketing strategy has a higher probability of achieving its planned profit if any adverse profit impact on any competitor is both small and well distributed among competitors. Thus, a very high competitor impact risk is where the adverse profit impact on a leading competitor is so great that it puts the continued existence of its business in doubt. Conversely, a very low competitor impact risk is where all the profit growth comes from growth in the total profit pool or from other levels in the value chain, so that the loss of profit to competitors is negligible, as is shown in Table 6.4.

It is fairly obvious that a marketing strategy that attacks the heartland product of the existing leading competitor is likely to receive a very aggressive response. Even if the strategy

Table 6.4 A graduated scale of competitor impact risk

Competitor impact risk is the risk that profit will be less than planned because of a single competitor reacting to the strategy. Risk is higher if the profit impact on competitors is concentrated on one powerful competitor and that impact threatens the competitor's survival. It is lower if the profit impact is relatively small, distributed across a number of competitors and has a non-survival threatening impact on each.

Competitor impact greatly increases the profit risk (very high competitor impact risk)	The profit loss to a leading competitor puts their business at risk.
Competitor impact increases the profit risk (high competitor impact risk)	The profit loss to leading competitors is significant but not sufficient to threaten their businesses.
Competitor impact does not significantly increase the profit risk (moderate competitor impact risk)	The profit loss to competitors does not threaten anyone's survival.
Competitor impact decreases the profit risk (low competitor impact risk)	The profit loss to any competitor is noticeable but relatively small.
Competitor impact greatly decreases the profit risk (very low competitor impact risk)	The profit loss to any competitor is negligible.

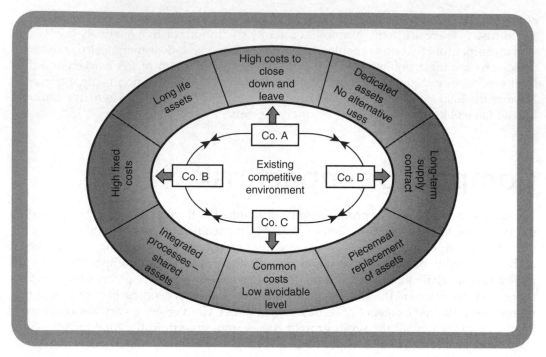

Figure 6.5 Exit barriers

is based on a major product innovation that generates a strong competitive advantage, the incumbent will fight hard to retain the current customer base that represents the major source of its profit stream. If the scale of the incursion into its current market share puts its continued viability at risk, then the reaction may cease to be economically rational as competitors facing death and destruction can lash out wildly in their fight for survival.

Of course, the marketing strategy may deliberately target such a competitor in an attempt to force it to leave the market. In this case, a sound analysis of the exit barriers, which are shown in Figure 6.5, faced by the competitor is required.

Exit barriers can mean that there are significant costs associated with leaving a market or an industry; this can mean that some competitors will remain despite their unacceptably low levels of financial return or even losses. It is important to predict how such a competitor will respond to the proposed marketing initiative before implementation, and to develop as many contingency plans as possible if the strategy targets large and powerful competitors.

The USA cigarette industry illustrates how small problems can rapidly develop into major strategic issues. As previously discussed, Philip Morris deliberately increased real prices and manufacturers' profit margins during the 1980s. As both prices and profit margins grew substantially, there were increasing opportunities for industry players to launch lower priced cigarettes that still generated perfectly acceptable margins. To Philip Morris, this did not make any sense, as it risked turning the industry into a commodity where competition was based on selling price alone. There was no evidence that lower prices would reverse the downward trend in cigarette consumption; thus, the total profit pool would be reduced. Philip Morris wanted consumer choice to be dominated by brand equity and image, not surprising as they were winning hands down under these rules of the game, with Marlboro having 25% market share while no other brand had over 5% share. Therefore, although extra-low-priced cigarettes were launched in 1981, Philip Morris stayed out of this new sector until 1992.

The first competitor to try to change the competitive game by launching much cheaper (i.e. almost half the retail price of Marlboro) cigarettes was Liggett, the smallest industry player. Back in the 1950s and even earlier, Liggett had been a major force in the industry, but it had declined to around 2% market share with no really viable brands. Unfortunately for all their competitors, the sheer profitability of the industry meant that Liggett was only dying very slowly; 2% of a $10 billion industry profit pool is still more than most businesses make in annual profit. It felt it had nothing to lose from a high-risk, aggressive strategy, as it was not able to compete against the big boys on brands. Its initial launch of a cheap commodity cigarette doubled its sales volumes within 18 months, but within four years its sales were back to their previous levels.

In a declining market, Liggett's volume growth all had to come at the expense of its larger competitors. The biggest losers all responded by launching equivalently priced cigarettes. Not only did they succeed in halting the growth of Liggett, but they were too successful and grew this extra-low-priced segment significantly. Not surprisingly, the profit margins on these much cheaper cigarettes were much, much lower than those achieved on the higher price segment. Also during this period, a number of retailer brands were launched, supplied by the major manufacturers, who had plenty of spare capacity.

The result was that, by 1989, the total mid- and low-price segments represented 30% of the total market, not too surprising given the large price differentials. In the early 1990s, growth of this segment continued and, for the first time, there was evidence that Marlboro smokers were switching to the very cheap alternatives. This brought Philip Morris into the segment, and their launch in 1992 took a sizeable segment share immediately. This merely increased the total segment size, as their now established competitors further discounted their own products to maintain their sales volumes.

Thus, in April 1993, Philip Morris was forced to reduce the selling price of Marlboro by 25% to close part of the gap with the extra-low-priced segment. This move forced all its competitors to reduce their full revenue brands by the same amount, but they were unable to reduce their much cheaper offerings so as to maintain the previous differential; the lower margins meant they would have been selling at a loss. Philip Morris regained the lost share with Marlboro, but the total industry profit pool was halved for 1993 and has still not fully recovered to its previous levels. However, Philip Morris has since grown the share of Marlboro significantly as it could also predict that, in the environment of falling profits, its competitors would drastically cut back on marketing support to try to restore short-term profitability. In view of this prediction, Philip Morris dramatically increased its own marketing support behind the new, lower priced Marlboro; this gave it a dramatically increased market share of the more image-conscious, younger adult smokers.

Once the new, lower priced segment started to attract consumers from the leading competitor's flagship brand, it was fairly predictable that this competitor would respond in order to protect its market share. The nature of that response reduced the profitability of *all* competitors dramatically, but it did enable it to retain the dominant market share in what is still a very profitable market. Predicting the potential losers from any proposed marketing strategy and their likely reactions is therefore a key element in assessing the associated risks.

Internal gross margin risk

The remaining two sub-components of profit risk examine the internally focused assumptions that are built into the marketing strategy. The first of these looks at the assumptions regarding the internal gross margins forecast to be made but, since the forecast selling prices are assessed in the market risk under the Marketing Due Diligence diagnostic process (as discussed in Chapter 4), the major variables considered here are the direct costs associated with the goods or services sold.

The marketing strategy has a higher probability of achieving its profit objectives if the internal gross margin assumptions are conservative relative to current products. Thus, a low level of gross margin risk is created by setting forecast gross margins at levels well below those being achieved for current similar products. Conversely, a high level of risk would result from a marketing strategy that forecasts higher future gross margins that are not justified by corresponding improvement in the value proposition offered to customers. The various possibilities are summarized in Table 6.5, but the need to justify any planned improvements in gross margins highlights a key element in this risk assessment.

Although the gross margin risk looks at the direct costs of producing the product or service, the risk assessment cannot be entirely internally focused. There is a need to use value analysis techniques to assess whether the value offered to customers has been improved or degraded by any changes proposed in the marketing strategy. Obviously, any costly major improvements may be reflected in higher selling prices, and this requires that this sub-component is closely integrated with the selling price element of the market risk

Table 6.5 A graduated scale of internal gross margin risk

Internal gross margin risk is the risk that the internal gross margins will be lower than planned because the core costs of manufacturing the product or providing the service are higher than anticipated. Risk is higher if the internal gross margin assumptions are optimistic relative to current similar products and lower if they are relatively conservative.

Internal gross margin risk greatly increases profit risk (very high internal gross margin risk)	Internal gross margin assumptions are significantly above levels for similar products.
Internal gross margin risk increases profit risk (high internal gross margin risk)	Internal gross margin assumptions are slightly above those for similar products.
Internal gross margin risk neither increases nor decreases profit risk (moderate internal gross margin risk)	Internal gross margin assumptions are in line with those for similar products.
Internal gross margin risk slightly decreases profit risk (low internal gross margin risk)	Internal gross margin assumptions are slightly below those for similar products, or all changes are justified.
Internal gross margin risk greatly reduces profit risk (very low internal gross margin risk)	Internal gross margin assumptions are significantly below those for similar products, or all changes are fully justified using externally validated evidence.

assessment. Thus, some cost increases may be shareholder value enhancing, while cost decreases that destroy customer value can have a negative impact on shareholder value.

Also, there can be ways of reducing costs that can have an indirectly negative impact on the long-term financial return from the marketing strategy. Many large groups are seeking to reduce their direct costs by utilizing common processes for as much of their total product range as possible. Thus, the 'value-adding' differentiation is added as late as practical in the total operational process. An example of this is the automotive industry, where the concept of sharing basic car components is now very well developed as it saves product development as well as manufacturing costs. However, there is clearly a risk associated with utilizing these common components in final products that have widely varying selling prices and brand positions. The Audi Volkswagen group now owns the Skoda brand and has done an excellent job of improving the build quality, driving performance and overall brand acceptability of Skoda since its acquisition. Part of this improvement has been achieved by the use of common parts from Volkswagen and Audi models, which has enabled quality improvements without dramatically increasing Skoda's manufacturing costs. However, the risk is that if this association becomes too strong in consumers' minds, some of them will no longer be willing to pay the premium for the group's higher priced and more prestiguously positioned brands.

However, the marketing strategies that demonstrate the highest levels of gross margin risk are in markets that have relatively low, tight gross margins and high levels of competition. In these circumstances, even small absolute increases in gross margin represent large proportionate increases that are likely to cause competitive responses and may face severe customer resistance. This is often seen by technology-led advances in existing, well-developed industries where the innovator may achieve a temporary increase in gross margins due to its cost decreases. Unless the defendability of the technology advance is very good, the competitors will rapidly copy, or circumvent, the new technology to match the new cost level. Similarly, this has been the case with outsourcing initiatives in many industries; the increased gross margin has not been sustainable, as competitors have implemented equivalent cost-reducing strategies and the industry-wide benefits have all been passed on to customers, due to the high level of competition within the industry.

Consequently, the focus of the gross margin risk assessment is to analyse both the causes and the sustainability of any proposed changes to existing gross margin levels and to understand the assumptions underlying the gross margins on any new products that are incorporated into the marketing plan.

Other costs risk

The remaining sub-component of profit risk considers the assumptions made in the marketing plan regarding all the indirect costs that reduce the planned gross margin to the net profit level that drives shareholder value creation. The marketing strategy has a higher probability of achieving its shareholder value objectives if assumptions regarding other costs, including marketing support, are realistically and conservatively based on existing costs for comparable products.

Where the marketing strategy only involves existing products and minor associated product amendments, the other costs risk can be stated as being very low level where other costs assumptions are significantly higher than current levels for comparable products.

Table 6.6 A graduated scale of other costs risk

Other costs risk is the risk that net margins will be lower than planned because other costs are higher than anticipated. Risk is higher if assumptions regarding other costs, including marketing support, are less than current costs and lower if those assumptions are more than current costs.

Other costs assumptions greatly increase profit risk (very high other costs risk)	The other costs assumptions are not supported by evidence from market research or other comparable products.
Other costs assumptions increase profit risk (high other costs risk)	The other costs assumptions are below those for comparable products.
Other costs assumptions neither increase nor decrease profit risk (moderate other costs risk)	The other costs assumptions are in line with comparable products.
Other costs assumptions decrease profit risk (low other costs risk)	The other costs assumptions are slightly above those for comparable products.
Other costs assumptions greatly decrease profit risk (very low other costs risk)	The other costs assumptions are significantly above those for comparable products.

This is summarized in Table 6.6. Any planned improvements in these other cost levels must be clearly justified in terms of both cause and sustainability. However, where completely new products and/or significant new markets form a material part of the marketing strategy, the other costs risk assessment may need to use a different basis of analysis.

Clearly, the first approach is to find comparable products and to analyse their cost levels both at the same stages of development and adjusted for the impact of inflation. If this is not achievable, then the Marketing Due Diligence diagnostic review looks at external evidence to support the assumptions made in the marketing plan. Thus, market research or competitor analyses can provide good estimates of the cost levels that are likely to be incurred in supporting these new products. However, sometimes senior managers still find it very difficult to accept cost levels that are materially different to their own experience. This is particularly true where the marketing strategy proposes moving the business into a completely new sector.

This was the case for a new business idea proposed by the Masterfoods division of the Mars group. Mars is a leading global player in the confectionery, pet food and processed convenience food industries, with the Masterfoods division focused on the latter group of products. In the UK, the company already had a business selling processed potato products in various forms, such as dehydrated, canned, etc. As part of this process, it obviously bought in raw potatoes that were graded, washed, peeled, cooked and appropriately processed for the final convenience products.

However, there was a rapidly growing market for graded, washed and pre-packed raw potatoes sold through the major supermarket chains, the market known as fresh pack potatoes. The divisional management saw an opportunity to get into this market with relatively small new capital expenditure, as most of the required machinery was already in place. Also, their manufacturing processes did not need this higher quality raw material;

therefore, grading out the larger, 'better-looking' potatoes for fresh pack would not increase input costs to existing products.

Clearly, it would be difficult to develop a strong Mars group branding strategy for this product, but it could be sold under the retailers' brands and the group was already experienced at producing for retailers in their own brands. The marketing strategy and business case were put together with the cost structures being developed from research into existing competitive operations. These competitors were primarily vertical moves further down the value chain by agriculturally based businesses whereas, for Masterfoods, the strategy represented a move further back up the industry's value chain.

A major difference was in the other costs element, as the agriculture-based businesses had much lower levels of infrastructure and overhead support than was typical for a Mars-style processed food operation. Masterfoods' management argued that the lower other costs were appropriate for this type of operation, but central group management decided that it was too big a risk to go with the much lower cost assumptions and insisted that normal group levels of overhead were incorporated. Not surprisingly, the new product plan was financially unattractive if much higher levels of indirect cost were included; thus, the group never entered this now very large and well-developed market.

The element of other costs that was most commonly found in our research to cause problems was marketing support. Many marketing strategies include assumptions about declining levels of marketing support in the future, even though the strategy requires the launch of new products, the development of new brands or entry into new markets. These strategies normally require investment in marketing expenditure in the early years and, as discussed in Chapter 3, this should be regarded as development marketing expenditure.

If development marketing budgets are reduced in an attempt to boost short-term profits, the long-term indicators that must be part of the overall performance measurement process should be reassessed. For brand development, there would be specifically identified brand health indicators that show the relative future strength of the key elements of a brand. However, it must also be remembered that marketing assets, such as brands, are developed in a competitive environment and the effectiveness of marketing expenditure is significantly affected by competitors' level of spending. This is shown diagrammatically in Figure 6.6, where the curve drawn is an extreme version to make the point clearly.

When a business spends too little on development marketing in a heavily supported market, the effectiveness of its spend will be minimal. Unless a critical mass of marketing support is spent, the business will not overcome the level of 'noise' that already exists in the marketplace and the targeted customers will not register the desired messages. Clearly, this critical mass level can be reduced if the targeted group of customers can be so highly segmented that they can be very specifically addressed, as was discussed in Chapter 5.

Once this critical mass point is passed, there is normally a very strong positive correlation between increasing marketing expenditure and its effectiveness. However, there is a point where the law of diminishing returns sets in and incremental development marketing expenditure has almost no additional impact. Some observers believe that the curve can actually turn down, as additional expenditure annoys existing customers so much that they stop buying!

Not surprisingly, this has led to the development of a relative marketing expenditure measure: share of voice. Share of voice (SOV) refers to the proportionate share of the total marketing expenditure spent on one product (e.g. brand). One increasingly common relationship compares this SOV to the relative value share of market (SOM) achieved by the

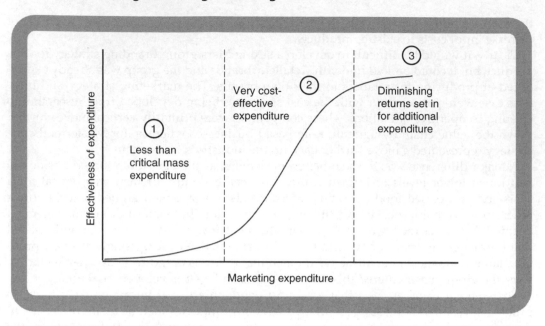

Figure 6.6 Relationship of marketing expenditure and effectiveness

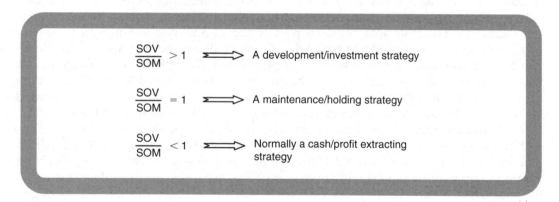

Figure 6.7 Share of voice (SOV) compared to share of market (SOM)

product. As shown in Figure 6.7, the ratio of SOV/SOM can be greater than 1, equal to 1 or less than 1.

If the marketing strategy implies proportionately outspending the current share of market (i.e. SOV/SOM > 1), then the business is investing in developing a marketing asset. If the marketing asset is already fully developed and the strategy is now to exploit it, the relative level of marketing support should be designed to be at around parity with the share of market (i.e. SOV/SOM = 1). There is, of course, one competitor in any market that may be able to maintain its share of market while spending significantly less than its proportionate share of marketing support. This is the market leader, because it may achieve economies of scale in its marketing expenditure that are not available to its smaller competitors.

In most cases, however, an SOV/SOM ratio of below 1 indicates that the marketing asset is not being properly maintained and its value is likely to reduce over time. This may be the appropriate marketing strategy if the asset is coming to the end of its economic life.

These issues indicate that the other costs risk assessment cannot focus exclusively on the internal costs assumptions in the marketing plan. Consideration of external issues, including competitive activity, needs to be included, particularly where the marketing strategy moves the business into new market segments where it has no previous experience of the cost structures involved.

Summary

It may be helpful to draw together the five sub-components discussed in this chapter to see what the overall profit risk assessment looks like. This can be done by considering the attributes of a weak marketing strategy that has a high profit risk, as outlined below.

What do weak marketing strategies look like?

1 They do not quantify the total profit pool
2 They do not specifically identify sources of profit growth
3 They do not quantify the impact on key competitors
4 They often assume higher levels of gross margin in the future
5 They frequently include significant improvements in other cost levels, even though the plans may require new product developments and launches.

The first three sub-components look at the total available profit pool and competitive reactions to marketing strategies that try to gain a larger share of this pool, while the last two consider the assumptions regarding the relative cost structure of the business. If the total profit pool is not quantified, the targeted sources of profit growth are not identified and the impact on competitors is not calculated; the overall effect can be disastrous. Implementing such a poorly developed marketing strategy can result in very aggressive but unexpected competitor reactions. The total profit pool generated by the market can be significantly reduced and competition can become much more based on selling price. The market often becomes considerably more volatile and unstable, with the result that the profit objectives of the strategy are not achieved, even if the total market value and market share are in line with the plan.

This part of the book has tried to set out in detail how the Marketing Due Diligence diagnostic process breaks down the assessment of the overall business risk associated with any proposed marketing strategy. The three fundamental components of this overall risk (market risk, share risk and profit risk, considered in this chapter) are each subdivided into five risk sub-components that can be assessed using well-researched techniques.

These 15 elements can therefore be quantitatively measured so that any required adjustment to the original marketing plan forecasts can be made. As was discussed in Chapters 2 and 3, the level of these adjustments depends on the way in which the original forecasts were prepared. The output from this diagnostic risk assessment process is ideally a 'potentially revised' projected financial return from the marketing strategy. This can then be compared, as set out in Chapter 3, against the required level of return on the assets employed in implementing the strategy to identify the level of any shareholder value that should be created.

However, as we stated earlier, an important aspect of the Marketing Due Diligence diagnostic process is that it can add considerable value to any marketing planning process, even if the outcome is not a quantified assessment of shareholder value creation. The requirement to break down the total risk profile associated with a proposed marketing strategy into individually assessable components means that the key elements of risk will be identified by the Marketing Due Diligence analysis. Thus, gaps in existing information may be found or unacceptable levels of risk for the potential level of return highlighted. These issues can then be addressed by using the Marketing Due Diligence therapeutic process that is discussed in Part 3.

The Marketing Due Diligence Therapeutic Process

Chapter 7
The key role of market definition and segmentation

Fast track

Successful commerce has always been the result of a careful matching of offers to needs. Only a fool would conclude that all women between the ages of 18 and 22 are the same, or that all people who live in the same neighbourhood are the same, etc. Nonetheless, it is such shallow thinking that has come to represent market segmentation over the years.

A market trader many years ago, on having it pointed out to him that exactly the same apples at opposite ends of his stall were priced at 20 cents and 25 cents, replied that the 25-cent apples were especially for customers who wanted to pay 25 cents!

This somewhat silly and elementary example is only intended to illustrate that, in life, as in business, people have different need sets and the authors find it incredible that, in the twenty-first century, so many organizations still haven't fathomed that the secret to success is correct market definition and segmentation as precursors to product development, positioning and branding.

A market must be defined as 'the aggregate of all the products or services that satisfy the same need'. Hence, in financial services, a pension is a product, not a market, as there are other financial products that can fulfil the same need set. It is crucial, therefore, to understand the specific demand for pensions. This is to ascertain whether other products are taking the place of pensions and whether pensions are growing, static or declining as part of the overall market.

Once this has been done, a quantitative method of market mapping is then essential to trace the flow of all goods and services from suppliers, through channels, right through to those who eventually use them. This market map (an example of which is given later in this chapter) is intended to ensure that the supplier fully understands the change and trends throughout the value chain and that, if they are in some way different in their distributor and value-adding patterns, it is for rational reasons known to the board. The second principal reason for drawing a market map is to ascertain which are the major decision points or leverage points that need to be influenced in favour of the supplier. It is here that the 80/20 rule often applies, in that up to 80% of volume or value is accounted for by 20% or less of the leverage points. These, clearly, will form a central part of any strategic marketing plan.

It is also at the leverage points that market segmentation needs to be carried out. For example, in the radiator heating market, architects are major influencers of which radiators go on which wall, but architects come in many different shapes and sizes and have many different needs and motivators.

The market segmentation process involves decomposing a market into a number of actual behaviour patterns according to what is bought, where it is bought, when it is bought, how it is bought and, finally, according to who buys, which are then understood in terms of why it is bought. This will result in a number of micro-segments, of which there could be around 20 or 30. It is then a comparatively simple process to cluster these micro-segments until there are seven or eight groups remaining. These are the final segments, on which all strategic decisions should be based.

Introduction

The preceding chapters have an underlying theme running through them, which is eluci-dated in this chapter. Correct market definition and market segmentation are the keys to all successful marketing and hence the creation of sustainable competitive advantage and shareholder value.

Some of the most famous business leaders in the world – people such as Sir Michael Perry (former Chairman of Unilever), Tom Peters and Philip Kotler – are agreed that the following are top of their list of what constitutes world-class marketing:

- A deep understanding of the market (hence our insistence in this book on drawing market maps, with a quantification of volume and value, from all suppliers through to all users).
- Correct market segmentation (hence our insistence in this book on moving away from silly, pointless and largely useless a priori segmentation schemes such as demographics and psychographics, to a purely needs-based segmentation).
- Product development, positioning and branding based on this correct segmentation (hence our insistence in this book that it is market understanding and market segmen-tation that are the cornerstones of winning marketing strategies).

There are, of course, others, such as:

- Effective marketing planning processes
- Long-term integrated marketing strategies
- Institutionalized creativity and innovation
- Total supply chain management
- Market-driven organization structures
- Careful recruitment, training and career management
- Rigorous line management implementation.

However, whilst anyone would recognize the inherent wisdom in these latter items, it is still interesting that some of the world's best-known gurus still put market understanding and segmentation ahead of all the others. This is simply because these latter points are important but consequent to and dependent upon the first three, and especially on market segmentation.

This chapter will therefore be constructed around these two pillars of marketing:

- Correct market definition
- Market segmentation.

Correct market definition

A crucial business discipline, not just a philosophical argument

We have already said quite a lot about the need for correct market definition in Chapter 4 so, rather than repeating ourselves, we will merely remind readers that markets are most correctly defined as:

> The aggregation of all the products that satisfy the same need.

Hence, as we have mentioned before, in the financial services sector, a pension is clearly a product and not a segment, as there are many other similar, alternative products that could be bought to satisfy the same benefits sought. Indeed, good marketers in this sector also consider those 'products' that can't be bought in the same way but that compete indirectly, such as those who 'self-insure' by saving what they might otherwise spend on insurance premiums.

The importance of this point is not some esoteric, philosophical thesis. We only need look back at Chapter 4 and the list of blue-chip companies who failed because they persisted in defining their businesses in terms of the products they made rather than in terms of the needs to be satisfied, to be reminded of the very real implications of getting this wrong.

By contrast, the following simple example illustrates the crucial importance of getting this right.

The authors were running a workshop with the board of a business book publishing company, who persisted in defining their market in terms of the books they commissioned and sold. Their market map looked as shown in Figure 7.1.

The problem with the market map resulting from their market definition is that their competitors were therefore other business book publishers when, in reality, the market of all book publishers was being taken by other forms of business knowledge promulgation. This particular publisher was not only fighting against other publishers, but against unknown enemies in the shape of more convenient forms of knowledge promulgation.

Once this became apparent and they realized that their market was not just book publishing, but knowledge promulgation, their redefined market map was as shown in Figure 7.2.

The significance of this soon became apparent in their strategy, with the setting up of new divisions devoted to electronic publishing and new briefs to authors, many of whom were stuck in the time warp of writing words on paper for a supposedly supine audience of executives with little else to do other than read their ever-increasing outpourings.

The result is that this particular publisher, now it realizes it has many and varied competitors other than book publishers, is embracing many other forms of knowledge promulgation and remains one of the world's leading publishers.

Market mapping

Nonetheless, companies still make, sell and distribute products and, having made themselves aware of other forms of competition, do have to understand this market and how it works. So, it is crucial to find some quantitative method for understanding precisely how

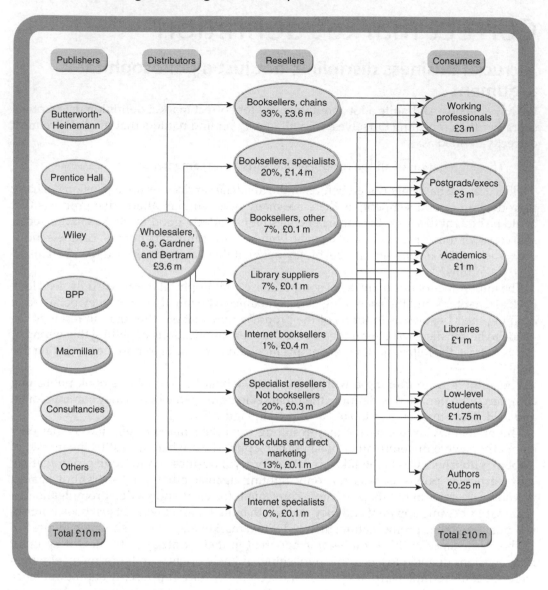

Figure 7.1 Original market map for XYZ book publisher. Copyright Professor Malcolm McDonald and Dr Hugh Wilson

goods and services get down the supply side to the end-use side, in order that important 'leverage' points can be identified for the purpose of informing strategic decisions. Leverage points are covered in more detail later in this chapter.

As we mentioned in the introduction to this chapter, correct market segmentation is perhaps the most important determinant of commercial success. A useful way of tackling the complex issue of market segmentation is to start by drawing a 'market map' as a precursor to a more detailed examination of 'who buys what'. An example of a very basic market map is given in Figure 7.3.

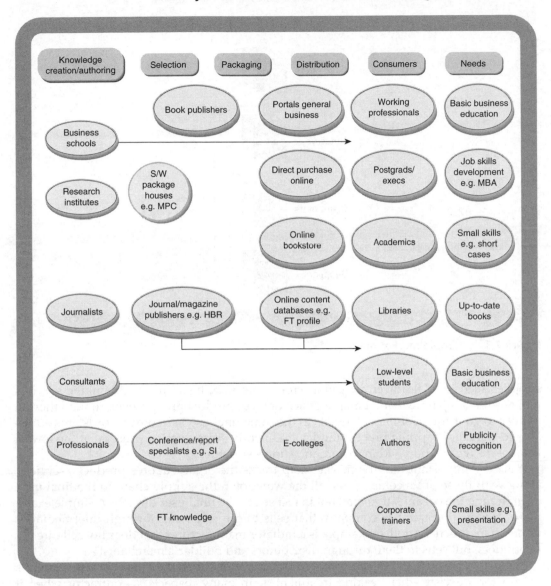

Figure 7.2   Revised market map for XYZ book publisher. Copyright Professor Malcolm McDonald and Dr Hugh Wilson

A market map portrays the distribution or supply and value chains that link the supplier and the ultimate consumer or final user. It takes into account the various buying mechanisms found in the market, including the part played by 'influencers'.

In general, if an organization's products or services go through the same channels to similar final users, then one composite market map can be drawn. If, however, some products or services go through totally different channels and/or to totally different markets, then more than one market map is needed to illustrate the full picture.

It is probably sensible to treat different business units individually, as their respective business value or volume justifies a specific focus. For example, a farming cooperative that

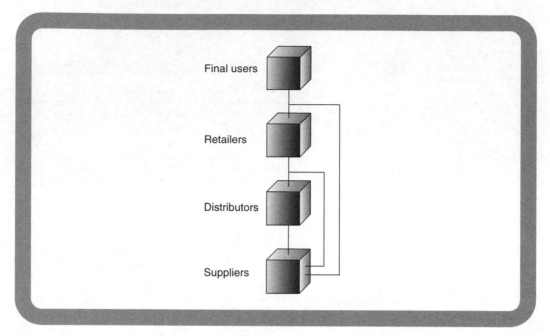

Figure 7.3 A simple market map

supplies seeds and fertilizer as well as crop protection, insurance and banking services will require a separate market map for each of these product groups, even though they all appear to go through similar channels to the same final users. In other words, it is advisable to start the mapping process (and subsequently segmentation process) at the lowest level of disaggregation within the organization's structure.

It is very important that the market map tracks the organization's products/services, along with those of its competitors, all the way down the supply chain to the final user, even though the organization may not in fact sell to the final user directly. A simple example of this is an insurance company that sells to the consumer through intermediaries rather than directly. Another example is a radiator manufacturer that does not sell directly to builders, but sells to them through distributors and builder's merchants.

In most markets, the direct customer/purchaser will not be the final user. For example, the doctor we visit when seeking treatment is, in many respects, a contractor when it comes to prescribing medicine. The doctor is the designated bridge between the pill maker and the pill taker. The distinction is important because, to win the commission, in this case the patients' custom, the doctor will have needed to understand the patients' requirements and, in treating them, would have addressed those requirements on the patients' behalf. To omit the final users (the patients) from the market map would, therefore, have ignored an array of needs of which the supplier (the pharmaceutical company) must be aware and include in its offer, to ensure that its name appears on the contractor's (doctor's) list of preferred suppliers. The inclusion of a contractor on a market map is illustrated in Figure 7.4.

Making certain that the market map follows through to the final user is also important in situations where products/services are purchased for final users by their company's purchasing department. In such instances, the market map should track the products/ services beyond purchasing to the departments where the final users are found. The

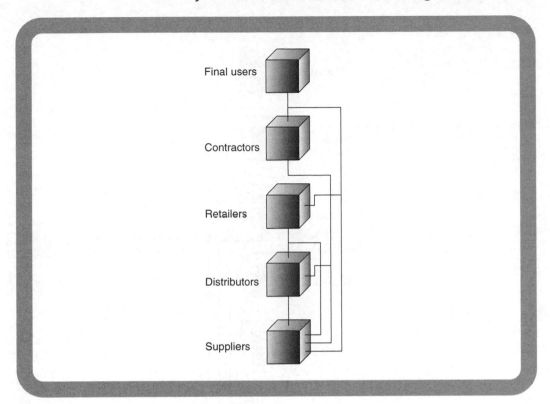

Figure 7.4 Market map with contractor

market map should also include, where appropriate, the existence of inherent purchasing procedures, such as committees, authorizations, sealed bids and so on. An opportunity to accommodate different purchasing procedures occurs later. As these diagrams demonstrate, most market maps will have at least three principal components:

● Consumers (final or end users)
● The channel
● Suppliers.

For many markets it is also essential that the map includes a fourth component, namely the role of influencers and/or providers of advice about which product to use, as shown in Figure 7.5. The involvement of influencers and/or providers of advice may not constitute a real transaction, but they should nonetheless appear on the market map as if they were. This will ensure that the market map incorporates all the transaction stages or 'junctions' en route that support the flow of products between suppliers and final users.

Be sure to draw a total market map, rather than just the part you deal with currently, to gain a comprehensive understanding of the market's dynamics. This covers both the distribution or supply and value chain and the routes through that chain.

With quantification playing an important role later on in the process, it is useful to mark along each 'route' the volumes and/or values that pass along that route (guesstimate if necessary) (Figure 7.6).

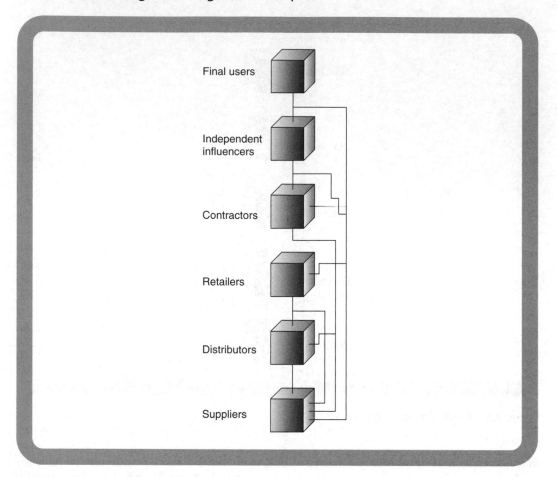

Figure 7.5 Market map with influencers

Each junction should be positioned hierarchically on the market map according to how close it is to the final user. The last junction along the market map would, therefore, be the supplier.

Note at each junction, if applicable, all the different types of companies/customers that occur there, as illustrated in Figure 7.7, and split the volume or value allocated to each junction between these different types. If you have included 'purchase procedures', this is where different purchasing procedures can be identified. At this point, the market mapping route may be challenging the traditional categories of company/customer types.

Leverage points

Leverage points are the fixed locations, or points, on the market map where power or influence may be exerted. To identify those junctions where decisions are made about which of the competing products/services should be purchased, highlight them with a thick bold outline and note how much they account for, as shown in Figure 7.8.

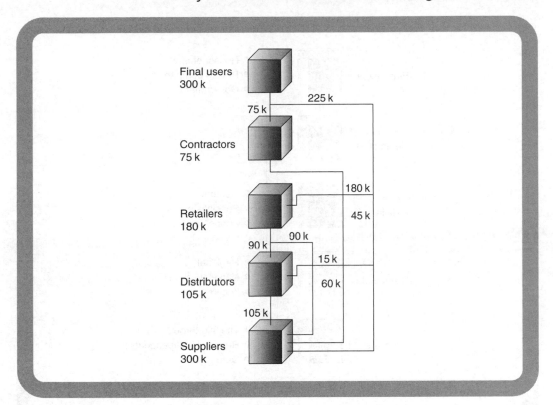

Figure 7.6 Market map showing volumes

Further details that can be added to the market map include attaching to each company/customer type the appropriate number of business units/individual purchasers it incorporates and your market share, if known. Market share figures can also be attached to the various routes through the market map.

Mapping out the different transactions that take place throughout the company's supply chain has revealed how the individual transactions relate to one another. Quantifying these various 'routes' and determining each company's share along them has served to identify the most important supply routes and the progressive changes in the company's market position.

By pinpointing where in the supply chain decisions are taken which consider the products/ services of competing suppliers, we can establish at which stages, or junctions, customers are expressing preferences, and thus where segmentation could occur. For most companies, it is recommended that segmentation should first be implemented at the junction furthest away from the supplier/manufacturer where decisions are made. Most importantly, however, market mapping provides a clearer understanding of the structure of the market and how it works.

A full explanation of market mapping can be found in *Market Segmentation: How to Do It, How to Profit from It* by Malcolm McDonald and Ian Dunbar (see References and further reading).

Figure 7.9 shows a partially completed market map for a company manufacturing radiators to warm domestic and commercial buildings. It is only partially completed, as can be

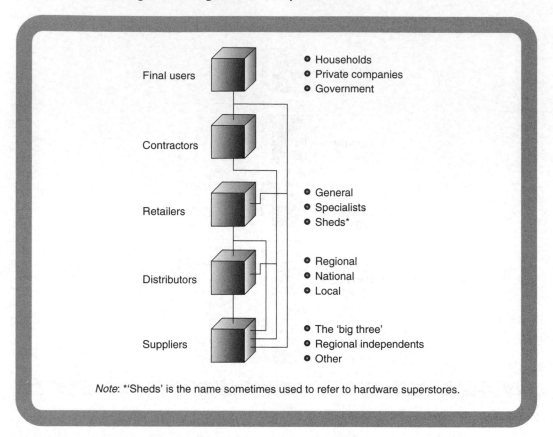

Figure 7.7 Market map with different company/customer types

seen from column 4 – the column quantifying who makes the decision about which radiator goes on which wall. The reason for putting this partially completed market map in this book is to illustrate that this particular company didn't know the full picture about decision-makers and had to do some market research to establish these facts. However, once completed, the manufacturer was better able to direct its sales force and other communications message to the right targets. This gave them enormous competitive advantage and they eventually went on to become extremely profitable market leaders.

Figure 7.9 also shows that, at the time, 70.2% of Company A's volume went through National merchants (column 2), who accounted for only 47.8% of distribution, whereas only 21.3% of Company B's sales went through the same type of outlet. It may be that it didn't matter at the time, but at least by knowing, both brands could have done something about it if necessary. Not knowing could possibly have led to serious strategic consequences.

Figure 7.10 shows a more recent market map for office equipment. It clearly illustrates that this major player (in red) was seriously out of step with what was happening in the total market. 'Other' was Internet sales, which the market leaders chose to ignore, along with 'Type C independents'. The biggest difference, however, between the market as a whole and this particular supplier was that 53% of its sales was made via their direct sales force, as opposed to only 14% for the market overall. The result of this lack of market alignment

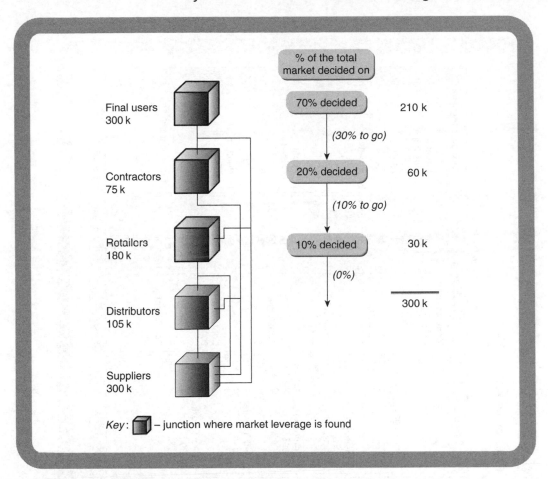

Figure 7.8 Leverage points at three junctions on a market map

was that this major player suffered extremely heavy losses whilst it aligned itself more closely to what was actually happening in its market.

Market segmentation

As Ted Levitt, one of marketing's founding fathers said, 'If you're not talking segments, you're not talking marketing.' Simply put, if you don't understand the way your market segments think, everything else you do is flawed – your company will only survive as long as your competitors remain similarly ignorant.

As relying on competitor incompetence cannot be described as sustainable strategy, learning how to test and improve market segmentation is a far wiser move.

As we have explained in detail earlier in this book, segments are groups of customers, not products or channels, who have the same, or similar, needs.

Customers clustered into descriptor groups – 'ABC1 males aged 18–35' or 'major accounts' – rarely all behave the same. Think of your friends. Even those in the same age, gender and income brackets probably behave very differently from one another when it

Radiator market map 2003

Radiator manufacturer

		Distribution	Sector share
Company A 2275 41.7%	1	1830	70.2
	2	360	17.3
	3	66	11.2
	4	Nil	Nil
Company B 860 15.8%	1	555	21.3
	2	280	12.8
	3	26	4.3
	4	Nil	Nil
Company C 605 11.1%	1	125	4.8
	2	450	20.5
	3	30	5.1
	4	Nil	Nil
Company D 480 8.8%	1	90	3.4
	2	270	12.3
	3	120	20.7
	4	Nil	Nil
Company E 300 5.5%	1	5	Nil
	2	255	11.6
	3	40	6.9
	4	Nil	Nil
Other imports 905 17.1%	1	Nil	Nil
	2	556	25.3
	3	300	51.8
	4	80	100.0

Total: 5425

Distributor

1. National merchants	2605	47.8%
2. Large independents	2190	40.1%
3. Small independents	560	10.6%
4. Sheds	80	1.4%

Total: 5435

Installer

5. British gas 465 8.5%	1	295		
	2	170		
	3	Nil		
	4	Nil		
6. Installer 2755 50.5%	1	1065		
	2	1360		
	3	360		
	4	Nil		
7. Contractor 1905 34.9%	1	1135		
	2	540		
	3	230		
	4	Nil		
8. Self-installer 80 1.4%	1	Nil		
	2	Nil		
	3	Nil		
	4	80		
9. Direct works 250 4.6%	1	120		
	2	130		
	3	Nil		
	4	Nil		

Total: 5455

Primary leverage point — Specification decision

Manufacturer 250	10	Nil	
	11	250	31.3
	12	Nil	
	13	Nil	
	14	Nil	
Local authority 1350	10	Nil	
	11	Nil	
	12	1050	95.4
	13	50	50.0
	14	250	27.8
Housebuilder 350	10	350	43.8
	11	Nil	
	12	Nil	
	13	Nil	
	14	Nil	
British gas 700	10	500	19.6
	11	100	12.5
	12	50	4.5
	13	Nil	
	14	Nil	
Contractor 200	10	Nil	
	11	100	12.5
	12	Nil	
	13	50	
	14	50	5.6
Consultant 550	10	100	11.1
	11	Nil	
	12	Nil	
	13	50	50.1
	14	500	55.6

Totals: 3400   420

End user segment

10. Private existing 2555 46.8%	5	385	
	6	2010	
	7	100	
	8	80	
	9	Nil	
11. Private new 800 14.7%	5	Nil	
	6	50	
	7	750	
	8	Nil	
	9	Nil	
12. Public existing 1100 20.2%	5	50	
	6	395	
	7	506	
	8	Nil	
	9	150	
13. Public new 100 1.8%	5	Nil	
	6	50	
	7	Nil	
	8	Nil	
	9	Nil	
14. Commercial 900 16.5%	5	50	
	6	300	
	7	550	
	8	Nil	
	9	Nil	

Total: 5455

Figure 7.9 Radiator market map

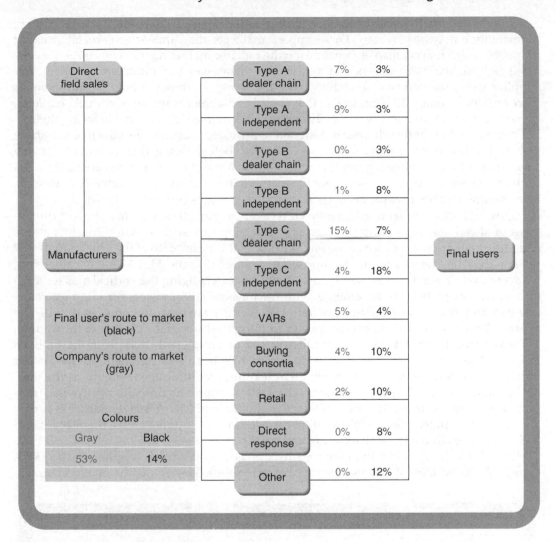

Figure 7.10   Office equipment market map

comes to buying a shirt, a car or a pension. If you took any of your organization's segments and asked if all the customers in that segment behave the same, would the answer be yes? Or would some be premium customers, some price sensitive, some loyal, some fickle? A segment is not a segment unless it passes the four classic tests. Ask yourself, are your segments:

1 Homogeneous? Are all the customers in that segment driven by the same motivations and needs, or are they simply grouped according to your data?
2 Distinct? Does each segment recognize itself as having distinct needs, or do some customers in that segment have more in common with those in other segments?
3 Accessible? Can you reach the segment you have identified via communication and distribution channels?
4 Viable? Is the segment big enough and stable enough for it to be worthwhile?

It should be clear by now that, at major decision-making junctions on the market map, segmentation may be necessary. For example, 'architects' may appear as a crucial group of influencers on a market map of radiators (on the radiator market map in Figure 7.9, they are listed as 'consultants'), even though they do not themselves buy radiators. However, any supplier who assumed that all architects are the same, or similar, would be mistaken, as there are clearly many different factors that appeal in different ways to individual architects. So, correct market segmentation of architects is clearly a major factor in influencing them.

The next section of this chapter is designed to provide an actionable, effective summary of best market segmentation theory and practice. Before doing this, however, for any finance directors or, indeed, general managers, who are still not convinced about the need for market segmentation, let us preface the methodology for doing it effectively with some brief comments about why it becomes so crucial as markets become established.

Figure 7.11 shows what would happen if we were to plot all cars against the two dimensions of speed and price, with the highest performing cars such as Aston Martins at one end and small, 'city' cars such as the Smart car or Fiat Cinquecento at the other end. It will be seen that the majority of cars fall into a 'fat' average (Mr and Mrs Average) category. If we were to do a similar exercise for, say, lawnmowers, changing the vertical axis to 'lawn size', a similar picture would emerge, with tractor-type lawnmowers for large estates at one end and small, hand-pushed lawnmowers for tiny lawns at the other end, with the average lawn size and average lawnmower forming the bulk of the market in the middle.

Transferring this market shape into Figure 7.12, it can be seen that, from the bulbous shape just described, the mass market in the middle begins to fragment as the market grows and as new models and new, different features are introduced. Finally, as the market becomes mature, the shape changes completely, as suppliers drop their prices in a frantic bid to retain their market share. Thus, the big, Mr and Mrs Average market is nearly always the one that suffers, whilst profitability declines as suppliers force themselves and their customers into a low-price culture and habit.

Figure 7.13 shows a situation enjoyed by a major photocopier supplier in the 1970s ('cpm' on the horizontal axis means 'copies per month'). This company enjoyed massive

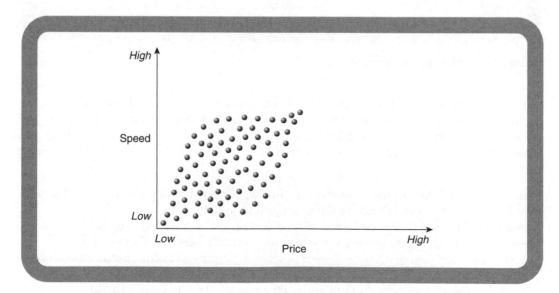

Figure 7.11 Basic market shape

market share and profitability but, gradually, the Japanese entered this growth market with small photocopiers, eventually populating the spaces on the graph with many different kinds of photocopiers to meet demand. Meanwhile, the market leader doggedly stuck to a 'one size fits all' policy, until finally their market share fell to 10% and they began to lose money. They eventually realized that their market was heavily segmented but, alas, it was too late; they had lost their pre-eminent position, never to regain it.

A more successful case history is that of ICI Fertilizers in the late 1980s. The company started to lose serious money when the market matured and overseas suppliers entered the market with low-price products. Being forced to drop their prices was disastrous, until they were finally convinced that not all farmers buy on price.

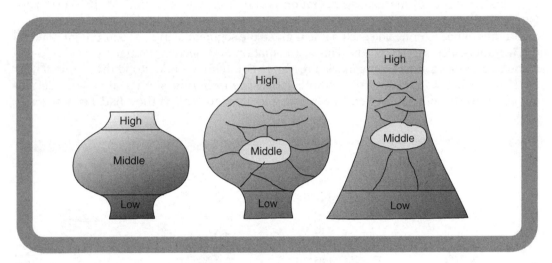

Figure 7.12 Fragmentation as markets mature

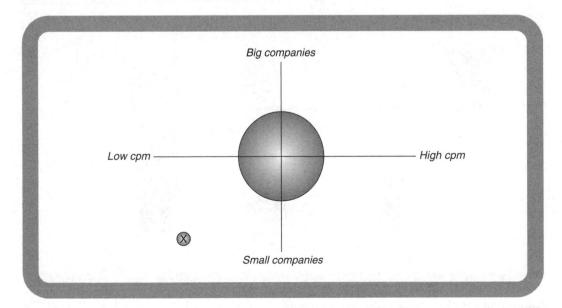

Figure 7.13 Photocopier market 1973

Seven distinct segments were identified (see Figure 7.14). After researching the needs of farmers, the seven segments which emerged were depicted as cartoon characters – Martin, David, Oliver, Brian, George, Arthur and Joe. Arthur was the only price-driven segment and accounted for a mere 7% of the total market. David was loyal to merchants, Martin was extremely interested in the appearance of his crops, Oliver was highly technical to the point of mounting a computer on his tractor attached to a satellite, etc. By carefully matching their offers to the different needs of these segments, ICI quickly regained their leadership position and became one of the few profitable fertilizer companies in the world. Meanwhile, their crude competitors made the incorrect assumption that all farmers were the same and therefore competed only on price.

A final example of market segmentation is shown in Figure 7.15. Like ICI Fertilizers, Global Tech gave names to each of the segments they identified, in this case naming them after types of bear. Alongside each name is given the segment's original equipment material (OEM) after-sales service needs. This segmentation and needs summary was elucidated through a piece of inexpensive market research. Before they understood the segmentation of their market, this major OEM supplier had been offering similar after-sales service packages to the whole market. The result was that, in reality, they had been severely

Figure 7.14 ICI Fertilizers' customer segments

under-servicing some segments and over-servicing others, with a consequent loss of market share and profitability. Having understood the real segments in their market, they were able to offer appropriately tailored levels of service to each segment. Only then did their customer satisfaction (CSI) survey become meaningful, because they were then able to measure CSIs by segment, instead of engaging in expensive and time-consuming omnibus surveys that revealed little of consequence about customer satisfaction, being, as they were, averages across the whole market.

Global Tech

Koala bears	Uses an extended warranty to give them cover. Won't do anything themselves, prefer to curl up and wait for someone to come and fix it.	
	Small offices (in small and big companies)	*28% of the market*
Teddy bears	Lots of account management and love required from a single preferred supplier. Will pay a premium for training and attention. If multi-site, will require supplier to effectively cover these sites (protect me).	
	Larger companies	*17% of the market*
Polar bears	Like Teddy bears except colder! Will shop around for cheapest service supplier, whoever that may be. Full third party approach. Train me but don't expect to be paid. Will review annually (seriously). If multi-site, will require supplier to effectively cover these sites.	
	Larger companies	*29% of the market*
Yogi bears	A 'wise' Teddy or Polar bear working long hours. Will use trained staff to fix if possible. Needs skilled product specialist at end of phone, not a bookings clerk. Wants different service levels to match the criticality of the product to their business process.	
	Large and small companies	*11% of the market*
Grizzly bears	Trash them! Cheaper to replace than maintain. Besides, they're so reliable that they are probably obsolete when they bust. Expensive items will be fixed on a pay-as-when basis – if worth it. Won't pay for training.	
	Not small companies	*6% of the market*
Andropov big bears	My business is totally dependent on your products. I know more about your products than you do! You will do as you are told. You will be here now! I will pay for the extra cover but you will ......!	
	Not small or very large companies	*9% of the market*

Figure 7.15 Global Tech's customer segments

The problem is, how companies can move from treating their market in an undifferentiated fashion (shown in Figure 7.16), beyond the highly fragmented stage (shown in Figure 7.17) to a segmented position (shown in Figure 7.18).

How customers vary: needs-based segmentation

If marketing is about matching customer needs to what we have to offer, its essence is treating different customers differently. We have therefore found that a grouping of customers into segments with broadly similar needs provides a fundamental and powerful tool for forming multi-channel strategy. This is explicated very clearly in 'The Multi-Channel

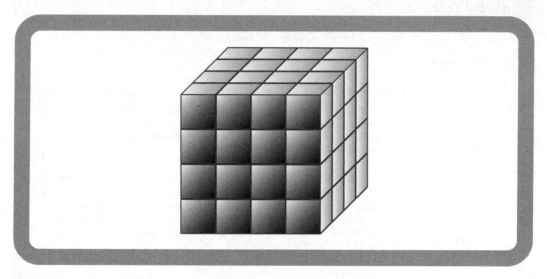

Figure 7.16 An undifferentiated market, but one with many different purchase behaviours

Figure 7.17 A highly fragmented market, but where an understanding of needs shows how it can be simplified

Challenge', an article produced by Dr Hugh Wilson and Matt Hobbs for Cranfield School of Management's Multi-channel Research Club in 2004 and summarized below.

Perceptual maps as a starting point

A common approach to presenting customer segmentation is in a two-dimensional perceptual map such as that illustrated in Figure 7.19.

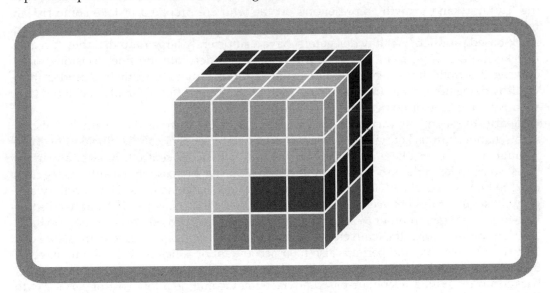

Figure 7.18   A segmented market

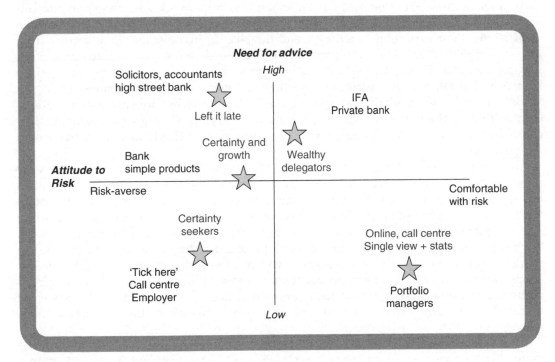

Figure 7.19   Perceptual map – retirement income

This perceptual map is for a financial services company and, in particular, its offering to those who are about to retire (with details changed to preserve confidentiality). The segments vary on two key dimensions: the customers' need for advice and their attitude to risk. The largest segment is 'certainty seekers', people who wish to convert their pension pot to a guaranteed income with the least possible trouble. This segment typically takes out an annuity with their pension provider. A slightly less risk-averse segment is that seeking 'certainty and growth', representing people who are prepared to take some risk in order to achieve a greater return – for example, by investing part of their pension pot in a stock-based product. 'Wealthy delegators' have a sufficiently large fund that they feel able to take more risk with an investment, and prefer to delegate the fine decisions to an adviser. 'Portfolio managers' may have similar funds, but vary in their attitudes from wealthy delegators, preferring to manage their own fund portfolio. Finally, the 'left it late' segment have little or no pension provision.

Clearly, the segments vary not just in what product propositions they want, but also in what channel to market will best suit them. Certainty seekers can be efficiently served through a simple 'tick here' form, perhaps backed up by a call centre to answer any questions, so as to keep the process as simple and reassuring as possible. Wealthy delegators need to be reached via advice-providing intermediaries such as IFAs. The 'certainty and growth' segment lies between the two: these people may not have an IFA but need some face-to-face contact in order to select the right product and provide reassurance. So bank distribution may form the main channel. People in the 'left it late' segment are also likely to turn to their bank, and perhaps also their accountant or solicitor. 'Portfolio managers', by contrast, want hard information rather than personal reassurance, and so the Internet backed up by skilled telephone-based advisers may combine a low cost of service with immediacy and a sense of control for the customer.

Another example that stemmed from one of the authors' work with an export consultancy is shown in Figure 7.20. This consultancy has seven segments, which vary on two dimensions: their exporting experience; and the level of involvement they require from any export consultant. For simplicity we have divided the segments into three main groups: 'confidents', who are experienced exporters; 'aspirants', who have as yet exported little or not at all, but who aspire to exporting as a key part of their business plan; and 'reluctants', who are similarly inexperienced to the aspirants, but are very different attitudinally, finding the notion of exporting risky and worrying. These macro-segments vary considerably in what kinds of channels are appropriate, as well as in their attractiveness to the organization.

Another example, a large IT company, is shown in Figure 7.21. Its customers vary on whether they are seeking 'relief' or 'reward', as well as on whether their focus is on business or technical issues. Again, some implications for channel strategy can be drawn fairly easily from the segmentation by a knowledgeable team of managers. A 'save my career' customer will need plenty of face-to-face reassurance from an account manager. A 'save my budget' customer may be perfectly prepared to buy at a distance in order to reduce the cost of sale and thus the price, as well as researching the best possible price by shopping around or holding reverse auctions. A 'radical thinker' may wish to be offered white papers and seminars with industry opinion leaders. A 'technical idealist' may want to see the company's technical staff, but as little as possible of the besuited account managers.

The following section shows, briefly, how to list what we call 'micro-segments', the many different need sets in a market shown in Figure 7.17 above, before forming them into segments.

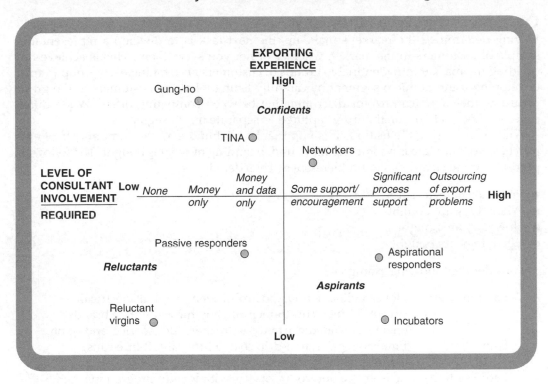

Figure 7.20 Perceptual map – export consultancy
Source: reproduced from a client report by PragMedic Ltd (www.pragmedic.com) by kind permission of UK Trade & Investment

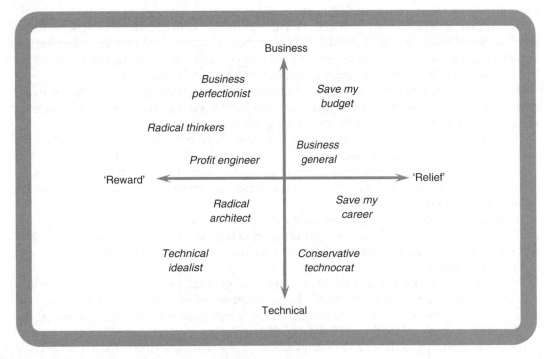

Figure 7.21 Perceptual map – IT company

Customers and what they buy

Having determined the market's make-up, the next task is to develop a representative sample of customers in the market, whether or not you serve them. This is achieved by dividing the market into identifiable groups of customers and, taking each group in turn, developing it into a micro-segment by carefully listing what the customers in the group regard as their key features for discriminating between competing offers. When differences are known to occur, these are captured as separate micro-segments.

When considering the features it is important to unbundle all the components of each purchase so that there is a comprehensive understanding of what is bought. The following product/service features should therefore be considered:

- Physical characteristics
- Where they are bought
- How they are bought
- When they are bought.

Consider the following examples:

Lawnmowers:	Hover, cylinder, rotary, petrol-driven, manual, electrically driven, 12-inch cut, 16-inch cut, any mower with a branded engine, extended warranty, with after-sales service, and so on.
Paints:	Emulsion, gloss, non-drip coat, 5-litre cans, 2-litre cans, environmentally friendly, bulk, and so on.
Petrol stations:	Self-service, forecourt service, with loyalty programme, and so on.

As part of this step of identifying the key features, take into account all the channels through which the range of products/services are bought.

Supply channels (where bought) might include: direct/mail order, distributor, department store, national chain, regional chain, local independent retailer, tied retailer, supermarket, wholesaler, mass distributor, specialist supplier, street stall, via a buying group, through a buyer club, door-to-door, local/high street/out-of-town shop and so on.

It may also be necessary to consider the different frequencies of purchase, such as every two years, at 50,000 miles, occasionally, as needed, only in emergencies, degrees of urgency, infrequency, rarely, special events, only during sales and so on.

Then consider the different methods of purchase (how bought) and, if applicable, the different purchasing organizations and procedures observed in the market.

Methods of purchase might include: credit card, charge card, cash, direct debit, standing order, credit terms, Maestro, outright purchase, lease-hire, lease-purchase, negotiated price, sealed bid and so on.

For each completed micro-segment, add some details describing who it represents using profiling characteristics such as demographics/firmographics, geography, geodemographics and so on. This is to ensure that there is information available to help identify who is found in the concluding segments.

This step often produces around 20 or 30 micro-segments, each of which should have a volume or value figure attached. When larger numbers of micro-segments are produced they can usually be reduced by ensuring they each represent real customers and that the features listed for them are those they use to discriminate between competing offers. A full explanation of this procedure can be found in *Market Segmentation: How to Do It, How to Profit from It* by Malcolm McDonald and Ian Dunbar (see References and further reading). Some preliminary screening at this stage is vital in order to reduce this long list of micro-segments to manageable proportions.

Why each micro-segment behaves the way it does

The third stage of analysing customer behaviour is to gain an understanding of why customers behave the way they do in order that we can better sell to them.

The most useful and practical way of explaining customer behaviour has been found to be that of benefit analysis, or the identification of the benefits customers seek in buying a product or service. For example, customer choice may be based on utility (product), economy (price), convenience and availability (place), emotion (promotion), or a combination (trade-off) of all these. For how else can the success of firms such as Rolls-Royce, Harrods and many others be explained? Understanding the benefits sought by different groups of customers helps us to organize our marketing mix in the way most likely to appeal to our target market.

Forming the micro-segments into larger segments

Following the above procedure will result in a list of micro-segments with details along the lines shown in Figure 7.22.

The final step is the culmination of all previous steps in the segmentation process: to look for clusters of micro-segments that share the same, or similar, needs and to apply to them the organization's minimum volume/value criteria in order to determine their viability. This process usually results in between five and ten main segments.

While this concluding step can be difficult and time-consuming, any care lavished on this part of the market segmentation process will pay handsome dividends at later stages

Key features	Micro-segments									
	1	2	3	4	5	6	7	8	9	10
What is bought										
Where										
When										
How										
Profile										
Who										
Why										
Benefits sought										
Size										
Volume/value										

Figure 7.22 The detail of micro-segmentation

of the marketing strategy development process. The following is a useful summary of the process of market segmentation:

What is bought	Physical characteristics
	Where bought
	When bought
	How bought
Who buys	Demographics
	Socio-economics
	Brand loyalty
	Heavy/light users
	Personality, traits, lifestyles
Why	Benefits
	Attitudes
	Perceptions
	Preferences

Some final thoughts

Successful commerce has always been the result of a careful matching of offers to needs. Only a fool would conclude that all women between the ages of 18 and 22 are the same, or that all people who live in the same neighbourhood are the same, etc. Nonetheless, it is such shallow thinking that has come to represent market segmentation over the years.

The complexities of customer segmentation are humorously illustrated in the following anecdote. A father whose daughter's small car had been stopped by the police for having bald tyres, on being told, obviously had to buy four new tyres. As he loved her deeply, he decided not to put on the four cheapest, nastiest, retreads he could find. Instead, he searched the Internet to find the cheapest Firestone tyres before making his decision. However, after a hectic week, he decided not to travel into the city to buy his Firestones, but to go to his local village garage. There, a heated discussion took place about the price of four Firestone tyres, but the grateful father paid the full asking price in return for the convenience of not having to travel to the city on a Saturday. Exactly one year later, the tyres were bald again but, this time, he decided to sell the small car and buy a new one for his daughter. Not surprisingly, before selling it, he put on the four cheapest, nastiest retreads that he could find!

Anyone who doesn't understand that the tyre market is segmented will have little recourse but to trade solely on price.

These somewhat trivial and elementary examples illustrate that in life, as in business, people have different needs sets. With the wealth of management education and publications available to us, it seems incredible that, in the twenty-first century, so many organizations still haven't understood that the secret to success is correct market definition and segmentation as precursors to product development, positioning and branding.

Given the importance of segmentation, and knowing the difficulties that many organizations face in understanding and elucidating the segments in their market, we cover this in more detail in Chapter 8 when we look at how to create strong, successful strategies.

Chapter 8

Creating strategies that create shareholder value

Fast track

Strategic marketing planning is made more difficult by the myriad different approaches suggested in textbooks. In truth, however, these differ in jargon and detail but not in principle; there is a core process of strategic marketing planning. This core process involves an iterative loop of understanding the market, choosing the strategy, implementing the plan and monitoring outcomes. It is supported by a raft of strategic management tools and techniques, and this technology of strategic marketing planning can be used to reduce the risk associated with the business plan. This reduction of risk and subsequent improvement in potential to create shareholder value forms the therapeutic process of Marketing Due Diligence.

- *Market risk* can be reduced by better understanding of the risks inherent in growth strategies and in poorly characterized markets. It can be reduced in practice by intelligent use of market research, understanding the implications of Ansoff's matrix and the predictive power of life cycle analysis.
- *Share risk* can be reduced by improving the choice of target customers and the value propositions we offer them. It can be reduced in practice by understanding market structure, market segmentation and the difference between a product or service and a value proposition. It can be further reduced by insight into strengths and weaknesses of the company and how they align to the market.
- *Profit risk* can be reduced by understanding the impact of strategies on competitors. It can be reduced in practice by the use of game theory to predict and avoid aggressive responses. Profit margin risk can be further reduced by making better informed assumptions about the costs of implementing the strategy.

For each area of risk, therefore, the tools of strategic marketing planning can be used to reduce risks identified by the Marketing Due Diligence diagnostic process and hence improve shareholder value creation. Even when markets are complex, data is incomplete and planning resources are limited, it is possible to significantly improve shareholder value creation by applying rigour to the strategy-making process.

Starting from where we are

There is an old joke, told in most places yet always tailored to mock gently another nationality or region, about asking for directions. Whatever the adaptation, it always involves a travelling stranger asking a local for directions to some place or other. In reply, the local responds along the lines of: 'Well, if I were you, I wouldn't start from here.' The joke, of course, contrasts the stranger's need for practical help and the local's well-meaning naivety. It is tempting, and easy, when writing a chapter like this to fall into the same error and to direct the reader to start from scratch and create an entirely new marketing strategy that minimizes market, share and profit risk. However, such a recommendation would be a mistake for four reasons.

Firstly, most, if not all, of our readers simply do not have the time to recreate their marketing strategy from scratch. To attempt to do so might paralyse the company for so long as to outweigh the benefits of the new strategy.

Secondly, even if time allowed, the other components of the company's strategy constrain the choice of target market and value proposition. For instance, a company that has invested heavily in R&D and flexible (but relatively expensive) cellular manufacturing facilities might find itself unable to profitably target a price-sensitive segment with a low-cost proposition.

Thirdly, strategy is not decided by rational planning alone. In most organizations, strategy emerges from a complex hybrid of intuitive and cultural as well as rational planning processes. Even if it reduced business risk, strategies which run counter to a company's embedded cultural assumptions stand little chance of successful implementation. Readers interested in how different hybrid processes of making strategy are differentially effective in different markets and with different company cultures are directed to Dr Brian Smith's article, 'Making Marketing Happen' (see References and further reading).

Finally, choosing the lowest risk strategy is not always the right thing to do. Most investment strategies follow the principle of portfolio management, in that they balance different investments of differing risk/return ratios. The investment strategy that funds your SBU, whether a corporate subsidiary, a venture capital start-up or a bank-funded SME, sees your strategy as part of a balanced portfolio. In that case, the need is not to minimize risk, but to ensure three things:

- To ensure the business risk is well understood. This is the value of the Marketing Due Diligence diagnostic process.
- To ensure that the risk inherent in the strategy is minimized by the detail of its implementation. That is the value of the Marketing Due Diligence therapeutic process and the subject of this chapter.
- To ensure that the risk is accurately allowed for in the calculation of likely returns and that this calculation indicates that shareholder value will be created. That is the value of the overall Marketing Due Diligence process and is discussed in Chapter 9.

This chapter, therefore, starts from here. It assumes that investors' strategies, cultural constraints and other functional strategies imply that the existing strategy must form at least the basis of the future strategy. It then assumes that the existing marketing strategy has emerged from the Marketing Due Diligence diagnostic process with a mixed profile, that some areas of risk are relatively low and some relatively high. The following sections of this chapter go on to consider how each area of risk might be reduced so as to lead to a lower overall level of business risk.

Understanding and managing market risk

Market risk is at once the largest potential source of risk in a business plan and the hardest to change. As the risk that the market may not be as large as is promised, it is rooted in the company's fundamental choice of which market to serve and, by extension, what kind of product or service area to work in. This fundamental choice is rarely made *ab initio*. In some cases, such as growth by acquisition in a new area, or in some early-stage R&D choices, the company has the choice as to whether or not to enter the market. More often, the managers of an SBU are faced with, to some extent, a *fait accompli*, in which the essentials of market choice have already been made. It is within this constrained context that managers must work to reduce market risk. Fortunately, two of the oldest tools of strategic marketing planning arose from the need to do just this and, although to some extent familiarity has led to neglect of these tools, they remain essential and irreplaceable techniques for reducing market risk. Ansoff's matrix guides the reduction of both product category risk and market existence risk, whilst product life cycle helps in the understanding and management of sales volume, forecast and pricing risks.

Understanding and managing product category and market existence risk

Earlier in this book we used the helpful idea, borrowed from Henry Mintzberg, that strategy is a pattern of resource allocation decisions. If we look at our marketing strategy that way, we can see that among the first of these decisions is that of which market to enter and what kind of product or service to make. These decisions are not the entirety of the marketing strategy, which involves focusing on particular customers and offering a complete value proposition. However, the market/product choice can be seen as the first iteration of the marketing strategy, which is then honed into something more focused and precise. As a first iteration, it sets the parameters or limits to what the marketing strategy can be. If, for instance, we target the public transport market with a traffic prediction software package we can't then decide to offer something that is nothing to do with software to people not involved in public transport. We can only refine the segments we target within public transport (e.g. road transport providers in metropolitan areas with congestion problems) and the nature of the offer (stand-alone or integrated, basic or extended support, etc.).

The risk associated with this first, broad choice of resource allocation is often the largest single component of business risk for a company, especially if it is a new market or new product. When we attack existing markets with proven products, we may reduce market risk but often at the cost of increased share risk or profit risk, as we try to win share in mature markets against strong, entrenched competitors. Many companies therefore accept the higher market risk associated with new markets and/or new products because they offer higher potential growth than existing markets and/or products that offer lower market risk.

The key to understanding market risk is therefore to understand the idea that newness in marketing strategy is roughly proportional to risk. Among the first to recognize this principle, and the first to codify it, was Igor Ansoff. Although he contributed greatly for many years to the development of strategic planning, his name is almost always associated

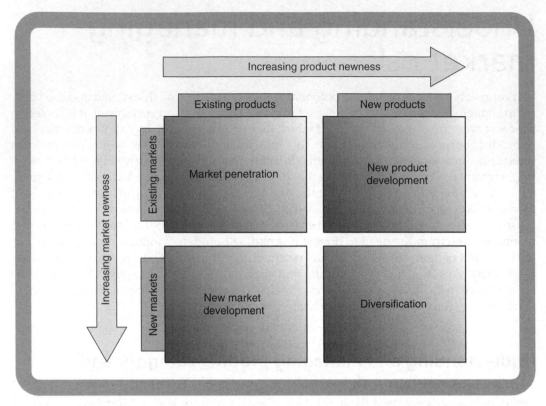

Figure 8.1   Ansoff's matrix

with the matrix in which he captured the relationship between the degree of newness in a strategy and its level of market risk.

The usual exposition of Ansoff's matrix is shown in Figure 8.1. This is the form in which it is most usually taught to marketers, although in his original work Ansoff used numerous variations around this theme to communicate the same idea that newness is usually proportional to risk. Unfortunately, the way marketers are often taught Ansoff's matrix can lead to something being lost in translation. Marketers, especially those with little understanding of strategic finance, can see the matrix as a kind of to-do list. First, get all the market penetration you can, then some market development and new product development, then some diversification. This interpretation of Ansoff misses out the key issue he was trying to communicate: risk. Finance people, by contrast, tend to see Ansoff's matrix as something akin to a medieval map, in which anything outside of market penetration is marked: 'There be dragons'. Interpreted too literally, this view of Ansoff neglects the other key theme of his work: growth. The reality of Ansoff's message, of course, is something between the two. You can and sometimes should look for growth from new products and markets, but only in the full knowledge that the further you stray from what you know, the greater risk you are incurring. Ansoff's point is actually very simple in principle. We are unconsciously ignorant; we don't know what we don't know. Hence any attempt to penetrate a market that is new to us or sell a product that is new to us opens up the possibility of making a mistake out of simple ignorance. Understanding this concept

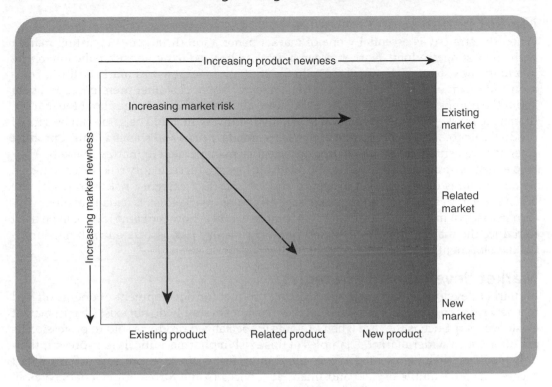

Figure 8.2   Ansoff's matrix – shaded interpretation

makes the two-by-two matrix too simple an interpretation of Ansoff's work. A more accurate and useful reading of Ansoff is that the newness–risk relationship is a continuum as we move from well-known strategies to related and partly understood strategies to entirely new ones. This more shaded interpretation of Ansoff's work is therefore summarized in Figure 8.2.

As Figure 8.2 indicates, our search for growth can lead in the direction of new markets or new products or both, and we can do so in incremental steps. There are no hard and fast borderlines in the degree of innovation in our strategy. Market penetration, market development, new product development and diversification are simply four stereotypes used to simplify a reality in which there are innumerable possible combinations of market and product innovation. This more nuanced interpretation of the growth/risk balance has two important implications for managing market risk. It means that:

● We can adjust the amount of newness in our choice of market and product or service (and therefore the level of risk) by degrees, without fundamentally changing the strategy.
● We can reduce the risk created by unfamiliarity with the chosen market or product by considering the lessons to be learned from related markets and products.

Ansoff's work dates from the mid 1960s and is often neglected on the grounds of its age, but a good understanding of his work leads us to a number of practical steps that can be taken to reduce market risk or to demonstrate the low-risk nature of our strategy. To do this, we need first of all to understand where in Ansoff's matrix our strategy sits. Our position in the matrix then determines what we might do to reduce risk.

Market penetration strategies

When the strategy is essentially one of market penetration (it targets an existing market with an existing product), market research data can be used to demonstrate the inherently low market existence risk associated with the strategy. In established markets, this is common and relatively easy. Demographic data, research about customer preferences and data about the number of customer organizations are all forms of knowledge about the market. In mature markets, such information is usually readily available. The same can be said of product category risk. Information about sales, trends, prices and shares within a product category are usually the staple of product category management in mature markets. They help to demonstrate and substantiate the relatively low product category risk. Taken together, demonstrations of low market existence and low product category risk help justify the business plan's assertions about market size. Of course, market risk is usually a minor concern in cases of market penetration. What is more useful is how the same ideas can be used to reduce the market existence risk and product category risk associated with new product development, market development or diversification strategies.

Market development strategies

In market development strategies an existing product (or development of one) is offered to a new set of customers. The risk is that these customers simply do not exist (that is, market existence risk). Such is the case when previously specialized products sold to professionals are offered to a wider market. Examples of this exist in pharmaceuticals (e.g. prescription-only medicines being presented in over-the-counter forms), in some areas of IT (broadband access was an example of this) and financial services (some forms of personalized asset management are examples of this). In cases such as these, market existence risk can be reduced by some combination of two approaches.

Firstly, we can reduce the newness of the customers we are looking at. Not all customers in the target market are the same and some are closer to our existing customers than others. If, within the market, we choose to target the segment that is closest to our existing customers in terms of needs or motivations, we are incurring less risk than if we target the whole market or segments that are very different from our existing customers. Two simple examples illustrate the point. Much of this book has been planned out using MindGenius, mind-mapping software. Seeking to grow beyond the existing market of professional users, the vendors of this package have attempted to target firstly home use by those professionals, rather than those not familiar at all with mind mapping. In effect, they have reduced the newness of their strategy and moved it, by intelligent targeting, to the borders between market penetration and market development. Contrast this with the approach of those US companies who operate in the 'wealth management' market. These companies wrap investment advice, equities management and other financial services into bundles for relatively wealthy individuals. Faced with increasing competition at home, many have attempted to move into Europe. However, their targeting, often based only on crude proxies for personal wealth, has led many of them to misunderstand the needs-based segmentation in the market. Culture and tradition means that the market for such products in the EU differs markedly from that in the USA. Perhaps they could have reduced risk by targeting either US market segments adjacent to their current customers or by uncovering and targeting a real European segment similar to their US customers, but most appear not to have attempted this.

In addition to reducing the newness of a market development strategy by selecting the target segment well, market existence risk can be reduced by using knowledge about related markets. This works best when the related market is well understood and its connection to the target market is strong. When Thor International, a company specializing in therapeutic laser technology, sought to move from its existing market (mainly physiotherapists and chiropractors working with soft tissue injury) it looked at the chronic wound-healing market, where its technology had clinically proven benefits but about which there was no data concerning market existence. There was, naturally, no market data about laser use in this area, since it was a new product category in this market. However, the market could be understood (and market existence risk reduced) by considering what was already known about the market for other wound-healing products, such as dressings. Not only is the wound-dressing market mature and well understood, the mechanism of its connection to laser therapy is clear, since the same professionals are involved in the purchase process for both. Hence Thor was able to intelligently apply knowledge of related markets to reduce the level of risk in this market development.

As we have seen, by understanding Ansoff's matrix we can identify two ways of reducing the market existence risk associated with market development strategies. By either careful targeting or by using knowledge of a related market, we can reduce this element of market risk and hence overall business risk.

Product development strategies

In product development strategies, a group of customers that are currently served is offered a new product or service. The risk is therefore that the offering fails to create a compelling value proposition to those customers – in other words, product category risk. This is the case when companies try to leverage their current knowledge of their customers and sell them a new product. Examples of this appear widely in branded FMCG products, but also in any market where the company holds a strong franchise with its customers. The research underpinning this book was carried out using a bibliographic software package called Reference Manager, which is widely used by scientists of various disciplines to index and cite their collections of academic literature. Recently, the makers of Reference Manager have launched RefViz, a software package that helps researchers to organize their databases visually. It is aimed at the same customers but is a completely different product category and offers different benefits. Interestingly, the makers, ISI Researchsoft, are a division of the academic publishers Thomson, so their entire software business is an example of product development to their existing book customers. In strategies such as this, product category risk can be reduced by a combination of two approaches. As with reducing risk in market development, these two approaches are to reduce the newness of the strategy and to use information from related markets.

Firstly, we can reduce the newness of the product or service being offered. The real or perceived originality of the offer can be varied, and we reduce the product category risk if we do so. Evian, famous for its bottled water, is an example of this. Part of its proposition has always been the health-giving, life-enhancing properties of their water. Leaving aside the questionable biochemistry, this is a central part of Evian's brand values. Seeking growth in the face of a maturing and competitive mineral water market, they attempted a product development strategy by launching an Evian moisturizing spray, which claimed to moisturize skin merely by spraying on Evian water. Clearly, this was aimed at existing customers but was an entirely new product category. In the event, the product failed when customers did not accept both the idea of moisturizing by spray and Evian as a cosmetics brand. Not ones to give up easily, Evian later made a second, more successful, attempt at this market with a relatively conventional moisturizing cream, branded Evian. In effect, this was the same growth strategy but with less risk, since it was able to learn from the mature skin care market and the product category data for moisturizers.

The second way to reduce product category risk is to learn lessons from related product categories and use knowledge of their markets. This lesson can be drawn from the success of 'portable jukeboxes' like the iPod. Although apparently brand new product categories, they are, in essence, developments of the Sony Walkman concept. In effect, Apple were taking much less risk with iPod than Sony had with the Walkman, because at the time of launch they could learn the market lessons of the technically different tape- and CD-based product categories and apply those lessons to hard drive-based products.

So, as with market development strategies, we can, by understanding Ansoff's matrix, identify two ways of reducing the product category risk associated with product development strategies. By either reducing the newness of the product category or by using knowledge of a related product category, we can reduce this element of market risk and hence overall business risk.

Diversification strategies

Diversification strategies are those in which the firm offers a new product category to a group of customers it does not currently serve. As such, they typically imply high market risk, both in terms of market existence risk and product category risk. Such strategies are accordingly quite rare, and those that do exist for long enough to be noticed tend to employ both the 'reducing newness' and 'using existing knowledge' tactics described above to reduce the risk associated with them. Examples of this include Dell's entry into the consumer electronics market. Although, on the face of it, this appears to be offering new product categories to customers not previously served, Dell seem to do all they can to reduce the newness of their value proposition and to piggy-back on knowledge of existing categories. The same can be said of Amazon's growth strategy into various sectors such as toys and house wares. In these cases, neither company is taking the risk of entering a wholly new market with an entirely new class of product. The lack of successful examples of such extreme diversification underlines the lessons of Ansoff's matrix and acts as a reminder that understanding it is crucial to reducing business risk.

Understanding and managing sales volume, forecast and pricing risks

The preceding section described how a good understanding of Ansoff's matrix allows us to understand and manage the two components of market risk that are most important when our strategy has a large degree of newness, either in the market we are attacking or in the product we are selling. For obvious reasons, the risks associated with market existence or the product category tend to be lower when our strategy is less than completely new. In these not entirely novel cases, the market risk factors of most concern are that we might inaccurately estimate the size of our sales, how they grow and the pricing levels we might achieve. In other words, even a strategy that focuses on an existing market still has risks associated with the uncertainty of how it will develop in the future. In the absence of a time machine, nothing can completely remove these risks by making our market predictions perfectly accurate. However, the technique of product life cycle analysis can, if understood well, greatly inform and improve our predictions. To gain those advantages, however, we need to have a better than superficial understanding of where this technique comes from and what it implies.

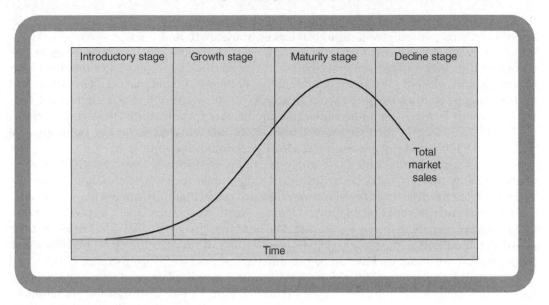

Figure 8.3   The product life cycle curve

Just like Ansoff's work, product life cycle analysis suffers from its familiarity. Almost every business person has heard of it and the technique no longer has any cachet of being new and trendy. This is a shame, since it remains woefully underused and poorly understood. Product life cycle is perhaps best thought of not as some cerebral academic theory but as an exercise in mass observation. Unlike the growth matrix, product life cycle analysis is not usually associated with the writings of any one person. Rather, it grew over several decades from the combined observations of many researchers. They noted that markets tend to follow patterns in which a new product is launched, followed by me-toos, and that this activity grows the market for this category or form of product. This growth in volume over time creates the well-known product life cycle curve, as shown in Figure 8.3. However, these observations also suggested several other patterns in the way the market develops as technologies converge, companies consolidate, growth slows and the form of competition between players changes over time. For a good understanding of product life cycle analysis, the reader is directed to Malcolm McDonald's book *Marketing Plans* (see References and further reading) on marketing planning. In short, the point to grasp is that product life cycle analysis applies to product forms or categories and not to particular products. For instance, consumer audio recording has had life cycles for wax cylinders, vinyl discs, cassette tapes, CDs, etc., not to mention short-lived episodes of eight-track cartridges, minidiscs, etc. Each product form usually follows the pattern of the product life cycle and thus the model, perhaps better described as product form life cycle, can be used to inform our judgement about what happens next.

Hence a careful and accurate judgement of whereabouts in the product form life cycle curve our product sits provides a valuable input into managing sales volume, forecast and pricing risks. At the embryonic stage, the curve tells us that volume estimates are necessarily difficult, although we can better inform them using the concepts discussed to reduce product category and market existence risk. On the other hand, a market at embryonic stage can reasonably be expected to grow quickly and with relatively high pricing, due to the absence of competitors. As the product form enters its growth phase, product life cycle analysis tells us to predict still rapid but less erratic growth and the entry of new players which, to some degree, curbs pricing aspirations. Perhaps the greatest danger lies in the turbulent transition phase from growth to maturity. At this stage, competitors vie to be one of the small handful of players that dominate, as happens in most markets. Growth slows and pricing aspirations become harder to achieve. In the mature phase itself, market volumes, growth and pricing all become more predictable from historic trends until, in the decline phase, we can anticipate that the market volume will decline; at this point growth will turn negative and pricing will be eroded by commoditization.

As with Ansoff, product life cycle analysis can be used in two ways. Firstly, it is very useful in allowing us to make better informed judgements about market volumes, growth and pricing. Secondly, it is a way of illustrating to investors that the business plan is thought out and that any risks have been allowed for. It is worth remembering at this point that our aim is not necessarily to minimize market risk, but rather to ensure that what risks we take are understood and managed. By using both Ansoff and product life cycle analysis in an intelligent manner, market risk can be minimized.

As already indicated, market risk is closely related to market or product newness. High market risk suggests that market size assertions are unrealistic and that the shareholder value creation claims of the plan are similarly optimistic. By careful application of Ansoff's matrix and product form life cycle, market size projections become better informed, more realistic and shareholder value creation becomes more assured.

Understanding and managing share risk

When a strategy contains a lower element of novelty in targets and value propositions, the level of market risk usually declines. However, reduction in novelty is usually accompanied by other aspects of market maturity and hence the level of share risk usually rises to compensate. The difficulty of achieving the intended market share decreases as competition intensifies and market growth rates decline and flatten. As already mentioned, share risk is, in essence, a function of strategy strength. Weak strategies lead to high share risk. It follows that understanding and managing share risk requires the appreciation and engineering of the chosen target customers and value proposition. As with other elements of the Marketing Due Diligence therapeutic process, a firm's efforts to this end are best focused and directed by the results of the Marketing Due Diligence diagnostic.

Reducing target market risk

Target market risk arises from poor definition of the target customers. More specifically it arises when the target group is heterogeneous in its needs and wants. As a consequence, any single value proposition will appeal to only some of the target, and that proportion of the target represents the upper limit on the possible share. Typically, target market risk is high when the strategy targets not true market segments but classifications of customers such as 'blue-chip companies', 'ABC1 males aged 25–35', 'the distributor market' or any target defined in terms of product or service. This kind of target definition is characteristic of weak strategies and is a contributing factor to other elements of share risk. Correcting this fundamental flaw takes more than superficial tweaking of the strategy, it requires the market segmentation to be well understood. Whilst it is beyond the scope of this book to explain the process in detail (the reader is directed to *Market Segmentation: How to Do It, How to Profit from It* by Malcolm McDonald and Ian Dunbar, see References and further reading). A quick summary of the process is given in Box 8.1.

By completing and acting upon a rigorous segmentation analysis of their market, companies refine the target or targets of their strategy. In doing so, they reduce the target market risk component of their share risk and hence the overall business risk.

Box 8.1 Creating real market segments

All good segmentation comes from the thoughtful execution of six steps. Try these for your own market as you read on.

1 *Define your market*
Markets and products are not the same thing. There is no such thing as the 'digital camera market' because cameras do not make purchase decisions. Markets are groups of people sharing a broad need, like capturing visual images. If your market definition is in product terms, try revising it to begin: 'Our market is those people who want …' and complete the sentence in terms of what needs the customer is trying to meet (e.g. 'Our market is those people who want to capture, modify and communicate images').

2 *Decide where the choice is made*
Two things are important here. Firstly, segmentation happens where the purchase decision is made. In most consumer markets, the consumer makes the choice, but if we need a hip replacement then we let someone else make the choice of implant. Good segmentation is done at the level of the purchase choice. In complex markets, this often requires a technique known as market mapping. (This technique was covered in detail in Chapter 7.) Secondly, the decision makers we segment might be individuals (I choose my own beer) or groups (we choose our house, car or power station). Before going further, try writing down: 'In our market, the choice is made at _____ level by _____'.

3 *Decide what drives the decision*
Markets are customers with needs, and needs come in two kinds: hygiene factors and motivators. Hygiene factors are things the offer must have just to be a possibility (we need drugs to be safe, lawyers to be qualified, etc.) and, since everyone does it, meeting these needs doesn't make a difference. Motivators are the needs that create segments. Critically, they are needs which differ between customers (you need status, I don't; I need ease of use, you don't). Typically, only two or three motivator needs determine the real segmentation in a market. Now try to write down: 'In our market, the hygiene factors are _____ and the motivators are _____'.

4 *Cluster your customers*
Armed with an understanding of where the purchase decision happens, who makes it and what motivators differentiate customers, segmentation becomes much clearer. Think about the customers you meet in terms of their motivations and it will become clear that customers cluster. In office software, one group may want multiple programs, another just word processing. Some want lots of clever functions, others want ease of

use. In most markets, customers cluster, driven by their needs, in an uneven fashion. These clusters of customers are, in essence, segments. Make a first attempt at writing down between two and six customer clusters, defined in terms of motivators, for your market. You should come up with groups like: 'always wants the latest thing and doesn't care much about price' or 'wants lots of support and isn't technically minded'.

5 *Find your segments*

Your initial, intuitive guesses at needs-based segments can and ideally should be refined and tested by both research and experience, but the next step is to move from the mind of the customer to the reality of implementation. Sadly, we can't look at a customer in the street and find a segment label stamped on his or her forehead. We can, however, use things that we can measure as loose approximations for his or her needs. Younger people tend to be driven more by fashion needs. Young families have high security needs. The public sector is often more price sensitive than the private and SMEs have less formal procurement systems than large companies. Making a strong match between these measurable descriptors (such as age, education, company size or sector) and motivations is the critical issue in implementing segmentation. We get it wrong when we start with the descriptors instead of understanding the motivators first. For each of the customer clusters you defined in Step 4, try writing down the most accurate set of descriptors you can. You should, to a good approximation, begin to find that real needs-based segments can be characterized in terms of things you can measure and see.

6 *Test your segments*

The needs-based segments that have emerged from the five steps above will be better than the classifications used by many marketers. It is worth remembering that your segmentation does not have to be perfect, just better than the competition. To improve your segmentation further, try applying the four classic tests of segmentation. For each of the segments you have defined, ask yourself:

● Is it homogeneous? Do all of the customers in that segment have pretty much the same needs and will they react similarly to the same value proposition?
● Is it distinct? Do the customers in each segment differ from the others in what they want and how they behave?
● Is it accessible? Can you reach the customers in this segment by promotional and distribution channels?
● Is it viable? Is the segment big enough, profitable enough and stable enough to be worth going after?

If the answer to any of these questions is no, then go through the process again, thinking more carefully about each step.

These six steps capture the fundamentals of how segmentation is done. Of course, the devil is in the detail, but effective segmentation gets the basics right first: markets not products; segments not classes; motivators before descriptors. Then the tests are used to make sure that the segmentation is right before going to market.

After segmentation come the next two steps in the differentiation process: deciding which segments to target and designing a tailored proposition for each segment. Often, tactically minded marketers rush on to building these next two important steps without having first got the foundations of segmentation right, with predictably poor results. But then, as Theodore Levitt might have said, they are not doing marketing.

Reducing proposition risk

Proposition risk is the risk that the value proposition does not appeal to the target customers. The most common cause of this is poor targeting and segmentation, as discussed previously. However, targeting a well-defined and homogeneous segment does not always lead to a compelling proposition; it is necessary but not sufficient. The other major cause of proposition risk is the internal conflict that occurs in most organizations between customization and mass production. Clearly, mass-producing a product is attractive because of economies of scale, and the same or similar rationale applies in services. What is conveyancing if not the standardized, computer-assisted, service to facilitate the sale of a property? Even when technology allows so-called mass customization, this is still more costly in efficiency and working capital than true mass production. Hence most organizations do, to some extent, expose themselves to some proposition risk by standardizing their product or service offering and offering that to more than one segment. By definition, this offering will be sub-optimal for one or more of the segments targeted. When the Marketing Due Diligence diagnostic suggests a high level of proposition risk, some way of reconciling the advantages of mass production with the need to tailor the offer to the segment must be found.

As with other risks, an established concept from strategic marketing planning helps to illuminate ways to understand and manage proposition risk. As shown in Figure 8.4, the augmented/extended product model explicates the implicit truth that the product or service is only a component of and not the entire value proposition. Especially in mature markets, it is the service, pricing, channels, packaging and design features that represent most of the value to the customer, whilst the core product is relatively taken for granted. Take

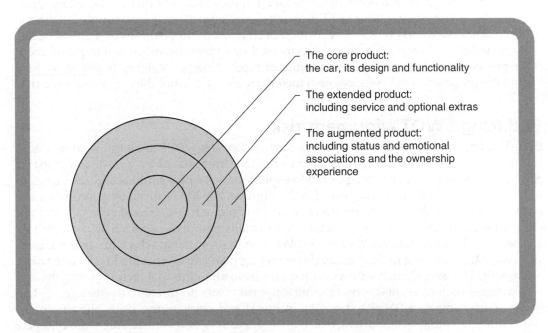

Figure 8.4   The extended/augmented product model: an automotive example
Source: PragMedic Ltd, taken from a consultancy project with a global car manufacturer. Reproduced with permission

for example cars, mobile phones, PCs, many classes of packaged consumer goods, most forms of professional services, financial products and so on. At the core, there is little difference between rival value propositions, and differentiation (and hence appeal to the customer) is derived from the extended and augmented components of the overall 'product'.

A clear understanding of the nature of the value proposition, its components and what parts drive the attractiveness to customers, helps resolve the dilemma of standardization versus customization and hence reduce proposition risk. This is especially important when the core of the product cannot easily be adapted to the needs of a segment. The MBA programmes delivered by business schools are an example of this. The knowledge that forms the core of the product is costly to generate and the constraints of external validation mean that adapting it to the needs of specific segments is difficult. Since the market for postgraduate-level knowledge in business subjects is very heterogeneous, any single MBA programme risks being non-specific to the needs of many potential students. To tweak the core product is difficult and costly. However, a consideration of the MBA as an extended, augmented product reveals the importance of channels, differences in content emphasis, delivery method (e.g. full/part time, modular), pricing mechanisms, etc. In the case of a university offering an MBA programme, therefore, the expensive parts of the value proposition (generating and packaging the core knowledge) can be standardized and produced at a manageable cost. The proposition risk is then reduced by tailoring the outer elements of the extended and augmented 'product'.

The same principle can be seen in all the various examples cited in the preceding paragraph and in almost any successful value proposition that is not mass-produced to compete simply on price. By way of contrast, consider the examples of firms that do not adapt their proposition significantly, such as the low-cost airlines or some patent-protected technology firms in IT or biosciences. The fact that they can only thrive by extreme price competition or from exceptional IPR protection, and even then in very imperfect (in the economist's sense) markets, is evidence of the need to adapt propositions to segment needs.

By completing a careful, extended, augmented consideration of the value proposition, therefore, companies can refine the tailoring of their value proposition. In doing so, they reduce the proposition risk component of their share risk and hence the overall business risk.

Reducing SWOT alignment risk

SWOT alignment risk is the risk that arises when a strategy fails to align the company to the market well by using the organization's relative strengths or by guarding against its relative weaknesses. Such strategies fail to exploit market opportunities and fall victim to market threats. As the name suggests, SWOT alignment risk is reduced by appropriate use of SWOT analysis although, to be effective, this technique must be used correctly and not simply be the subjective listing of factors that so many companies call a SWOT analysis.

The key difference between a valuable SWOT analysis and that which many companies put under that heading in their strategic marketing plan can be summed up in one word: alignment. The SWOT analysis process requires us to align internal factors (strengths and weaknesses) with relevant external factors (opportunities and threats) so as to suggest key issues. For example, a BMW's strengths in brand and engineering skills align with the opportunity created by a segment which sees cars as less of a vehicle and more of a personal status symbol. The key issue for BMW, then, is that their choice of strategy leverages those strengths against that segment. In the same way, Sony's strengths in innovation imply that they should target innovative segments. To do otherwise would be to waste strengths and create SWOT alignment risk. Hence the SWOT alignment process, and acting on the resulting key issues, is the appropriate corrective action to high levels of SWOT alignment risk indicated by the Marketing Due Diligence diagnostic process. Whilst it is beyond the scope of this book to explain the process in detail, Box 8.2 gives a brief illustration of the process.

Box 8.2   Achieving SWOT alignment

There are four key steps to executing a SWOT analysis:

1 Gather strengths, weaknesses, opportunities and threats from the outputs of your market audit. Typically, strengths and weaknesses emerge from comparisons against competitors, such as value chain benchmarking or relative competitive strength analysis. Opportunities and threats emerge from analysis of customer segmentation, mapping of routes to market and broader market analyses.
2 Test and filter your potential strengths and weaknesses. Many companies mistake these internal factors due to lack of objectivity. Two simple mnemonics help.
   a Strengths are only strengths if they are VRIO:
      ● Valuable to the customer, in that the customer is willing to pay for them
      ● Rare, in that they are not possessed by the competition
      ● Inimitable, in that the strength is hard or costly for the competitors to reproduce
      ● Organizationally aligned, in that the company is organized to use this strength.
   b Weaknesses are only weaknesses if they are MUDU:
      ● Meaningful to the customer, in that they care about this weakness
      ● Uncommon, in that they are not weaknesses of the competition
      ● Difficult or costly to correct
      ● Uncompensated for by other factors.
Only strengths and weaknesses which pass these tests should be used in the subsequent SWOT alignment.
3 Align the tested, filtered strengths with market opportunities and weaknesses with market threats to reveal key issues for the strategy. For instance:
   a Strength in superior performance technology protected by IPR aligns with opportunity of performance-seeking, price-insensitive segment to imply that a key issue is to leverage that technology to create a compelling value proposition for that segment.
   b Weakness in high relative costs aligns with threat of low-cost inferior copies to imply that the key issue is to minimize that threat by avoiding price-sensitive, performance-indifferent segments.

A number, typically six to ten, of alignments like this is the normal output for a SWOT analysis and clearly provides strong guidance for the design of marketing strategy.

Reducing uniqueness risk

Uniqueness risk is the risk that arises from going head-on with the competition, offering the same value proposition, to the same customers, in the same way. In such cases, the result is proportional to relative resources and any strategic advantage is dissipated. Such

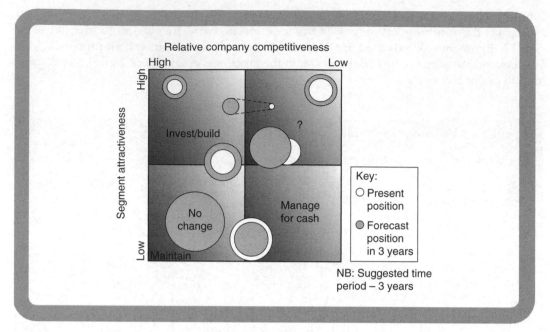

Figure 8.5 A directional policy matrix

head-on competition is very common and is usually excused by managers' claims that, with similar products in similar markets, it is inevitable. This, however, is not the case. Going head-on and the consequent uniqueness risk is usually the result of failing to target correctly. In particular, it results from failing to allow for customer needs, competitor strategies and our own capabilities in the targeting decision.

There is a whole category of tools in the strategic marketing planning process that can help inform targeting. Broadly, they are all methods of portfolio management and involve directing resources according to both how attractive each segment is and how strong we are in that segment. The directional policy matrix (DPM) is probably the most practically useful of these techniques and is described in detail in Malcolm McDonald's *Marketing Plans* (see References and further reading). An example of a DPM is shown in Figure 8.5.

The value of DPM and similar methods lies in the way segment attractiveness and our competitive strength for a segment is calculated. Both are multifactorial, involving the consideration of several factors internal and external to the company, but both rely on judgements particular to the firm's situation. Hence segment attractiveness is its attractiveness to the firm in question (i.e. not to firms generally) and often varies according to the particular goals of the firm (e.g. profit-driven and volume-driven firms are differentially attracted to profitable and large segments respectively).

In the same way, our competitive strength is that segment's view of us and our particular value proposition. What this 'company specificness' means in practice is that no two companies are likely to prepare identical DPMs for the same market. This is even more true if the two companies take different views on how the market is segmented. In short, the particular objectives, strengths and views of a firm combine to lead it, via DPM, to target different customers compared to its rivals. For instance, *The Economist* targets different people in the same market as *Business Week*. The targeting of especially reflective business people by

The Economist aligns well to its brand and editorial strengths. In the same way, this book is based on sound research and practical experience and targets senior and reflective executives, whilst most marketing books target either students or 'airport readers' with a need for quick, superficial, panaceas. Hence careful and rigorous use of the directional policy matrix is a good approach to reducing any high uniqueness risk identified from the Marketing Due Diligence diagnostic process.

Reducing future risk

Future risk is the possibility that our choice of target market and value proposition, however strong in today's market situation, will be weakened by changes in that situation. In our research, we found this to be a particularly insidious risk, which could be hard to identify and correct, given the complexity and turbulence of many markets. It seems to be particularly threatening to large, multifaceted and successful companies. In these cases, a combination of complexity and complacency can blind a company to changes in the marketplace that render its historically successful strategy less effective.

Of course, constant or periodic re-examination of the external microenvironment (that is, customers, competitors and channels) is partial protection against this, but our evidence suggests that this is insufficient. Simply put, by the time changes in a company's microenvironment are clear, it may be too late to react to them. Evidence of this is provided by the suffering of companies that once dominated their market. The changes in the UK retail market have rendered obsolescent the once-strong strategies of Sainsbury, C&A and many others. In IT, financial services, pharmaceuticals, construction, defence and many other sectors, the consolidation of the industry is partly driven by the failure of many companies' strategies to realign to a changed market.

If the Marketing Due Diligence diagnostic reveals a high level of future risk, then the need is to predict likely changes in the marketplace and build that future scenario into the selection of target segments and intended value propositions. That this does not happen in many companies would seem to be due to two reasons. Firstly, directors and others like to stay in their comfort zone, dealing with the here and now and the foreseeable short-term future. Correcting this requires not a new management technique but a new board, since anticipating the future is a core responsibility of the board. Secondly, the impossibility of anticipating the future market conditions accurately leads many firms to think it worthless to try. Whilst understandable, this is a case of the best being the enemy of the good. It is simply not necessary to predict the detail of the future market with any accuracy. What is necessary is to resolve the broad trends in the market and draw from those strategic implications, not detailed data. For instance, it is not necessary to predict the exact size of the market for products for the retired in the developed markets; it is sufficient at this stage to predict that it will grow and involve more active, discerning and wealthy customers.

The primary tool for achieving this insight into the future is SLEPT analysis (an acronym of Social, Legal, Economic, Political and Technological). The technique is variously named PEST, STEP, PESTLE, etc., but the nomenclature is inconsequential as all versions amount to the same thing. Again, this is a tool that is much devalued by its misuse in many companies, in which it is degraded into a simplistic listing of thoughts with no analysis and therefore little management value. Doing SLEPT analysis well is both more rigorous and more useful than what passes for it in some companies. As with the other techniques of strategic marketing planning, space does not allow for a detailed exposition of the SLEPT process here. The principles are, however, straightforward and can be summarized in four steps, described in Box 8.3.

> **Box 8.3   An outline process for SLEPT analysis**
>
> 1 *Gather possible SLEPT factors*
> This requires the collation of all possible macroenvironmental factors which might have an impact on the market and the firm. The SLEPT acronym acts as a good mnemonic and it should be remembered that the aim is to make a comprehensive collection of macroenvironmental factors. Microenvironmental considerations about customers, competitors and channels are not relevant at this stage, and nor are internal factors. For a single SBU, typically 20–50 SLEPT factors might be identified.
> 2 *Draw out the implications of each SLEPT factor*
> This stage requires the thinking through of what each SLEPT factor means for the market under consideration. If the SLEPT factors have been clearly stated, most of them will have a simple implication for the market, either positive or negative. It should be remembered at this stage that the aim is to draw out the broad implications for the market and not detailed implications for the company. Although some SLEPT factors might have no discernible implications, this stage will usually result in a list of implications about the same size as the list of SLEPT factors.
> 3 *Combine the implications*
> This stage requires the consideration of all the implications and how they might combine to impact on the market. There is no quick and easy process for this; it requires careful thought and an understanding of how the market works. In particular, it should be remembered that the classification of factors and their implications into one of each of the five SLEPT categories is purely notional and implications combine across these categories. The aim at this stage is to create a list of combined implications for the market, usually much fewer than the original number of uncombined implications.
> 4 *Translate into opportunities or threats*
> It is at this stage when the analysis starts to consider the more localized effects of the SLEPT factors and their combined implications. Each combined implication will usually translate into a likely and meaningful macroenvironmental trend in the market. Where these are positive, they are labelled opportunities, where negative, threats. It is these outputs that are added to the SWOT analysis to detect if it and the key issues it produces are likely to change in the future.

A worked example of a real SLEPT analysis, from the market for organ transplantation therapies, in shown in Table 8.1. It is simplified for clarity and adapted to protect the firm's confidentiality. Even so, it illustrates the process of SLEPT analysis.

The outputs of a rigorous SLEPT analysis feed into the SWOT analysis and enable an informed review of the way the strategy will align the company to the market in the future. To the extent that the firm allows for this in its strategy, it has effectively managed any notable future risk that was identified in the Marketing Due Diligence diagnostic process.

Other components of share risk

As discussed in Chapter 2, the five principal components of share risk make up most of the share risk and, in growing and mature markets, often constitute the major element of business risk. However, there remain a number of other factors that may contribute to

Table 8.1 SLEPT analysis example from the organ transplantation therapy market

SLEPT factor	Implication	Combined implication	Opportunity or threat
1. Ageing demographics	Greater volume demand	1 + 2 + 3 + 4 + 5 + 6 + 8	Threat of price pressure on undifferentiated propositions
2. Higher social expectations for treatment	Greater volume demand and less tolerance of low-performing products	Increased motivation to control costs of transplant therapies	
3. Lifestyle factors such as obesity and drinking	Greater demand and more awareness of avoidance		
4. Political aversion to increasing the tax burden	Limitations on rate of growth of funding		
5. Macroeconomic trends towards GDP growth in 2–4% region	Limitations on rate of growth of funding	7 + 9 + 10 + 11 + 12 + 13	Threat of reduced volumes from indiscriminate treatment
6. Technological development of product for wider applications	Increase in volume demand by market development, above natural growth	Greater motivation to be more selective about therapy application	Opportunity for more secure, targeted segments
7. IT developments allowing better use of data by customers	Greater enforcement of centralized prescribing policies		
8. EU trade regulations enabling greater cross-border trading	Increase in level of PI	7 + 11 + 13	Opportunity for value-added proposition extending up and down provider value chain
9. Development of the web as a patient information source	Increase in level of patient influence	Greater motivation to control transplantation value chain, rather than simple product costs	
10. Emergence of Patient Advocacy Groups	Increase in level of patient influence		

(Continued)

Table 8.1 (Continued)

SLEPT factor	Implication	Combined implication	Opportunity or threat
11. Political shift towards establishment of foundation hospitals	Greater attention to costs beyond product costs	12 + 10 + 2	Opportunity for an extended, augmented transplantation therapy proposition
12. More litigious environment	Greater fear of litigation	Greater demand for more personalized and augmented treatment regimes	
13. Development of better management processes within the NHS	Greater attention to overall cost management		

share risk. These arise from the resourcing of the strategy, its proportion to the objective, and the creation of internal and external synergy within the strategy. These factors are not always insignificant and are described in more depth in Brian Smith's *Making Marketing Happen* (see References and further reading). However, the application of thoughtful and rigorous strategic marketing planning to reduce the principal components of share risk will usually, as a serendipitous side-effect, also manage these secondary components. To discuss them at length here, however, might risk giving them more prominence in the reader's mind than is appropriate.

As already indicated, share risk is closely related to strategy strength and becomes especially important as the market becomes less novel and competition intensifies. High share risk suggests that current market share goals are unrealistic and that the shareholder value creation claims of the plan are similarly optimistic. By careful application of these various techniques of strategic marketing planning, share projections become more likely to be achieved and shareholder value creation becomes more assured.

Understanding and managing profit risk

In broad terms, the most important component of business risk varies in relation to the maturity of the market. As already discussed, market risk tends to be highest when the market and product category are relatively new. As markets mature, more is learned about them and market risk declines. However, markets that have moved beyond the embryonic stage often see battles between a number of competitors for market share. In these circumstances, share risk is often important and success is closely related to strategy strength. Once market shares and positions are well established and settled, the major component of business risk is often profit risk, and success depends on optimizing profit rather than share alone. These patterns are, of course, generalizations and therefore imperfect, but they are useful broad indicators of when to anticipate different kinds of business risk.

In the case of, usually, mature or declining markets where profit risk is an issue, the five components of profit risk can be grouped into two categories: risks that the planned price may not be obtained and risks that the planned costs may be exceeded. When the Marketing Due Diligence diagnostic results suggest high levels of profit risk, the diligent board is required to find ways of reducing that risk and optimizing the probability that the business plan will deliver its profit promises. As with other elements of the Marketing Due Diligence therapeutic process, a firm's efforts to this end are best focused and directed by the results of the Marketing Due Diligence diagnostic and are aided by the use of various strategic management tools.

Reducing profit pool risk

Profit pool risk is the risk that the planned profit may not be achieved because the overall profit in the market is smaller than anticipated. It is important to note that the term profit pool is not simply the same as the margin available to the company, although it is related to this. The profit pool is the total profit available to all competitors in a sector. When the

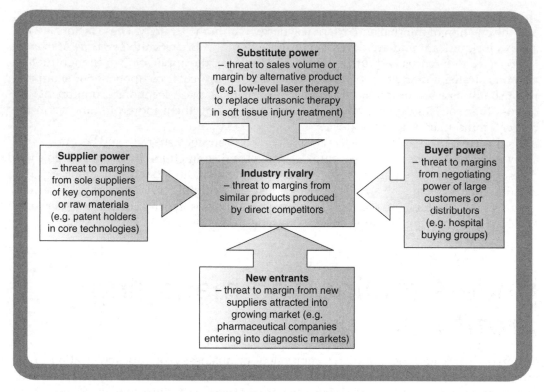

Figure 8.6 Porter's five forces model: an example for wound dressings

trend in this amount is downwards, profit pool risk is higher and vice versa. It is therefore important to understand the current and future profit trends in the industry. Profit pool risk can therefore be better understood by understanding the competitive pressures on the market as a whole, since these largely determine the profit trends for the market.

Perhaps the most well-known tool for better understanding the competitive forces acting on a market is Porter's five forces model, as outlined in Figure 8.6. Porter's model describes a situation in which the profit in an industry is reduced by one or more of the five forces acting upon it. The greater this combination of forces, the more likely that the profit pool will decrease and hence that this component of risk will increase. The great value in Porter's model lies not only in its description of these forces, but in identifying the conditions in which these are likely to increase. A summary of these conditions is given in Table 8.2.

It is rare for all of these forces to act strongly on any single market at one time. However, the use of Porter's model does allow a wider understanding of competitive forces than the narrow assessment of direct competition. In doing so, it allows firms to better predict changes to the profit pool. A good example of a shrinking profit pool is the situation faced by farmers in many developed markets. Low market growth rates and a handful of major retail customers, together with mostly undifferentiated commodity products and high exit barriers, mean that the overall profit available in the market is shrinking. Similar patterns are seen in large parts of the car market, in which a few evenly matched competitors who cannot afford to exit their market operate in a relatively small profit pool.

Table 8.2 Conditions leading to an increase in competitive forces

Competitive force	Conditions leading to an increase
Industry rivalry	Industry rivalry increases when the market contains a number of evenly balanced competitors following similar strategies with high exit barriers and when there are low market growth rates and little differentiation between value propositions.
Supplier pressure	Supplier pressure increases when suppliers of critical components are few and much larger than the industry player.
Customer pressure	Customer pressure increases when customers are relatively few and large in relation to the industry players and when there is little differentiation between value propositions.
New entrants	New entrant pressure is likely when barriers to entry are low and when the market is attractive (e.g. growing and profitable).
Substitutes	Substitute pressure is likely when new technologies or changes in regulation allow the entry of alternative ways of addressing the needs of the market.

In most cases, there is relatively little that can be done to reduce profit pool risk. It can be ameliorated to some extent by market leaders concentrating on differentiation strategies and avoiding price wars, but this discipline is hard to maintain in free markets. Even when the traditional competitive set maintains discipline, new entrants can initiate a price war. In most cases, therefore, an assessment of high profit pool risk contributes to decisions to focus on other markets or helps to inform more realistic assessment of likely profits. On the other hand, Porter's model does allow, in more profitable markets, the explication and evidencing of low profit pool risk to potential investors.

Reducing profit source risk

Profit source risk arises from the threat of a generalized competitor response to the strategy either in terms of price or some other response, such as increased advertising or product improvement. As described in Chapter 6, such a response from competitors is most likely when the strategy damages their business in some noticeable way. Such is the case when the business plan calls for growth that exceeds that of the market and therefore eats into competitor share.

The most useful tool for understanding and managing profit source risk is a form of gap analysis, in which future profit goals are considered in terms of their origin. In most business plans, profit growth comes from a variety of sources, such as increased pricing, reduced costs, changes to product mix, natural market growth and share gain. When the profit aspirations of a business plan represent an increase over historical performance, a graphical representation of the plan indicates a gap between a simple extrapolation of historical performance and the intended profit. Gap analysis is simply the detailed consideration of how this gap is to be filled by the various sources of profit, as shown in Figure 8.7. When this gap analysis indicates that share gain is a large contributor to profit growth, it is an indication of likely competitor reaction and hence profit source risk.

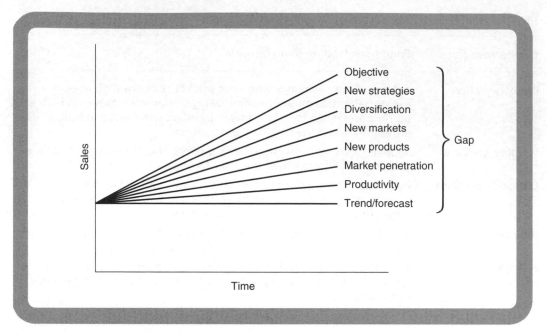

Figure 8.7 Gap analysis chart

There are two general ways in which profit source risk can be reduced. The first is simply to lower the profit growth aspirations to a level which is less likely to provoke a generalized competitor response. Whilst this may seem self-defeating, it is, in effect, trading a higher but unstable level of profit growth for a lower but more predictable one. As such, it may be a perfectly reasonable approach to reducing profit risk. The second is to adjust the mix of profit sources so that future profit growth relies more on cost management, price increases and changes in product mix than on winning share from competitors. In reality, the two approaches are often combined when a firm wishes to avoid an aggressive competitor response. Such is the case in the current strategy of many mobile telecoms operators. In addition to moderating their previously aggressive growth, they are now reducing costs, modifying pricing structures, and adding new products and services to generate profit growth. In doing so, they seek to avoid an aggressive competitor response that would threaten their planned profit.

Reducing competitor impact risk

Competitor impact risk is a special case of profit sources risk, in which the threat to profit aspirations comes not from a generalized competitor response, but instead from the response of a single, powerful competitor. Unsurprisingly, the risk of this happening is increased when one or more of the following things are implied by the business plan:

- The plan involves taking a relatively large amount of profit from a single competitor
- That your profit would be severely damaging to the competitor, in extremis threatening that firm's survival
- The threatened competitor is well resourced and able to respond

- The activity of the business plan is clearly and visibly targeted at the threatened competitor.

Clearly, these factors are combinatorial and a strategy that implies all four has a high level of competitor impact risk. In the same way, however, these factors indicate ways of managing high levels of this risk. Firms seeking to reduce competitor risk typically amend the implementation detail of their business plan to:

- spread the impact of any profit growth across a number of competitors
- avoid having a survival-threatening impact on any one competitor
- where significant damage must be done to a competitor, choosing to damage that competitor least able to respond aggressively
- make the activity of the business plan as difficult as possible for competitors to discern and recognize.

The strategic management tool that best informs efforts to reduce competitor impact risk is game theory, which was discussed in some detail in Chapter 6. In this approach, the impact of the plan and its possible implementation approaches are modelled with respect to competitor impact. By modelling both impact and response, games theory tries to avoid 'win–lose' strategies that might evoke powerful responses. Procter & Gamble use just such techniques to predict the price and promotion responses of their competitors, such as Unilever, in mature packaged goods FMCG markets. Such modelling techniques typically lead away from traditional 'warfare' type strategies in which one player wins at the expense of another. Instead, models of 'coopetition' arise in which the activities of each competitor are intended to maximize profits of each and avoid damaging price wars. It should be noted that this is not the same as cartel behaviour and does not involve explicit cooperation between rivals, which is illegal in most markets. Instead, it involves carefully predicting rivals' behaviour and the signalling of strategic moves to the market. Even without explicit use of game theory, however, many industries demonstrate behaviour between rivals that is designed to minimize competitor impact risk.

Reducing internal gross margin risk

The concept of profit risk is, in essence, a simple one. There is a risk that the firm may not deliver on its profit promises because it may not realize the planned prices, or it may exceed planned costs, or some combination of both. The preceding three sections on profit pool risk, profit sources risk and competitor impact risk all considered the management of the former, the risk that prices may not be realized as a result of competitive action or reaction. This and the following section deal with the risk of exceeding planned costs.

Although exceeding costs and coming in below target on price have the same net effect, there is an argument to be made that exceeding costs is a less forgivable sin. A strategy can, as described above, minimize the threat of competitor response but price levels remain only indirectly controllable by the firm. In comparison, cost levels are less removed from a board's sphere of control, especially if we ignore industry-wide labour or material costs that affect all players more or less equally. In our research, errors in cost predictions could be traced back to two principal sources. The less common of these was in the case of very new products or services where there were few or no reference points for calculation. Much more common was the effect of political bargaining in the business planning process. In the course of fighting for resources, boards and managers are pressured to optimism on both prices and costs. The optimism on costs leads to two components of profit risk, internal gross margin risk and other costs risk, which are often revealed in the course of the Marketing Due Diligence diagnostic process.

Internal gross margin risk is, in simple terms, the risk that the product or service will cost more to make than was expected and planned for. In other words, it arises from an error in estimating the direct costs of the product or service, rather than the indirect costs or overheads. As already mentioned, this error is, to some extent, understandable when the product is very new and the only reference points are the costs of prototypes. Except in this relatively rare situation, however, internal gross margin risk is reduced by careful comparison with analogous products and processes. Even for a very new product or service, there are often close comparisons to be made with other products in terms of material, labour and manufacturing costs, and the same can be done with services. This deeper understanding of costs is not merely an accountant's panacea; it can be very significant in managing the profit of some businesses. In the case of Volkswagen, the search for better understanding of costs has partly driven their acquisition strategy. By buying into a car-leasing firm, they acknowledge that part of the benefits they seek are an understanding of the running and maintenance costs of their own and other makes of cars. In doing so, they allow more accurate costing and pricing of their entire value proposition, of which the vehicle is merely the core.

Hence the appropriate response to a high indirect gross margin risk is to seek more and better information about likely direct costs. Where these are not easily available from direct experience of other very similar products or services, they can be 'synthesized' from other experiences which are similar in part. For instance, the provision of an added-value CRM software product, even if very new, might learn from the development costs of both data-mining and call-handling software. At the same time, the delivery costs of the value proposition might be extrapolated from experience with ERP (enterprise resource planning) packages such as SAP. In this way, even a complex, new product can be more accurately costed and the politically pressured aspirations of the business plan tested. Such testing is a necessity if the Marketing Due Diligence diagnostic suggests a high level of internal gross margin risk.

Reducing other costs risk

Other costs risk is the risk that profits will fail to meet plan because of an overshoot of other, indirect costs. Although the precise definition of 'other costs' varies between companies, distribution and selling costs are typically a major component of this. The nature of these also varies between markets. B2C firms usually spend most heavily on advertising and trade promotions, whilst B2B firms also often employ trade promotions but spend heavily on sales teams. In either case, these costs threaten profitability and, to the extent that they are inaccurately assessed, represent other costs risk.

As with direct costs, there are two principal factors to consider in assessing and forecasting other costs. Whilst both are explained at length in more specialized books, such as *Marketing Finance* by Keith Ward (see References and further reading), they can be summarized as allocation and prediction.

Clearly, the allocation of other costs is a perennially difficult problem, often ignored by marketers and left in the hands of cost accountants. However, it is not difficult to see how inaccurate or inappropriate allocation can have a strategic impact. This is especially true when resources such as a sales team are shared between different products or services. Such was exactly the case for one, anonymous, company which supplied routers, hubs and other equipment for Internet infrastructure. By allocating other costs on an arbitrary basis it effectively disguised the true costs of its several product groups. This cost allocation went unchallenged by marketing and the resultant overall costs strongly influenced the company's management of its product portfolio. When, as inevitably happened, the poor SBU profitability came under scrutiny it was found that the cost allocation policy, a seemingly trivial accounting issue, had in fact impacted heavily on the bottom line.

The prediction of other costs is the second important factor in reducing this component of profit risk. Two issues contribute to the incorrect prediction of other costs. The first is underestimating the size of the task. Other costs are often set using purely internal reference points and historical trends. This can ignore the true determinants of the cost. For example, one manufacturer of specialized recording studio equipment costed the sales and marketing costs of an important new product on the basis of current activity. This failed to recognize that the new product was technically much different and aimed at a different customer group. The sales and marketing resources required to support the launch and introductory phases of the product turned out to be much larger than planned and this, of course, reduced profitability considerably.

The second issue is an external one of competitor response. As described above, some strategies risk invoking competitor response which reduces the price achievable in the marketplace. In the same way, that competitor response can require additional promotional spending which increases other costs. In the direct experience of one of the authors, timely and targeted response to a competitor launch can force that competitor to change their promotional allocation, reduce their profitability and ultimately shift focus from the product.

As we have seen, then, the appropriate response to high other costs risks is one of diligent cost allocation and intelligent cost anticipation. Allocations of other costs must be challenged, the calculation of other costs must be based on the nature of the task as well as history, and likely competitor response must be allowed for.

Summary and conclusions

This chapter has considered what to do when the Marketing Due Diligence diagnostic process suggests significant levels of business risk. Such risk is not a monolithic entity. It is the sum of market, share and profit risk, and the relative proportions of these three risks vary between markets. New markets generally face high market risk, growing and maturing markets high share risk, mature and declining markets high profit risk. In any case, the nature and composition of the risk is amenable to detailed analysis and understanding by the use of existing and well-proven tools of strategic marketing planning. This understanding then informs corrective action that can, in most cases, significantly reduce both the component risks and overall business risks.

Whilst probably the majority of strategies have significant business risk that can be managed in this way, there remain cases of much higher risk. In these cases, the size of the assets at risk and the intrinsic level of risk in the market mean that careful management of the strategy is necessary but not sufficient. In these important cases, some way must be found of reducing the assets at risk as well as simply managing the risk. It is to these cases that the next chapter is addressed.

Chapter 9
Managing high-risk marketing strategies

Fast track

Most marketing plans do not explicitly take account of the risks associated with proposed marketing strategies. The diagnostic phase of the Marketing Due Diligence process not only highlights all of these associated risks, but also identifies the critical risks that could have the greatest impact on the predicted financial outcomes.

The therapeutic part of the Marketing Due Diligence process concentrates on these critical risks and assesses whether modifications to the originally proposed marketing strategy could significantly reduce them and, as a result, increase the shareholder value created. This focused, detailed approach to altering a marketing strategy is only possible because the overall risk profile has been disassembled into its constituent parts so that the critical areas of risk are highlighted. There may be costs incurred in reducing the level of these critical risks, but the resulting reduction in the level of the required financial return can make this expenditure shareholder value enhancing.

The risks assessed in the Marketing Due Diligence process include both controllable and uncontrollable risks. Even though uncontrollable risks cannot, by definition, be directly controlled by the business, they can normally be predicted and, in many cases, can also be indirectly influenced by modifying the marketing strategy. Shareholder value creation is impacted by both types of risks and hence economic performance measures include both controllable and uncontrollable items. At the very top of a company, i.e. the main board of directors, this is fine as they are held accountable by their shareholders for the strategic decisions both as to which products to sell and which customers to sell them to.

However, at lower levels of the organization, the level of managerial discretion is normally more constrained in that many divisional managers are given responsibility for a geographical region and/or range of products, and/or specific types of target customers. A key element in assessing managerial performance is that managers should only be held accountable for areas where they can exercise influence, i.e. exert some degree of control. In many organizations the rigorous implementation of this concept has meant that uncontrollable elements have been excluded from the metrics used to assess performance.

As a consequence, these same uncontrollable elements are either not included in the marketing planning process or the risks associated with them are not properly evaluated as they will not be taken into account in the assessment of managerial performance. This can create a significant gap between the assessment of managerial performance and the overall economic performance that drives shareholder value creation. One way round this problem is through the use of contingency planning, where potentially material, but unlikely, outcomes are predicted and 'what-if' plans are prepared 'just in case'. Managers are not held accountable for the unlikely uncontrollable event occurring, but they are expected both to have predicted it and to have prepared a contingency plan to take account of it.

The use of probability assessments in managing risk was discussed in Chapter 3, but even sequential probabilities do not fully value the flexibility that can be built into sophisticated marketing strategies. Where the next stage of marketing expenditure is made dependent upon the success of the previous stage, the company is creating for itself an option as to whether or not it will proceed with the strategy. These 'real' options can be valued using a modified form of the option theories developed in the financial markets.

The financial mathematics can appear complex but the underlying logic is very straightforward; there is a financial value for increasing the flexibility incorporated within a marketing strategy so that the company can adjust to cope with a new competitive environment. The value of such flexibility can be extremely important in very-high-risk marketing strategies, where none of the possible final outcomes is clearly the most probable. Also, the option value can enable companies to justify marketing expenditure to 'explore' potentially attractive opportunities without having to waste time developing completely spurious business cases.

Allowing for risk

As stated clearly in Chapter 3 and mentioned throughout the book, the normal focus of marketing planning is on predicting outcomes, not assessing the associated risks. These predicted, financially evaluated outcomes are often presented as single value, apparent certainties rather than being expressed as the expected value that has been derived from the range of possible outcomes of the proposed marketing strategy.

The focus of our Marketing Due Diligence process is explicitly to take account of all the risks associated with marketing strategies and to highlight the likely impact of the key risk factors. The diagnostic phase of the process therefore assesses the risk profile of any marketing plan by breaking down the overall risk into the three major components and then further subdividing each of these into five specific risk factors. Thus, the market value, market share and profit risks are all closely interlinked, and together give the overall risk profile of any specific strategy. Further, as has already been discussed, it is very unlikely that they will have equal impacts on the financial outcome of such a specific marketing strategy.

Consequently, in the therapeutic part of the Marketing Due Diligence process that is the focus of this part of the book, the emphasis is on gaining a very detailed understanding of those critical elements within the overall risk profile that could have the greatest impact on the shareholder value creation potential of the proposed marketing strategy. It is very often the case that relatively minor modifications to the proposed strategy can have significant impacts on these critical risk factors, without compensating reductions in the potential success-based assessment of financial returns. A common, simple example is the phasing of marketing expenditure so that better information on market size or potential market share is obtained before the commitment of most of the marketing money is made.

The identification and highlighting of these most important components of the total strategy risk is only made possible through a structured analysis process such as Marketing Due Diligence.

Risk equals volatility

We have already demonstrated, in Chapter 3, how financial markets assess risk through the volatility in the financial returns generated by a business. Thus, any increase in volatility results in an increased risk perception which leads, inevitably, to the compensating requirement for a higher return on the part of the external investor. Of necessity, this has to be taken into account internally within any large organization through its resource allocation decision process. Any ability to respond to potential volatility so as to mitigate its impact will reduce the risk perception of a marketing strategy and thus increase the potential shareholder value creation of the expected financial outcome. This may still be true even if the volatility reduction involves some expenditure, as long as the direction of the move is in the direction of the arrow in Figure 9.1.

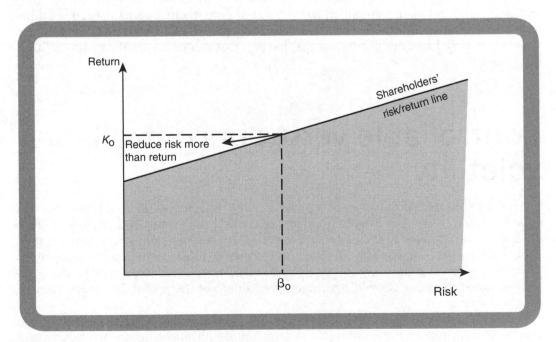

Figure 9.1   Shareholder value-adding strategies

The easiest way to illustrate this value-enhancing relationship is by using the example of insurance. Taking out an insurance policy against the risk of the company's factory, office block, distribution centre or computer centre burning down does not actually reduce the probability that such an event will occur. However, what it does achieve is to mitigate the financial consequences to the company of the event occurring. Hence, the company's financial performance will be much less volatile, if and when such a calamitous happening were to take place, than it would be if it were uninsured. Effectively, the company has swapped a certain small reduction in financial return (the cost of the annual insurance premium) for the relatively low probability (it hopes) of a massively large reduction in financial return.

Clearly, it is not normally possible to insure with outside third parties for most of the risks assessed in the Marketing Due Diligence process. However, many companies no longer automatically externally insure all of their business risks, as they believe for some of these risks the cost incurred outweighs the value of the potential reduction in volatility. They therefore consciously choose to self-insure themselves for a portion of their insurable risks and may decide only to take out true catastrophe cover with external insurers.

The therapeutic part of the Marketing Due Diligence process allows businesses to go through a similar process when assessing the risks associated with any proposed marketing strategy, as was discussed in Chapter 8. A proportion of our 15 risk categories will normally be assessed as being perfectly acceptable to the company, e.g. the market size risk for a well-established, stable product. Some others may be seen as mutually offsetting, e.g. high projected market growth but very conservative pricing assumptions, in terms of their financial impact. The company may be quite willing to absorb any volatility resulting from these elements but there may be some other elements, such as proposition specificity risk or competitor response risk, that are much more worrying.

This chapter focuses on these areas of high risk to try to identify the marketing equivalent of the external insurance policy, i.e. removal of potentially severe financial volatility at an acceptable cost to the business. This can be quite challenging when the potential volatility is very high, but this means that the cost that can be incurred can also be quite significant.

Controllable versus uncontrollable volatility

The concept of external insurance as a proxy example is quite useful, as it highlights that volatility can be caused by externally driven, uncontrollable events. Your factory or office block may burn down due to an internal problem or because a jumbo jet crashes onto it. In either case, the potential financial impact can be equally disastrous unless the company is adequately insured. Indeed, not surprisingly, the insurance premiums charged by the external insurance company depend upon their assessment of the probability of the insured event occurring.

These probability assessments are applied to both the internally controllable events (e.g. provision of sprinklers, fire protection and dampening equipment, nature of products produced and raw materials used) and externally driven, uncontrollable events (e.g. physical location on flight paths near major airports). The same process must be followed in the assessment and management of the key risks associated with a marketing strategy.

The statement that 'this risk is externally determined and therefore cannot be controlled' does not decrease its financial impact. Shareholder value creation is impacted by both controllable and uncontrollable risks, which means that all types of risks should be both assessed and managed. An uncontrollable risk may not be *directly* controllable by the company, but it almost certainly can be predicted and it probably can be influenced or even indirectly managed.

A good example of this is the competitive response that is predicted as a result of implementing a high-growth strategy in a mature, stable, highly profitable market segment. The profit sources risk and competitor impact risk, which are sub-components of profit risk, as discussed in detail in Chapter 6, would indicate the probability of aggressive competitor reaction. They consider not only which competitors lose, but also what the impact on them will be of the predicted level of loss. If the current marketing strategy targets an existing leading player to the extent that their financial viability is threatened, an aggressive response is almost guaranteed!

It may be possible to modify the marketing strategy so that market share gains are more widely spread, but this clearly depends upon the particular market segment that is being targeted and the nature of the specific proposition that is to be used. Alternatively, the planned rate of growth could be moderated so that the company has time to establish and then strengthen its position in this market segment, before the dying competitor starts a serious price war or uses some other tactic that could destroy a lot of the total market value added.

In any case, a clear understanding of the interlinked set of risks in any marketing strategy enables both controllable and uncontrollable risks to be predicted. After all, external shareholders tend to hold boards of directors accountable for all volatility in their financial returns, whether the board would classify it as controllable or not. At the very top of the organization this may be perfectly acceptable as the board can, over time, fundamentally change the nature of the underlying businesses either through acquisition and divestment or by organic restructuring.

Therefore, it is not unreasonable to use primarily economic performance measures to assess the performance of the managers directing the overall strategy of the business. There is normally also a deliberate attempt to link this economic performance to the rewards received by these directors through the use of stock options and long-term incentive plans linked to total shareholder returns and earnings per share growth, etc. However, at lower levels in the organization, managerial discretion is normally more constrained as the group is subdivided into divisions and strategic business units. Marketing Due Diligence has to be carried out at this lower level, as this is where the business develops real, competitive strategies in terms of competing with identified competitors for specific groups of customers.

In most groups, there are restrictions placed on these lower-level business subdivisions in terms of product range, market segments, target customer groups, channels of distribution, etc. that they can utilize. This means that they cannot always fundamentally 'change the nature' of their business, even if they do not find their future external environment to be particularly attractive. As a consequence, many organizations do not hold divisional managers fully accountable for the overall economic performance of their divisions. Indeed, it is very well accepted that managerial performance measures should only include areas over which the managers concerned can exert influence, i.e. can exercise at least some degree of control.

Unfortunately, omitting such uncontrollable factors from managerial performance measures can mean that they do not receive rigorous evaluation by these same managers when they are developing their marketing plans. In some organizations consideration of these uncontrollable factors is left out of the marketing strategies completely, despite their potentially significant impact on shareholder value creation. If the value creation potential of the proposed marketing strategies is to be properly evaluated, it is vitally important that all the factors that impact on the relative risk versus return profile of each strategy are taken into account.

This does not mean that managers should be held responsible for the actual outcome of any uncontrollable factors but they *can* be held accountable for identifying both the likelihood and the impact of such potential outcomes. They should also be held accountable for developing contingency plans that mitigate the negative financial impact of significant adverse outcomes. Contingency planning, which is also sometimes known as scenario analysis, is becoming increasingly popular and is diagrammatically illustrated in Figure 9.2.

The basis of contingency planning is that the base strategic plan is built around the most probable set of outcomes, with the emphasis on those items with the greatest potential impact. However, there are also some significantly less likely outcomes that would have a material impact on the value generated by the strategy if they actually occurred. These require contingency plans to be developed, so that the management team has decided what it should do as soon as it knows that the unlikely, but material, outcome will actually occur. The types of event that are often covered by contingency plans include a material currency devaluation, the launch of a new or improved product by a competitor, the entry of a new competitor, the loss of a major customer and the onset of a significant price war. Of course, the identification of the specific issues for contingency planning and the assessment of their relative probabilities are much easier if a Marketing Due Diligence process has been carried out.

Scenario analysis first came to widespread public attention when it became known that Shell had used it to predict the possibility of the dramatic increase in the world price of oil that could result from the concerted actions of the major oil-producing countries. This had led it to prepare a contingency plan that enabled the group to respond very rapidly once such an event actually occurred in the early 1970s.

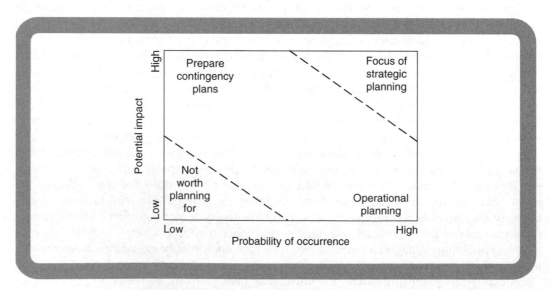

Figure 9.2   Contingency planning/scenario analysis techniques

Since then, many companies have adopted some form of contingency planning, but there are still many examples where it has not been applied when it would have proved useful. One such example relates to consumer-based businesses in Argentina at the end of the 1990s. During the 1980s, the Argentine economy had been ravaged by rampant inflation, but the introduction of the currency convertibility plan in 1991 had resulted in a dramatic decline in the rate of inflation by the mid 1990s. This period had also seen rapid growth in national income per head, so that Argentine consumers were feeling much better off. In consumer goods markets this created a high level of uptrading into more expensive, premium products; the potential demand had been there for a long time, but consumers could not afford these goods during the hyperinflation period.

Unfortunately, but not surprisingly, it proved impossible for the government to manage a completely 'soft landing' from an annual inflation rate of over 2000% and the economy moved into recession in 1997. This could have been managed but, throughout this period, Argentina had failed to generate a strong trade balance surplus and its foreign currency reserves were dependent on capital inflows. However, the fundamental basis of the convertibility plan was that the Argentine peso was held at parity to the US dollar and was freely convertible. This required foreign currency reserves to be held to back all the local currency in circulation. By the end of the 1990s it had become clear that the central bank was running out of these critical foreign currency reserves, but the newly elected President stated that he had no intention of devaluing the peso.

Thus, it apparently came as a complete surprise to most companies operating in the country when the Argentine peso was significantly devalued and local bank deposits were frozen. The impact on the economy was dramatic, with consumer purchasing being hit immediately. Consumption levels fell but, even more noticeably, consumers downtraded to much cheaper brands and products wherever they were available. Amazingly, several of the supposedly sophisticated, international, fast-moving consumer goods companies operating in the country had not prepared contingency plans to allow for the impact of such a devaluation. One argument used in their defence was that the government had stated that it was not going to devalue the currency, even though all the economic data indicated that such an action was highly likely, if not inevitable! A few of these companies had also been very slow to respond to the rapid uptrading that had resulted from the earlier growth in the economy, so that they had only just got their premium brands fully launched into the market when the devaluation happened.

Contingency planning can therefore become a key element in marketing planning, irrespective of whether the critical event can be controlled by the company. This is particularly true where the adverse event is a specific action by a competitor, which is likely to be triggered by predictable and traceable other events. A classic example is the major price reduction of Marlboro by Philip Morris in the USA in 1993, which was discussed in Chapter 6. It should have been predictable that Philip Morris would respond, in order to protect Marlboro's leading market share, if and when the new lower-priced products gained smokers from Marlboro rather than from the other weaker brands in the market. This prediction could have been turned into a contingency plan so that the competitors had already decided what they would do once Philip Morris had reduced the effective selling price of Marlboro. These competitors may not have been able to stop it happening, but such an important, uncontrollable, but predictable event can still be planned for.

Therefore, the outcome of a sound, strategically oriented, marketing planning process is not only a base marketing plan but a number of contingency plans that indicate how the business should respond to significant differences in both controllable and uncontrollable

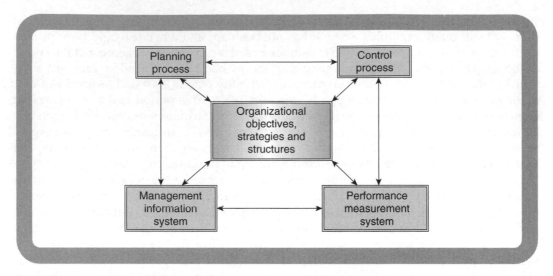

Figure 9.3   An integrated process

key factors. In order to ensure that managers take full cognizance of the uncontrollable factors for which they are not personally held accountable, the marketing planning process needs to be integrated into the financial control process and the performance measurement system, as shown in Figure 9.3.

This can most easily be achieved by their all using the same management information system. It is quite astonishing that, at the beginning of the twenty-first century, there are still many organizations that prepare plans outside their normal accounting system. Some of these businesses then spend a lot of time trying to reconcile the inputs to their planning processes with those used by their monthly 'control' focused reporting systems, so that the performance measures (which are normally based on their plans) can meaningfully assess the relative actual performance against their plans. Other businesses in this position have given up trying to reconcile their plans with their actual results, which means that the performance measures used are based on one or the other or, in some cases, something else altogether.

Using real option analysis

As mentioned earlier in the book, it is very common for companies to adjust for these specific risks by altering the discount rate that is applied to the expected future cash flows arising from the proposed marketing strategy. This is not only conceptually flawed, but also turns the sophisticated discounted cash flow technique into a very blunt instrument for taking account of risk, as it applies a uniform adjustment to *all* the expected cash flows, irrespective of how they are affected by the specific risk being evaluated.

As discussed in detail in Chapter 3, using probability assessments focuses attention on the key risk elements and can highlight the financial impact of each risk factor. However, even using cumulative probabilities in these sequential strategic investment decisions does not fully reflect the potential value of some high-risk opportunities, as it does not apply a financial value to any flexibility that may exist regarding subsequent investment

Five parameters

1) Current price of the underlying asset (P)
2) Exercise price of the option (E)
3) The instantaneous variance of the asset returns (σ^2)
4) The time to expiry of the option (t)
5) The risk-free interest rate (r_f)

Figure 9.4 Option value drivers

decisions. Each major decision point in the marketing strategy may create an option for the company to continue or not, and these options can have significant value. This is particularly true where additional information can be gained during the intervening period for which the rest of the expenditure can be deferred.

An option is *a right*, but not an obligation, *to buy or sell* an asset *within a specified period* of time *at a given price* (the exercise or striking price of the option). A 'call option' is the right to buy an asset; a 'put option' is the right to sell an asset. Over the last 30 years, finance theory has developed very sophisticated models for valuing financial options (e.g. those relating to stocks and shares, foreign currencies, etc.). More recently, there has been a growing awareness that this methodology can be applied to valuing the real options created as part of major strategic investment decisions. Space in this book does not allow a comprehensive discussion of option valuation techniques, but all the normal valuation models are based around the five basic value drivers of options. These are set out in Figure 9.4 and are amazingly logical. Options are valuable only where the value of the asset involved is volatile; thus, an option to defer for a year the decision to buy a house or a share etc. is valuable if you think house prices etc. may change significantly during this year. This makes volatility a key driver of option values, but the volatility *must* make the option exercisable if it is to generate value.

Therefore, the relationship between the current asset price and the exercise price is another key driver of option value; the closer the exercise price is to the current asset price, the more valuable is the option, as it is more likely that it will ultimately be exercised. If the exercise price of a call option is already below the current asset price, the option is said to be 'in the money'; for a put option, this happens when the exercise price is above the current asset price. Logically, an option with two years to run is more valuable than an option with an unexpired life of two weeks and therefore the time to expiry of the option is also important as an option value driver.

The last factor, the risk-free interest rate, relates to the fact that the exercise price does not have to be paid until the option is exercised, which is normally at the end of its life. If the asset was actually bought or sold, the value would be paid immediately; therefore, the comparison should be made between the asset price and the present value of the exercise price. This means that the exercise price of the option is discounted back to its 'certainty' present value by using the risk-free discount rate.

Each of these option value drivers has an equivalent for strategic marketing investment decisions so that the methodology can be applied to real options, as is shown in Figure 9.5. In strategic marketing investment decisions, the option does not relate to buying or selling

Option value drivers ~ Applied to real options

Five parameters

1) Current price of the underlying asset (P) – Present value of investment's cash flow
2) Exercise price of the option (E) – Subsequent expenditure required to acquire the total investment
3) The instantaneous variance of the asset returns (σ^2) – Volatility of the investment's returns
4) The time to expiry of the option (t) – Length of deferment period
5) The risk-free interest rate (r_f) – Time value of money

Figure 9.5   Valuing real options

an asset but rather to carrying on with the investment programme. Hence the current asset price is normally the present value of the marketing strategy's expected cash flows, while the exercise price of the option is the subsequent expenditure required to finish the marketing programme and consequently generate these expected cash flows. The life of the option is clearly the potential length of deferment for these subsequent expenditures and the time value of money is the same as for financial options, although several companies seem to prefer to use their own cost of capital rather than the more appropriate risk-free rate.

The most difficult issue in most cases is the volatility of the investment's returns, but this can be quite simply assessed by considering the range of the potential outcomes. It is not necessary to try to get over-sophisticated to generate continuous ranges and statistical distributions. Many practitioners in this area prefer to exercise commonsense judgements rather than spurious complex calculations. A logical frame of reference for volatilities in high-risk strategic marketing investments can be gained by considering the annual volatility of the relevant stock market sector; the overall USA stock market index has had an annual standard deviation (which is the square root of the variance) of $\pm26\%$ over the past five years. This is the volatility for an index containing thousands of individual companies that may move in opposite directions, thus smoothing the movement of the overall index. Most individual strategic marketing investments will therefore have annual volatilities significantly in excess of this!

The main advantage of incorporating the real option value drivers is that it can highlight how flexible and phased, but high-risk, marketing investments can be financially worthwhile even if the current net present value of the investment is negative, using the probability-adjusted expected cash flows. The cumulative volatility value impact from the real options built into the investment may *more than offset* the current negative net present value. This type of investment would not be accepted under traditional discounted cash flow analysis, even using cumulative probability factors. A very simple initial example may make this clearer and this is given in Figure 9.6.

Under traditional discounted cash flow analysis, this marketing investment would not be started, since it shows a negative NPV of £4 million. At first sight, it looks even more absurd to spend £1 million to acquire a one-year option on a negative NPV project. However, Figure 9.6 also shows that the expected returns have quite a high volatility (assessed to be 30% per year) and could therefore be significantly higher than the current 'expected' present value of £100 million. This means that the investment *could* have a substantial positive net present value (e.g. £130 million minus the less volatile investment

Present value of expected, but volatile, returns (P) = £100 m
Present value of required investment (E) = £104 m
Volatility of returns (per year) (σ^2) = 30%
Risk-free interest rate (r_f) = 6%
*It is possible to defer the investment for 1 year (t) at a cost of £1 m. Should the £1 m option fee be incurred?
The company's cost of capital is 10%

Traditional DCF analysis

NPV today = £100 m − £104 m = −£4 m

Figure 9.6 Valuing real options – a simple example

However, the investment of £1 m purchases an option to go ahead, or not, at the end of 1 year.

This option can be valued by using option tables:

$\sigma\sqrt{t}$ and $P/Ee^{-r_f t}$

$\Rightarrow$ $0.3\sqrt{1}$ and $\left[\dfrac{100}{1.1}\right] \times \left[\dfrac{1.06}{104}\right]$

$\Rightarrow$ 0.3 and 0.93 = 9%

This represents the option value as a percentage of the underlying asset value.
Thus, the option value is £100 m × 0.09 = £9 m

Figure 9.7 Valuing real options – a simple example (continued)

costs of £104 million). Equally, the cash inflows could turn out to be much less valuable than the expected £100 million, but it could be worth spending £1 million to find out.

The one-year deferral option is valued in Figure 9.7 by applying the well-known Black and Scholes option pricing model to these particular values. As stated before, the details of the valuation are beyond the scope of this book, but it should be clear that it is well worth spending £1 million to acquire an option that is valued at £9 million. It must be clearly understood that paying the £1 million option fee does not mean that the £104 million investment will automatically be undertaken in one year's time. This investment will be reassessed prior to the expiry of the option, when a better assessment of the likely returns may be possible.

The use of real options is therefore particularly relevant where the total marketing investment can be made on a phased basis and the subsequent investments depend on the situation at the particular time when they are to be made. The company is effectively creating its own real options, and these need to be valued appropriately. There are several common types of strategic investment decision-created options and these are summarized

Type of decision	Real option created
Phased investments	Call option on subsequent stages
Abandonment	Put option on value of abandoned assets
Learning by waiting (timing/deferment)	American call option, but with dividend flows (i.e. early exercise may be worthwhile)
Varying outputs/methods (e.g. sourcing/location)	Flexibility options – values dependent on volatility of costs (e.g. supplier prices/exchange rates and labour costs, etc.)

Figure 9.8   Examples of real options

Project cash flows – expected results if second phase goes ahead

£m

Year	0	1	2	3	4	5	6–15 (p.a.)	Perpetuity (p.a.)
Investments	(10)	–	–	(150)	–	–	–	
Cash inflows – from first phase	–	(4)	(2)	–	2	2	2	1
– from second phase	–	–	–	(10)	8	14	20	15

N.B. Company cost of capital = 10%

Figure 9.9   A simplified phased investment example – project cash flows

in Figure 9.8. One of the most common examples is a new market entry where the initial entry can be done on a phased basis, while much greater information is gained about the particular market. Thus, the benefits of phasing and learning by waiting are obtained. A slightly more detailed example of such a decision is given below.

Real option example

An initial market entry requires an upfront investment of £10 million and losses are expected for the first two years. If the sales growth targets and other success indicators are being met, a significant second-phase investment of £150 million will then be made in Year 3. Subsequently, significantly enhanced profits and cash flows are anticipated. These are shown in Figure 9.9.

There is a currently assessed 50% probability that the second-phase investment will be made. Probabilities on all subsequent cash inflows are ignored to keep the analysis relatively

Overall DCF evaluation (applying 50% probability factor to second phase)

£m

Year	0	1	2	3	4	5	6–15	Perpetuity
Investments	(10)			(75)				
Cash inflows	–	(4)	(2)	(5)	6	9	12	8.5
Net cash flows	(10)	(4)	(2)	(80)	6	9	12	8.5
Discount factors @10%	1	0.909	0.826	0.751	0.683	0.621	3.82	2.39
Present value	(10)	(3.64)	(1.65)	(60.08)	4.10	5.59	45.84	20.32

NPV = £0.48 m, i.e. the overall project generates a nil NPV

Figure 9.10   A simplified phased investment example – overall DCF evaluation

simple. The volatility of the second-phase investment's cash flow projections is estimated to be 40% per year.

The discounted cash flows for the combined project are shown in Figure 9.10 using a 10% discount rate (the company's cost of capital) and applying the 50% probability factor to all the second-phase cash flows. This shows that the overall project generates a nil net present value (i.e. it has an internal rate of return of 10%), but there is a potential real option as to whether to undertake the second phase of the investment.

A better way, therefore, of evaluating this investment is to consider it as a first-phase investment of £10 million that acquires for the company an option to make a subsequent £150 million investment. The financial evaluation is consequently the sum of the net present value of phase 1 plus the net present value of the option to do phase 2.

Phase 1 can be evaluated using conventional discounted cash flow and this is shown in Figure 9.11. The resulting negative net present value (£2.66 million) means that phase 1 is not worth doing just for itself. To this, we need to add the value of the option and this uses our five option value drivers, as shown in Figure 9.12.

The expected present value of the cash flows resulting from the second-phase investment can be calculated from a discounted cash flow, as is done in Figure 9.13. Care is needed to ensure that the present value of these cash inflows is then compared to the present value of the required second phase investment (the £150 million is the amount to be spent in Year 3) discounted at the risk-free rate of 6%. This discounted present value of the investment (£125.94 million) is higher than the expected present value of the inflows but this is not critical because these expected inflows are highly volatile, and we are going to value that volatility as is done in Figure 9.14.

The high volatility (40% p.a.) and the long deferment period (three years) when combined with the relative closeness of the current asset value and the option exercise price make for a very valuable option. The £30 million option value easily outweighs the small negative NPV (£2.6 million) generated by phase 1 of the investment. Thus, the £10 million

Phase 1 can be evaluated using conventional DCF

Year	0	1	2	3	4–15 (p.a.)	Perpetuity (p.a.)
Cash flows	(10)	(4)	(2)	–	2	1
Discount factors	1	0.909	0.826	0.751	5.12	2.39
Present values	(10)	(3.64)	(1.65)	–	10.24	2.39

NPV = £(2.66)m, i.e. phase 1 is not worth doing as a stand-alone project

Figure 9.11 A simplified phased investment example – introducing option values (1)

To evaluate phase 2 as an option, we need the five option value drivers:

P = the present value of the cash inflows from the extra investment
E = the required new investment (£150 m)
σ = the volatility of this investment's returns (assessed to be 40%)
t = the deferment period (3 years)
r_f = the risk-free interest rate (6%)

Figure 9.12 A simplified phased investment example – introducing option values (2)

Year	0	1	2	3	4	5	6–15 (p.a.)	Perpetuity (p.a.)
Cash inflows	–	–	–	(10)	8	14	20	15
Discount factors @10%	1	0.909	0.826	0.751	0.683	0.621	3.82	2.39
Present values	–	–	–	(7.51)	5.46	8.69	76.4	35.85

Present value = £118.89 m

[N.B. This is still less than the true present value of the required new investment (£150 m); if this is discounted at the risk-free interest rate (6%) it has a present value of £125.94 m. If discounted at 10%, this is reduced to £112.7 m, which is how the overall project evaluation was done to generate the combined NPV of £0.48 m.]

Figure 9.13 A simplified phased investment example – cash inflows (for phase 2)

Applying the option value drivers and option tables

$\Rightarrow$ $\sigma\sqrt{t}$ and $P/Ee^{-r_f t}$ $\Rightarrow$ Option value

$\Rightarrow$ 0.69 and 0.94 $\Rightarrow$ (approx.) 25%

Therefore, the option has a value of 25% of £119 m = around £30 m

This significantly outweighs the small negative NPV on phase 1

Figure 9.14   A simplified phased investment example – valuing the option

The revised evaluation of the current investment shows a positive NPV of £27.4 m (£30 m OPTION VALUE − £2.6 m PHASE 1 NPV)

When this is placed in the context of an initial investment of £10 m, by calculating the Profitability Index, the attractiveness of this flexible investment is highlighted.

$$\text{P.I.} = \frac{\text{NPV}}{\text{Original Invt.}} = \frac{£27.4\,m}{£10\,m} = 2.74$$

$$\text{Adjusted P.I.} = \frac{\text{NPV}}{\text{P.V. of Cum. Invt.}} = \frac{£27.4\,m}{£15.3\,m} = 1.79$$

Figure 9.15   A simplified phased investment example – reassessing the investment

investment should be undertaken as shown in Figure 9.15. However, it should be re-emphasized that this does not mean that the second-phase investment will automatically be undertaken. This will depend on a reassessment of the financial evaluation using the improved understanding of the expected returns that should be gained during the first three years of market entry.

The application of real options to this strategic marketing investment has enabled the initial entry into the new market to be financially justified, without the need to come up with completely spurious long-term projections of market shares before any real information has been obtained. This type of approach also focuses management attention on the critical areas of marketing information that need to be resolved in the first three years of market entry. As more information about the market and the success of the initial launch is obtained, the company should be able to make a much less volatile assessment of the potential financial return from the large-scale second-phase investment. As already stated, this reassessed financial return will form the basis for the second-phase investment decision.

Summary

The diagnostic phase of the Marketing Due Diligence process will highlight which, if any, of the 15 categories of risk should be classified as high risk. These particular high risks may need a specific risk management approach that is unnecessary for the normal risk categories, which can be managed using the approaches set out in Chapter 8.

In this chapter, we have argued for using contingency planning and real option techniques as ways of coping with the high-risk elements of a marketing strategy. These risk management techniques should be applied whether the risk factor can, or cannot, be directly controlled by the company. The determining criterion is the potential impact on the financial return that will be generated from the marketing strategy.

The application of these techniques, along with the strategic marketing processes discussed in Chapters 7 and 8, should enable any deficiencies in the marketing strategies identified by the Marketing Due Diligence diagnostic process to be properly evaluated and removed where relevant.

Chapter 10
Fast track

Why Chief Executive Officers must demand a revolutionary new approach from their Chief Marketing Officers

Many CEOs despair of their senior marketing colleagues. There is a disparity between what boards see marketing doing and what they need from this critical function. CEOs and senior non-marketers perceive marketing's focus to be on promotional activities rather than on the key issues of strategy which create shareholder value. What they need is good decisions about which customers to target and with what value propositions in order to create sustainable competitive advantage. Above all else, boards need to know if the planned marketing strategy is going to make returns, above the cost of capital, that take account of the risks associated with the strategy. Marketing as a discipline has failed during the past 50 years by concentrating on promotion rather than on developing world-class marketing strategies. The result is that, in most companies, marketing has been relegated to running promotional campaigns and designing T-shirts and does not deserve a place at the high table, i.e. the board of directors.

The result of this sad lack of marketing leadership is the demise of many of our erstwhile famous organizations. Most of the highest earning Return on Investment plcs during the decade up to 1990 have since gone into liquidation or were acquired in desperate circumstances, while many of the leading companies in different sectors up to the year 2000 also got into financial difficulties or were acquired.

All of this happened against a background of three major challenges that industry was facing during this period and still faces.

The first is maturity in demand in many markets. Since most consumers already have most things, market growth is no longer a natural expectation and suppliers have been forced to understand the needs of their customers as a route to growth in sales and profits. Alas, since their so-called marketing colleagues were obsessed with promotion, many failed in this fundamental task and subsequently went bust. This sad trend began first and is clearest in consumer markets, but the same argument applies and will apply in business-to-business markets.

The second challenge is globalization, the result of mature national markets combined with political and macroeconomic change. Today, we have a situation of a declining number of global mega-companies, with only eight car companies in the world, only four major firms of accountants whilst, in the UK, only four supermarkets account for nearly 80% of all grocery product sales. The result of this is that many second-tier companies face a bleak future, having to compete with companies whose global reach gives them enormous economies of scale and scope. Again, the only hope for such companies is an increasing focus on customer needs.

Finally, all of this has resulted in a massive shift of power to customers away from suppliers. Today, customers are destroying old make/sell business models, whilst entrepreneurial, technology-enabled competitors unfettered by the baggage of legacy bureaucracy, assets, cultures and behaviours have raised customers' expectations. Technology has empowered customers to have more information about their suppliers than their suppliers have about them. This customer pressure is, of course, in addition to new business metrics and pressures from institutional shareholders to report meaningful facts about corporate performance. Other stakeholders demand exemplary corporate behaviour. All these pressures have resulted in a need for strategies other than downsizing and cost-cutting as a route to increased profitability. Never before has the need for real marketing professionalism been greater and the challenge facing Chief Executives is to drag their marketing colleagues away from the trivia they are engaged in, to a central, board-driven, strategic role.

This raises the question of what marketing is. It is a function, just like finance, with its own professional standards, institutes and body of knowledge. The role of marketing is to define markets and to understand the needs of the segments within these markets, then to formulate strategies for meeting these needs. Furthermore, they need to do this in a way that enables the company to create long-term, net free cash flows which, having taken account of the associated risks, represent a financial return over and above the cost of capital, thus creating shareholder value.

CEOs need a way of holding marketing accountable, despite the obvious complexity of the process. At the lowest level of promotional effectiveness, tools for this have existed for decades. They can, however, only tell us about the effectiveness of promotional activity, which is far removed from understanding the effectiveness of the entire marketing process. It is perfectly possible to communicate effectively with the right customers and still fail to improve sales or profit. At the next level of assessing the degree to which the whole mix of tactics creates advantage, existing and new tools allow us to predict and measure the degree to which that mix creates customer preference and hence sales and profits. It is, however, perfectly possible to create sales and profits whilst destroying shareholder value. What CEOs and the board need is a way of measuring the risk associated with a marketing strategy and hence its likely shareholder value creation. That is the aim of Marketing Due Diligence.

A process of Marketing Due Diligence

Despite what many non-marketers think, marketing is much more than just promotion. It is much more, even, than designing and delivering the 'marketing mix' of promotion, product, pricing, place (distribution), process, people and physical evidence. As stated above, methods for measuring the effectiveness of these more obvious marketing activities have been in place for years. Whilst these tactical measures have their place, they tell us little about the effectiveness of the marketing strategy, that part of the marketing process that concerns itself with understanding the market and deciding what parts of it to focus upon and with what value propositions. It is this aspect of marketing that the Marketing Due Diligence process concerns itself with.

Marketing, in this broad strategic sense, is closely correlated to shareholder value. It is the choice of which customer segments to focus upon and what to offer them that lies at the root of sustainable competitive advantage. Good choices create customer preference which, in turn, creates better return on investment. Looked at through the lens of business risk, as investors do, strong strategy reduces the risk associated with a promised return. To investors, it is the risk-adjusted rate of return that matters, and managing risk is as important as managing returns, sometimes more so.

The Marketing Due Diligence process involves both diagnostic and therapeutic stages. The first evaluates business risk and assesses whether the plan creates or destroys shareholder value. The second, building on the outcomes of the first, adapts the business plan to improve its risk profile and enhance shareholder value creation.

Marketing Due Diligence begins with explicating the strategy, which is often implicit and unclear even to those who need to implement it. This explication results in a clear definition of which customers are to be served and what products, services and overall value proposition are to be offered to them. This explicit strategy is then assessed for market risk, share risk and profit risk.

Market risk arises from the possibility that the market may not be as large as hoped for in the business plan. It is, to a large degree, a function of the novelty of the business plan. Strategies involving new customers and/or new products are more likely to have high market risk than those involving existing products and customers.

Share risk arises from the possibility that the plan may not deliver the hoped for market share. It is the corollary of the competitive strength of the strategy. Share risk is reduced when homogeneous segments are targeted with specifically tailored value propositions which leverage strengths, negate weaknesses, avoid direct competition and anticipate future trends.

Profit risk arises from the possibility that the plan may not deliver the intended profits. It is a function of the competitor reaction engendered by the plan and of the aggressiveness of cost assumptions.

Significant levels of market, share or profit risk, or some combination of the three, suggest that the returns delivered by the plan are likely to be less than promised. The final stage of shareholder value creation is therefore to calculate whether this risk-moderated return represents the creation or destruction of shareholder value. This involves calculating the full value of the assets put at risk, including intangibles. Only if the likely return is greater than the cost of this capital is shareholder value created. In addition to shareholder value creation or destruction, a third possible outcome of this diagnostic phase is that the plan is insufficiently thought out to make a judgement about its value-creating potential.

The Marketing Due Diligence therapeutic process uses the tools of strategic marketing management to manage and reduce the risk associated with the strategy. Using the results of the diagnostic stage to direct efforts, it suggests improvements to the marketing strategy. Hence the implications of using Marketing Due Diligence are to improve the marketing strategy in terms of its ability to create shareholder value.

The implications of implementing Marketing Due Diligence

The key objective of the Marketing Due Diligence process, then, is to link marketing strategies directly to the creation or destruction of shareholder value. This requires an assessment of the particular risks associated with any proposed marketing strategy, as risk and the corresponding required rate of return are directly linked.

Unfortunately, the normal financial focus of marketing strategies and plans is on predicting outcomes, not assessing the associated risks. These potential financial outcomes are often presented as single point, apparent certainties rather than being expressed as a range of the possible outcomes that may result, given the volatility of future business environments.

Where risk is taken into consideration, this is normally done by altering the discount rate that is applied to the predicted future cash flows; thus, higher risk strategies have a higher discount rate applied to all these cash flows. This can give a false result particularly, as is the case for many marketing strategies, where the strategy depends on the successful completion of a sequence of individually somewhat risky activities, such as are involved in the development and launch of a new product or the entry into a new market.

The Marketing Due Diligence process looks at the specific risks associated with each element of the marketing strategy, so that individual probability assessments of success/failure and the consequent impact on financial outcomes are identified. This enables these predicted financial outcomes to be directly adjusted, where necessary, in the light of identified risks. The level of any adjustment that is required clearly depends on how the forecasts were originally prepared. Thus, plans that include extremely optimistic stretch targets ('best case' plans) will normally need more adjustment than more conservative plans that already allow for expected risks and consequent volatility in financial returns ('most likely' plans).

In order to produce a shareholder value 'figure' from the Marketing Due Diligence diagnostic process, this probability-adjusted set of expected future cash flows is then compared to the financial return required by the business. This is done by assessing the true capital tied up in implementing the proposed marketing strategy. The true capital includes the critically important, and often highly valuable, intangible marketing assets as well as the more obvious tangible assets of the business.

As the specific risks of the proposed marketing strategy have already been taken into account in the diagnostic review, the return required on this capital employed can be calculated by reference to the company's normal cost of capital. In other words, there is no need arbitrarily to increase the required rate of return to try to take account of the complex myriad of risk factors.

There can be one additional adjustment to the predicted financial return if the proposed marketing strategy places any existing assets at risk. This concept of 'capital at risk' is used to highlight strategies that leverage off existing marketing assets, such as umbrella branding. Often this is done to reduce the required marketing expenditure, but the expected financial returns do not normally include the potentially offsetting decrease in value of the existing asset, if the strategy is not completely successful. This adjustment is made as part of the full Marketing Due Diligence review.

Even if the existing marketing planning information is not sufficient to enable a numerical value to be calculated, the Marketing Due Diligence diagnostic process will still highlight the key risk areas of any proposed strategy and show up the specific deficiencies in the current marketing plan. In many cases these deficiencies can be remedied by applying the therapeutic process within Marketing Due Diligence, which reviews and improves the marketing planning process.

The application of Marketing Due Diligence clearly has significant implications for both internal and external stakeholders in any business. The rigorous review of proposed marketing strategies should be a key element in any sound corporate governance process. Marketing Due Diligence provides a methodology to do this consistently across even a diversified group and through time. Indeed, the knowledge that all marketing plans and strategies will be subjected to this type of analysis will rapidly improve the quality of the processes used internally within the marketing function.

Thus, the critical resource allocation decisions at board level should be based on much better and more validly comparative information. Knowing this should provide great reassurance to external analysts and shareholders, as they can be more confident that future marketing strategies will be shareholder value enhancing.

Assessing market risk

Despite the loose use of the terms by some, markets and products are not the same thing. Markets are groups of people with related needs; products are bundles of benefits that might meet those needs. Market risk arises when a company attempts to match one to the other.

Market risk is the risk that the market size will not be as large as hoped for by the plan, as a result of which the intended shareholder value would not be created. It is distinct from, but aggregates with, share risk and profit risk. In short, market risk arises when the market projections turn out to be wrong. This happens for a number of reasons: the targeted market is very new; the product category is very new; the product enters a new stage in its life cycle; or the uncertainty arising from this 'newness' is not compensated for by effective research and analysis.

Market risk is the cumulative risk of five component risks:

- *Product category risk*. This is the risk that the entire product category may be smaller than planned. It is higher if the product category is novel and lower if the product category is well established.
- *Market existence risk*. This is the risk that the target segment may be smaller than planned. It is higher if it is a new segment and lower if the segment is well established.
- *Sales volumes risk*. This is the risk that sales volumes will be lower than planned. It is higher if sales volumes are 'guessed' with little supporting evidence and lower if the sales volumes are well supported by evidence such as market research.
- *Forecast risk*. This is the risk that the market will grow less quickly than planned. It is higher if forecast market growth exceeds historical trends and lower if it is in line with or below historical trends.
- *Pricing risk*. This is the risk that the price levels in the market will be lower than planned. It is higher if pricing assumptions are optimistic and lower if they are conservative.

Two important, but often neglected and abused, techniques of strategic marketing planning are Ansoff's growth matrix and the product life cycle. Used correctly, these tools are critical to understanding, assessing and managing market risk. For all marketing strategies, but especially those that involve new markets or products, assessing market risk is a necessary step in creating shareholder value.

Assessing share risk

Share risk is the risk that the strategy will not create the degree of customer preference or competitive advantage that is needed to create the planned market share and hence fall short of creating shareholder value. It is distinct from, but aggregates with, market risk and profit risk. In short, share risk arises when what is offered to customers is not, in their eyes, valuable enough to them. This happens for a number of reasons: the wrong customers are targeted, they are offered the wrong things, or the strategy involves going head-on with a bigger, stronger competitor.

Share risk is the cumulative risk of five component risks:

- *Target market risk.* This is the risk that the value proposition will appeal only to a minority of the customers targeted. It is low when each target segment is homogeneous in its needs and high when each segment is heterogeneous in what it seeks.
- *Proposition risk.* This is the risk that the value proposition will not be quite right for any of the customers targeted. It is low when the strategy involves making specific offers to each target segment and high when the strategy involves a single offer to the whole of a segmented market.
- *SWOT risk.* This is the risk that the strategy does not make use of the company's strengths and does not compensate for its weaknesses. It is low when the targeting reflects the distinctive competencies of the company and high when it fails to understand them.
- *Uniqueness risk.* This is the risk that the strategy competes head-on with powerful rivals. It is low when the strategy involves targeting different customers and offering different value propositions and high when it offers the same thing to the same customers as do the competitors.
- *Future risk.* This is the risk that the strategy is designed for yesterday's market and not today's. It is low when the company understands the combined implications of the forces acting on the market and high when it ignores or neglects what is happening in the business environment.

For each of these sub-components of share risk, it is possible to make a rigorous assessment of risk level against a comparative scale. Each component has a different weighting according to the company and market context in which the strategy is to be implemented and the components can then be aggregated into an overall measurement of share risk. In addition, a number of other, minor, but interesting components of share risk can be assessed in a qualitative way to colour and inform the overall judgement.

Taken overall, a careful assessment of market share risk enables the strategist to do two things. Firstly, to adjust market share projections to allow for the strength of the marketing strategy. Secondly, to identify actions that will improve the strategy and the shareholder value creation potential of the business plan.

Assessing profit risk

It is still by no means certain that a marketing strategy will create shareholder value even if, when implemented, the strategy achieves the predicted market share of a market that generates the planned total sales revenue values. There are other risks that need to be assessed, and these are covered in the Marketing Due Diligence diagnostic process by the assessment of profit risk. Profit risk assessment considers the probability of creating the anticipated financial return from the predicted market share of the planned market value.

Not surprisingly, therefore, the profit risk is normally most important in relatively mature markets where established competitors, and other stakeholders in the total industry value chain, are often fighting to obtain a larger share of a static or even declining total profit pool.

As before, the total profit risk assessment has been subdivided into five elements, which are separately assessed in order to generate an overall view of the probability of achieving the planned level of profitability.

- *Profit pool risk*. This assesses the probability that the future total profit pool will be less than planned. This risk is clearly higher if the existing profit pool is static or shrinking and lower if the targeted profit pool is high and growing. Another factor impacting on this risk is the relative proportion of this total available profit pool that the marketing strategy aims to take; the higher the proportion, the higher is the associated risk. The other major component of this risk assessment is the likelihood of significant changes within the total value chain that may impact on the potential profit attainable from the marketing plan.
- *Profit sources risk*. This assessment looks specifically at whether overall competitors' reactions to the proposed marketing strategy are likely to reduce the profit below that planned. The profit sources risk is higher if the planned profit growth comes directly at the expense of competitors and lower if it comes from growth in the total profit pool. The highest level of this risk is therefore seeking to grow profits aggressively from a high existing base in a highly competitive market with a declining total profit pool and increasingly sophisticated customers.
- *Competitor impact risk*. Many marketing strategies will have a disproportionate impact on one competitor, or a few specific competitors, while the remaining competition will be largely unaffected. The level of competitive response will therefore be determined by the scale of this impact on those most affected, and can be much greater than if the 'financial pain' is shared more widely across competitors.

   This assessment focuses specifically on the impact of the marketing plan on individual competitors, rather than considering them in total. This element evaluates the risk that profits will be less than planned because of a single competitor reacting aggressively to the marketing strategy. The competitor impact risk is higher if the profit impact on competitors is concentrated on one competitor and this impact threatens the competitor's survival.

The remaining components of profit risk examine the assumptions made regarding the internal cost structure of the business.

- *Internal gross margin risk*. This assesses the probability that gross margins will, in reality, be lower than planned. As the risks associated with forecasting selling prices will have already been assessed under the market value risk section, this component concentrates on the costs of manufacturing the product or providing the service. The risk is higher if the internal gross margin assumptions are optimistic relative to current similar products, or if the business has no previous experience or validated information on which to base its assumptions.

- *Other costs risk*. This assesses the probability that net margins will be lower than planned because other costs are higher than anticipated. A commonly important component of these other costs is marketing support, and this is the most frequent cause of adverse profit impact, due to overspending against plan. Very often, the overspending is 'required' in order to achieve the targeted market share, but this still results in profit being lower than planned. This other costs risk is higher if assumptions regarding other costs, including marketing support, are optimistic, e.g. lower than current costs, or where the business has no previous experience in similar product areas.

The key role of market definition and segmentation

Successful commerce has always been the result of a careful matching of offers to needs. Only a fool would conclude that all women between the ages of 18 and 22 are the same, or that all people who live in the same neighbourhood are the same, etc. Nonetheless, it is such shallow thinking that has come to represent market segmentation over the years.

A market trader many years ago, on having it pointed out to him that exactly the same apples at opposite ends of his stall were priced at 20 cents and 25 cents, replied that the 25-cent apples were especially for customers who wanted to pay 25 cents!

This somewhat silly and elementary example is only intended to illustrate that, in life, as in business, people have different need sets and the authors find it incredible that, in the twenty-first century, so many organizations still haven't fathomed that the secret to success is correct market definition and segmentation as precursors to product development, positioning and branding.

A market must be defined as 'the aggregate of all products and services that satisfy the same, or similar, needs'. Hence, in financial services, a pension is a product, not a market, as there are other financial products that can fulfil a similar need set. It is crucial, therefore, to understand the specific demand for pensions. This is to ascertain whether other products are taking the place of pensions and whether pensions are growing, static or declining as part of the overall market.

Once this has been done, a quantitative method of market mapping is then essential to trace the flow of all goods and services from suppliers, through channels, right through to those who eventually use them. This market map (an example of which is given in Chapter 7) is intended to ensure that the supplier fully understands the changes and trends throughout the value chain and that, if they are in some way different in their distributor and value-adding patterns, it is for rational reasons known to the board. The second principal reason for drawing a market map is to ascertain which are the major decision points or leverage points that need to be influenced in favour of the supplier. It is here that the 80/20 rule often applies, in that up to 80% of volume or value is accounted for by 20%

or less of the leverage points. These, clearly, will form a central part of any strategic marketing plans.

It is also at the leverage points that market segmentation needs to be carried out. For example, in the radiator heating market, architects are major influencers of which radiators go on which wall, but architects come in many different shapes and sizes and have many different needs and motivators.

The market segmentation process involves decomposing a market into a number of actual behaviour patterns according to what is bought, when it is bought, how it is bought, why it is bought and, finally, according to who buys. This will result in a number of micro-segments, of which there will usually be at least 30. It is then a comparatively simple process to cluster these micro-segments until there are seven or eight groups remaining. These are the final segments, on which all strategic decisions should be based.

Creating strategies that create shareholder value

Strategic marketing planning is made more difficult by the myriad different approaches suggested in textbooks. In truth, however, these differ in jargon and detail but not in principle; there is a core process of strategic marketing planning. This core process involves an iterative loop of understanding the market, choosing the strategy, implementing the plan and monitoring outcomes. It is supported by a raft of strategic management tools and techniques, and this technology of strategic marketing planning can be used to reduce the risk associated with the business plan. This reduction of risk and subsequent improvement in potential to create shareholder value forms the therapeutic process of Marketing Due Diligence.

- *Market risk* can be reduced by better understanding of the risks inherent in growth strategies and in poorly characterized markets. It can be reduced in practice by intelligent use of market research, understanding the implications of Ansoff's matrix and the predictive power of life cycle analysis.
- *Share risk* can be reduced by improving the choice of target customers and the value propositions we offer them. It can be reduced in practice by understanding market structure, market segmentation, and the difference between a product or service and a value proposition. It can be further reduced by insight into strengths and weaknesses of the company and how they align to the market.
- *Profit risk* can be reduced by understanding the impact of strategies on competitors. It can be reduced in practice by the use of game theory to predict and avoid aggressive responses. Profit margin risk can be further reduced by making better informed assumptions about the costs of implementing the strategy.

For each area of risk, therefore, the tools of strategic marketing planning can be used to reduce risks identified by the Marketing Due Diligence diagnostic process and hence improve shareholder value creation. Even when markets are complex, data is incomplete and planning resources are limited, it is possible to significantly improve shareholder value creation by applying rigour to the strategy-making process.

Managing high-risk marketing strategies

Most marketing plans do not explicitly take account of the risks associated with proposed marketing strategies. The diagnostic phase of the Marketing Due Diligence process not only highlights all of these associated risks, but also identifies the critical risks that could have the greatest impact on the predicted financial outcomes.

The therapeutic part of the Marketing Due Diligence process concentrates on these critical risks and assesses whether modifications to the originally proposed marketing strategy could significantly reduce them and, as a result, increase the shareholder value created. This focused, detailed approach to altering a marketing strategy is only possible because the overall risk profile has been disassembled into its constituent parts so that the critical areas of risk are highlighted. There may be costs incurred in reducing the level of these critical risks, but the resulting reduction in the level of the required financial return can make this expenditure shareholder value enhancing.

The risks assessed in the Marketing Due Diligence process include both controllable and uncontrollable risks. Even though uncontrollable risks cannot, by definition, be directly controlled by the business, they can normally be predicted and, in many cases, can also be indirectly influenced by modifying the marketing strategy. Shareholder value creation is impacted by both types of risks and hence economic performance measures include both controllable and uncontrollable items. At the very top of a company, i.e. the main board of directors, this is fine as they are held accountable by their shareholders for the strategic decisions both as to which products to sell and which customers to sell them to.

However, at lower levels of the organization, the level of managerial discretion is normally more constrained in that many divisional managers are given responsibility for a geographical region and/or range of products, and/or specific types of target customers. A key element in assessing managerial performance is that managers should only be held accountable for areas where they can exercise influence, i.e. exert some degree of control. In many organizations the rigorous implementation of this concept has meant that uncontrollable elements have been excluded from the metrics used to assess performance.

As a consequence, these same uncontrollable elements are either not included in the marketing planning process or the risks associated with them are not properly evaluated as they will not be taken into account in the assessment of managerial performance. This can create a significant gap between the assessment of managerial performance and the overall economic performance that drives shareholder value creation. One way round this problem is through the use of contingency planning, where potentially material, but unlikely, outcomes are predicted and 'what-if' plans are prepared 'just in case'. Managers are not held accountable for the unlikely uncontrollable event occurring, but they are expected both to have predicted it and to have prepared a contingency plan to take account of it.

The use of probability assessments in managing risk is discussed in Chapter 3, but even sequential probabilities do not fully value the flexibility that can be built into sophisticated marketing strategies. Where the next stage of marketing expenditure is made dependent upon the success of the previous stage, the company is creating for itself an option as to whether or not it will proceed with the strategy. These 'real' options can be valued using a modified form of the option theories developed in the financial markets.

The financial mathematics can appear complex but the underlying logic is very straightforward; there is a financial value for increasing the flexibility incorporated within a marketing strategy so that the company can adjust to cope with a new competitive environment. The value of such flexibility can be extremely important in very-high-risk marketing strategies, where none of the possible final outcomes is clearly the most probable. Also, the option value can enable companies to justify marketing expenditure to 'explore' potentially attractive opportunities without having to waste time developing completely spurious business cases.

Afterword: what to do now

On reading this book entirely, the reader will have gained an overview of and an insight into a vast mountain of research about the connections between strategy and share price. Further, you will understand the need for Marketing Due Diligence, how to carry out the diagnostic process and how to act on its findings. Looked at as one body of work, the concept and process of Marketing Due Diligence can be daunting and may prompt the reader to ask 'What now? Where do I start?'

In our experience, where to start with Marketing Due Diligence depends on the role you play in the organization. Both the inputs and the outputs of the process mean that it can only be addressed at the level of Strategic Business Unit (SBU) leadership or above. In simple terms, directors have to drive this process and managers have to support it. Further, whilst non-marketing leaders need the results of Marketing Due Diligence, the implementation of it falls to those whose role it is to develop and communicate the company's marketing strategy. In short, therefore, we recommend the following actions regarding Marketing Due Diligence, depending on who you are:

- Non-marketing leaders, such as CEOs, CFOs and the leadership team of any SBU, should demand the results of a Marketing Due Diligence diagnostic from their most senior marketing colleague, such as the Marketing Director. They should then support the diagnostic process and any changes to strategy that are implied by its results.
- Marketing leaders such as Marketing Directors or Chief Marketing Officers should execute a Marketing Due Diligence diagnostic, report the results to their peers and recommend actions to improve the shareholder value creation of their business.
- Marketing managers should both consider those parts of the Marketing Due Diligence process that impact on their responsibilities and bring the overall concept and process to the attention of their functional leader. They should then support the implementation of both diagnostic and therapeutic processes.
- Similarly, non-marketing managers should bring the overall concept and process to the attention of both their functional leader and their marketing peers. They should then support the implementation of both diagnostic and therapeutic processes.

Whether you are a director or manager, marketer or otherwise, we urge you to adopt the Marketing Due Diligence process. Choosing not to, given the research and knowledge it embodies, is a dereliction of your duties to shareholders. Choosing to will benefit not only them but also you, your firm and, by creating wealth, the broader society in which we all live.

References and further reading

This book is based on many years of research by the three authors and in our choice of references and further reading, we have had to tread a thin line. On the one side, we are keen to demonstrate the substantive support for the Marketing Due Diligence concept. On the other, we are loath to burden the practising manager with an unselective and impenetrable list which trades length for utility. We therefore provide a selective list and would welcome any further questions on our work. In the first instance, please contact Dr Brian Smith at brian.smith@pragmedic.com

Baker, S. (2000). Defining the Marketing Paradigm – The View of Senior Non-Marketers: A Report on Work in Progress. Cranfield Internal Report.

Fournier, S., Dobscha, S. and Mick, D. G. (1998). Preventing the Premature Death of Relationship Marketing. *Harvard Business Review*, **76**:42–44.

Kelly, S. (2005). *Customer Intelligence – From Data to Dialogue*. Wiley, London.

Kotler, P., Armstrong, G., Saunders, J. and Wong, V. (1999). *Principles of Marketing*, 2nd European Edition. Prentice-Hall, Englewood Cliffs, NJ.

Lilien, G. L., Kotler, P. and Moorthy, K. S. (1992). *Marketing Models*, 1st Edition. Simon & Schuster, Englewood Cliffs, NJ.

Lukas, B. A., Whitwell, G. J. and Doyle, P. (2005). How can a shareholder value approach improve marketing's strategic influence? *Journal of Business Research*, **58**(4):414–423.

McDonald, M. H. B. (2002). *Marketing Plans: How to Prepare Them, How to Use Them*, 5th Edition. Butterworth-Heinemann.

McDonald, M. H. B. and Dunbar, I. (2004). *Market Segmentation: How to Do It, How to Profit from It*, 2nd Edition. Butterworth-Heinemann, London.

McDonald, M. H. B. and Wilson, H. N. (2002). *The New Marketing*. Butterworth-Heinemann.

McGovern, G. J., Court, D., Quelch, J. and Crawford, B. (2004). Bringing Customers into the Boardroom. *Harvard Business Review*, **82**(11):70–81.

McGrath, R. G. and Nerkar, A. (2004). Real Options Reasoning and a New Look at R&D Investment of Pharmaceutical Firms. *Strategic Management Journal*, **25**:1–21.

Pascale, R. T. (1990). *Managing on the Edge*. Simon & Schuster, New York.

Peters, T. and Waterman, R. (1982). *In Search of Excellence*, 1st Edition. Harpers & Row, New York.

Reichheld, F. F. and Sasser, W. E. Jr (1990). Zero Defections: Quality Comes to Services. *Harvard Business Review*, **5**:105–111.

Rogers, E. M. (1976). New Product Adoption and Diffusion. *Journal of Consumer Research*, **2**(4):290–302.

Smith, B. D. (2003a). Making Marketing Happen: How Great Medical Companies Make Strategic Marketing Planning Work For Them. *International Journal of Medical Marketing*, **4**(2):129–142.

Smith, B. D. (2003b). Success and Failure in Marketing Strategy Making: Results of an Empirical Study Across Medical Markets. *International Journal of Medical Marketing*, **3**(4):287–315.

Smith, B. D. (2003c). *The Effectiveness of Marketing Strategy Making Processes in Medical Markets*. Ph.D., Cranfield School of Management.

Smith, B. D. (2003d). An Empirical Investigation of Marketing Strategy Quality in Medical Markets. *International Journal of Medical Marketing*, **3**(2):153–162.

Smith, B. D. (2003e). The Effectiveness of Marketing Strategy Making Processes: A Critical Literature Review and a Research Agenda. *Journal of Targeting, Measurement and Analysis for Marketing*, **11**(3):273–290.

Stahl, H. K., Matzler, K. and Hinterhuber, H. H. (2003). Linking Customer Lifetime Value with Shareholder Value. *Industrial Marketing Management*, **32**:267–279.

Stiles, P. (2001). The Impact of the Board on Strategy: An Empirical Examination. *Journal of Management Studies*, **38**(5):627–650.

Ward, K. R. (2003). *Marketing Finance*. Elsevier, Oxford.

Wyner, G. A. (2004). The Journey to Marketing Effectiveness. *Marketing Management*, **March/April**:8–9.

Index

MS005 22